Studies in Diversity Linguistics

Chief Editor: Martin Haspelmath

Consulting Editors: Fernando Zúñiga, Peter Arkadiev, Ruth Singer, Pilar Valenzuela

In this series:

1. Handschuh, Corinna. A typology of marked-S languages

2. Rießler, Michael. Adjective attribution

3. Klamer, Marian (ed.). The Alor-Pantar languages: History and typology

4. Berghäll, Liisa. A grammar of Mauwake (Papua New Guinea)

5. Wilbur, Joshua. A grammar of Pite Saami

A grammar of Pite Saami

Joshua Wilbur

Language Science Press
Berlin

Language Science Press
Habelschwerdter Allee 45
14195 Berlin, Germany

langsci-press.org

This title can be downloaded at:
http://langsci-press.org/catalog/book/17
© 2014, Joshua Wilbur
Published under the Creative Commons Attribution 4.0 Licence (CC BY 4.0):
http://creativecommons.org/licenses/by/4.0/
ISBN: 978-3-944675-47-3

Cover and concept of design: Ulrike Harbort
Typesetting: Joshua Wilbur
Proofreading: Joseph Farquharson, Tom Gardner, Richard Griscom, Jorge Emilio Rosés Labrada, Linda Lanz, Michelle Natolo, Stephanie Natolo, Jörn Piontek, Benedikt Singpiel

Storage and cataloguing done by FU Berlin

Language Science Press has no responsibility for the persistence or accuracy of URLs for external or third-party Internet websites referred to in this publication, and does not guarantee that any content on such websites is, or will remain, accurate or appropriate. Information regarding prices, travel timetables and other factual information given in this work are correct at the time of first publication but Language Science Press does not guarantee the accuracy of such information thereafter.

Muv vienagijda Árjepluovest

Contents

Acknowledgements • xi

Symbols and abbreviations • xiii

1 **Introduction** • 1
   1.1 The Pite Saami language and its speakers • 1
      1.1.1 Linguistic genealogy • 1
      1.1.2 Names for Pite Saami • 1
      1.1.3 Geography • 2
      1.1.4 The state of the Pite Saami language • 6
   1.2 Linguistic documentation of Pite Saami • 7
      1.2.1 Previous studies • 8
      1.2.2 The Pite Saami Documentation Project corpus • 10
      1.2.3 Using this description • 15
   1.3 Typological profile • 22

2 **Prosody** • 25
   2.1 Monosyllabic word structure • 25
   2.2 Multisyllabic word structure • 25
      2.2.1 Word stress • 26
      2.2.2 Relevant prosodic domains • 28
      2.2.3 Syllabification • 30
      2.2.4 A note on syllables and feet • 34
   2.3 Utterance-level prosody • 35
      2.3.1 Intonation in utterances • 35
      2.3.2 Utterance-final weakening • 36

3 **Segmental phonology** • 37
   3.1 Consonants • 37
      3.1.1 Consonant phonemes and allophonic variations • 37
      3.1.2 Consonant clusters • 58

	3.2	Vowels		63
		3.2.1	Vowel phonemes and allophonic variations	64
		3.2.2	Epenthetic schwa	70
4	**Morphological patterns and word classes**			**73**
	4.1	Overview of morphology		73
		4.1.1	Linear morphology	74
		4.1.2	Non-linear morphology (morphophonology)	74
	4.2	Overview of word classes		81
5	**Nominals I: Nouns**			**83**
	5.1	Number in nouns		83
	5.2	The nominal case system		84
		5.2.1	Nominative case	84
		5.2.2	Genitive case	85
		5.2.3	Accusative case	85
		5.2.4	Illative case	86
		5.2.5	Inessive case	87
		5.2.6	Elative case	88
		5.2.7	Comitative case	89
		5.2.8	Abessive case	90
		5.2.9	Essive case	91
	5.3	Number and case marking on nouns		92
		5.3.1	Nominal suffixes	92
		5.3.2	Non-linear noun morphology	95
		5.3.3	Problematic case/number marking in abessive case	97
	5.4	Inflectional classes for nouns		98
		5.4.1	Class I	100
		5.4.2	Class II	104
		5.4.3	Class III	105
		5.4.4	Summary of noun classes	107
	5.5	Possessive suffixes		108
6	**Nominals II: Pronouns**			**113**
	6.1	Personal pronouns		113
	6.2	Demonstrative pronouns		115
	6.3	Reflexive pronouns		117
	6.4	Interrogative pronouns		119
		6.4.1	Interrogative pronouns with human referents	119

		6.4.2 Interrogative pronouns with non-human referents	120
		6.4.3 Interrogative pronouns concerning a selection	120
		6.4.4 Non-nominal interrogative pro-forms	123
	6.5	Relative pronouns	125

7 Adjectivals — 127

- 7.1 Attributive adjectives — 128
  - 7.1.1 Attributive adjectives in elliptic constructions — 129
- 7.2 Predicative adjectives — 130
- 7.3 A note on attributive and predicative adjectives — 134
- 7.4 Comparatives and superlatives — 135
- 7.5 Comparing NP referents — 137
- 7.6 Restrictions on *smáva* and *unna* 'small' — 138
- 7.7 Quantifiers — 140
- 7.8 Demonstratives — 142
- 7.9 Numerals — 143
  - 7.9.1 Basic numerals — 143
  - 7.9.2 Complex numerals — 145
  - 7.9.3 Numerals and morphosyntax — 147

8 Verbs — 149

- 8.1 Finite verbs and inflectional categories — 149
  - 8.1.1 Person and number — 149
  - 8.1.2 Tense — 150
  - 8.1.3 Mood — 151
- 8.2 Non-finite verb forms and periphrastically marked verbal categories — 153
  - 8.2.1 Future — 155
  - 8.2.2 Aspect — 155
  - 8.2.3 Negation — 157
- 8.3 Passive voice — 158
- 8.4 Morphological marking strategies on verbs — 159
  - 8.4.1 Inflectional suffixes for verbs — 160
  - 8.4.2 Non-linear morphology in verbs — 161
  - 8.4.3 The potential mood: inflection or derivation? — 165
- 8.5 Inflectional classes for verbs — 168
  - 8.5.1 Class I — 170
  - 8.5.2 Class II — 171
  - 8.5.3 Class III — 173

		8.5.4	Class IV	175
		8.5.5	Class V	176
		8.5.6	Other possible verb classes	178
		8.5.7	The verb *årrot* 'be'	178
		8.5.8	The negation verb	179
		8.5.9	Summary of verb classes	180

9 Other word classes — 183
9.1 Adverbs — 183
9.1.1 Derived adverbs — 183
9.1.2 Lexical adverbs — 184
9.2 Adpositions — 187
9.2.1 Postpositions — 188
9.2.2 Prepositions — 189
9.3 Conjunctions — 190
9.4 Interjections — 192

10 Derivational morphology — 195
10.1 Nominal derivation — 196
10.1.1 The diminutive suffix *-tj* — 196
10.1.2 The general nominalizer suffix *-k* — 197
10.1.3 The action nominalizer suffix *-o* — 199
10.1.4 The agent nominalizer suffix *-däddje* — 200
10.1.5 The state nominalizer suffix *-vuohta* — 201
10.2 Verbal derivation — 202
10.2.1 The diminutive verbalizer suffix *-tj* — 202
10.2.2 The verbal derivational suffix *-st* — 204
10.2.3 The verbal derivational suffix *-d* — 204
10.2.4 The verbal derivational suffix *-dall* — 205
10.2.5 Passivization with the derivational suffix *-duvv* — 205
10.3 Adjectival derivation — 207
10.3.1 Adjective derivation — 207
10.3.2 Ordinal numeral derivation with *-át* — 208
10.4 Adverbial derivation — 208
10.5 Summary of derivational morphology — 208

11 Phrase types — 211
11.1 Verb complex — 211

11.2		Nominal phrases	215
	11.2.1	NPs in adverbial function	219
11.3		Adjectival phrases	219
	11.3.1	APs in adverbial function	222
11.4		Adverbial phrases	222
11.5		Postpositional phrases	223

12 Overview of the syntax of sentences — 225
12.1	Grammatical relations	225
12.2	Constituent order at clause level	226
	12.2.1 Information structure	229

13 Basic clauses — 231
13.1		Declarative clauses	231
	13.1.1	Basic intransitive declaratives	231
	13.1.2	Basic transitive declaratives	233
	13.1.3	Existential clauses	234
	13.1.4	Copular clauses	235
	13.1.5	Multi-verb declarative clauses	237
13.2		Interrogative clauses	242
	13.2.1	Constituent interrogative clauses	242
	13.2.2	Polar interrogative clauses	244
13.3		Clauses in the imperative mood	245
13.4		Clauses in the potential mood	246

14 Complex clauses — 249
14.1		Clausal coordination	249
14.2		Clausal subordination	250
	14.2.1	Complement clauses	250
	14.2.2	Adverbial clauses	254
	14.2.3	Other subordinate clauses with non-finite verb forms	256
	14.2.4	Relative clauses	256

Appendix: Inventory of recordings — 261

Bibliography — 271

Name index — 275

Subject index — 277

Acknowledgements

This grammar of Pite Saami began as a part of my PhD project at Christian-Albrechts-Universität zu Kiel, which I successfully completed in August 2013. To a large extent, its contents are the same as the final version of my dissertation (hosted by the university library in Kiel), but a number of revisions and improvements to content and structure have been made, thanks mainly to many useful comments from anonymous reviewers, editors and proof-readers, but also due to my own ever increasing understanding of the language.

A number of individuals played a vital role in enabling the research for and the writing of this grammar.

Above all, I am indebted to the Pite Saami community in Arjeplog not only for graciously permitting me to document their fascinating language, but also for allowing me – initially just a random but curious stranger – to intrude into their lives. I would particularly like to thank Nils-Henrik Bengtsson, Inger and Sven Anders Fjällås, Anders-Erling Fjällås, Elsy Rankvist, Edgar Skaile[†] and Dagny Skaile. *Gijtov adnet!*

My PhD supervisor, Ulrike Mosel, agreed to the task of guiding me quite late in my PhD project leading up to this book, even after much of the data for the corpus had already been collected; she provided invaluable criticism and played an essential role in the development of this grammar.

My sincere thanks are also due to Michael Rießler for his motivation, comments and support, particularly concerning Saami linguistics, and to the Hans Rausing Endangered Languages Project for supporting the Pite Saami Documentation Project for five years.

Many thanks also to: Rogier Blokland, Yvonne Ericson, Ciprian Gerstenberger, Martin Haspelmath, Martin Hilpert, Elena Karvovskaya, Erica Knödler, Kristina Kotcheva, Bruce Morén-Duolljá, Stefan Müller, Maarten Mous, Sebastian Nordhoff, Stanly Oomen, John Peterson, Christian Rapold, Robert Rißmann, Florian Siegl, Peter Steggo, Mulugeta Tsegaye, Riitta-Liisa Valijärvi, Øystein Vangsnes and Marijn van 't Veer.

Furthermore, I am grateful to the staff at Language Science Press and numerous dedicated volunteers, all of whom have spent their valuable time helping in

Acknowledgements

the review and publication process in support of the idea of true open-access publishing, free of charge to both authors and readers. I am pleased to be included in this unprecedented project.

And last but far from least, my appreciation and love go out to Rebecca, Miranda, Eliah, Reuben, Shirley and Lee for their love and support in the past, present and future!

Of course, I take full responsibility for any omissions, mistakes or faults found within this work.

Joshua Wilbur
Freiburg, July 2014

Symbols and abbreviations

-	segmentable morpheme boundary
\	morpheme via stem alternation (not segmentable)
+	compound boundary
=	clitic boundary
.	syllable boundary
σ	syllable
Σ	morphological stem
*	ungrammatical form; reconstructed form
?	uncertain form
<	source language
/ /	phonological representation
[ ]	phonetic form
< >	orthographic representation
~	variation between forms

ABESS	abessive	cl. sx.	inflectional class suffix
ACC	accusative	COM	comitative
ADJZ	adjectivizer	COMP	comparative
AdvP	adverbial phrase	CONNEG	connegative
ADVZ	adverbializer	DEM	demonstrative
agr. sx.	agreement suffix	DIM	diminutive
AP	adjectival phrase	DIST	distal
approx.	approximant	DU	dual
ATTR	attributive	ELAT	elative
C	consonant segment	e	elicitation session
CC	two-segment consonant cluster	ESS	essive
		GEN	genitive
CCC	three-segment consonant cluster	ILL	illative
		IMP	imperative
C-grad	consonant gradation	INESS	inessive

Symbols and abbreviations

INF	infinitive	PRS	present
n/a	not available	PST	past
NEG	negation verb	Q	question marker
NMLZ	nominalizer	REFL	reflexive
NOM	nominative	REL	relative pronoun
NP	nominal phrase	RMT	remote
ORD	ordinal number	SG	singular
PASS	passive	str	strong grade
PL	plural	SUBORD	subordinator
PP	postpositional phrase	SUPERL	superlative
POSS	possessive	V	vowel segment
POT	potential	VBLZ	verbalizer
PRED	predicative	VC	verb complex
PRF	perfective	VH	vowel harmony
PROG	progressive	wk	weak grade
PROX	proximal		

1 Introduction

This description of the grammar of the Pite Saami language is intended to provide a general linguistics audience with an overview of phonological and morphosyntactic structures found in the language. It is based on a corpus of spoken language data collected over several years, including both free speech and elicited data. It covers the phonology, morphology and phrasal structures, and how these interact with each other, while also providing a sketch of the clausal phenomena.

The present chapter provides background information on Pite Saami. It includes an overview of the language and its speakers in §1.1, then provides details about the documentation project on which this study is based in §1.2, and finally presents a typological profile in §1.3.

1.1 The Pite Saami language and its speakers

1.1.1 Linguistic genealogy

The Saami languages form a sub-branch of the Uralic language family. Pite Saami is classified as the southern-most Western Saami language in the Northern group. Together, the Saami languages form a dialect continuum; Pite Saami is therefore most closely related to Lule Saami and Ume Saami, the two languages spoken directly to its north and south, respectively.[1] Figure 1.1 on the following page shows the Saami sub-branch of the Uralic family tree.

1.1.2 Names for Pite Saami

While *Pite Saami*[2] is the term used in the present study to refer to the language spoken by the Pite Saami people, the language also has other names. It is also called *Arjeplog Saami* (cf. Lehtiranta 1992), referring to Arjeplog, the main mu-

---

[1] Cf. Sammallahti (1985: 151, 1998: 20–24) and Larsson (1985: 161–162) for more discussion on the linguistic features which motivate the division of the dialect continuum into ten Saami languages.
[2] In English, Saami is also spelled *Sámi* or *Sami*.

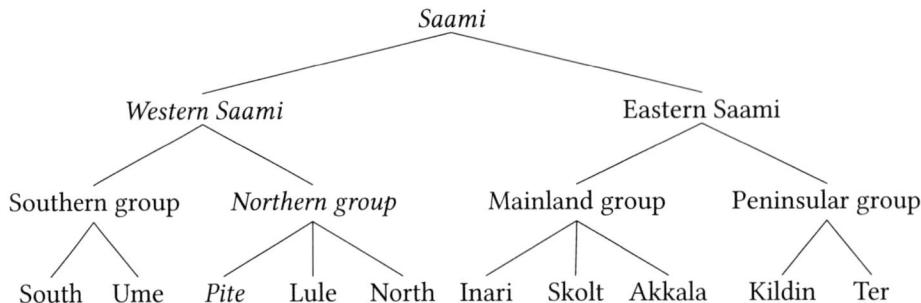

Figure 1.1: Pite Saami within the Saami sub-branch of the Uralic language family (based on Sammallahti 1998: 1–34)

nicipality it is spoken in. The endonym is *bidumsáme giella* or *bisumsáme giella*, which literally mean 'Pite Saami's language', as shown in example (1).

(1) *Bidumsáme giella*
    bidum+sáme giella
    Pite+Saami\GEN.SG language\NOM.SG
    'the Pite Saami language' [pit080621.41m10s]*e*

Nonetheless, speakers of Pite Saami (as is true for speakers of other Saami languages) generally refer to themselves and the individual language they speak simply as 'Saami', without further specification. This is likely the reason why there is no consensus concerning the endonym, which has two forms (see above); indeed, some speakers are quite unsure that an endonym exists at all.

Germanic cultures have often referred to Saami peoples using the exonym *Lapps* (cf. the place name *Lapland*), and thus the language has also been referred to as *Pite Lappish* in the past. This term is no longer considered respectful by many Pite Saami individuals; the name *Saami* is preferred, as it is borrowed from the endonym *sábme* or *sáme*. Nonetheless, a number of speakers I have worked with still refer to their own language as *lapska* when speaking Swedish.

1.1.3 Geography

The Saami languages are spoken in an area traditionally referred to as *Sápmi*; this covers a territory stretching from south-central Norway and central Sweden, across northern Norway, Sweden and Finland and over most of the Kola Peninsula in the Russian Federation, as illustrated in Figure 1.2 on the next page.

There is no official geographic or political unit defining any Pite Saami linguistic or ethnic area, but the individuals (including both speakers and non-speakers)

1.1 The Pite Saami language and its speakers

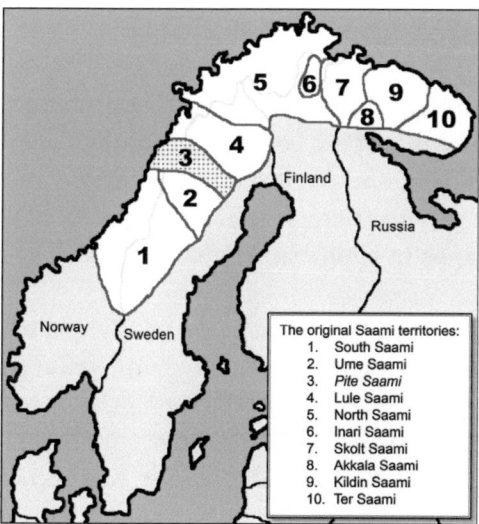

Figure 1.2: A map of Sápmi, the territory in which the Saami languages were traditionally spoken, with Pite Saami shaded in (borrowed from Bull et al. 2007, with permission)

I have met, worked with or heard about who consider themselves to be Pite Saami (regardless of language abilities) all come from an area based roughly on the Arjeplog municipality[3] in Swedish Lapland and bordering areas in Norway. On the Swedish side, this has traditionally been referred to as *Pite lappmark* 'Pite Saami territory'. For instance, Ruong, himself a native speaker of Pite Saami, claims that the "most genuine form" (Ruong 1943: iii; my translation) of the Pite Saami language is spoken by members of the Luokta-Mavas *sameby*,[4] whose summer reindeer grazing lands are located along the headwaters of the Pite River, and by settled Saamis in the same area.[5] Manker's ethnography of the Saami populations in the Swedish mountains (Manker 1947) outlines the three *samebyar*

---

[3] Note that Arjeplog *municipality* (*kommun* in Swedish) refers to the larger administrative district of ca. 15,000 km², while the town of Arjeplog is the main village in the municipality.

[4] A *sameby* (Swedish, literally 'Saami village'; *samebyar* in plural) is a group of reindeer herding families who tend their reindeer together in the same territory.

[5] However, speakers from Semisjaur-Njarg *sameby* to the south were also included as sources in Ruong (1945), indicating that Ruong was clearly aware of the difficulty of drawing distinct language borders in the Saami dialect continuum. He indicates that some areas on the north side of the Pite River drainage speak Lule Saami, while speakers along the Skellefte River drainage are more under the "influence of Southern Saami" (Ruong 1945: iii; my translation).

Luokta-Mavas, Semisjaur-Njarg and Svaipa as part of *Pite lappmark*.⁶ Sammallahti (1998: 22) corroborates this, and adds the forest *sameby* Ståkke to the list. Collinder and Bergsland also help delineate the southern border of Pite Saami territory. Collinder writes that the border "goes along the Pite River between the parishes of Jockmock [sic] and Arvidsjaur, and farther west through the parish of Arjeplog" (1960: 23), while Bergsland further specifies that Ume Saami is spoken by "the forest Lapps in southern Arjeplog [...] and by the mountain Lapps in Sorsele" (1962: 27).

As for the Norwegian side, some Pite Saami reindeer herding families had their summer reindeer grazing lands in the Norwegian territory adjacent to the international border (cf. Manker 1947). The Finno-Ugrian scholar Eliel Lagercrantz worked with Pite Saami speakers whose families originated in the Arjeplog municipality but had resettled to the Beiarn area in Norway (cf. Lagercrantz 1926). Ethnic Pite Saami individuals still live in Norway, and are, for instance, still active in the local Pite Saami association there, *Salten Pitesamisk Forening*.

As a result, one can say that Pite Saami was traditionally spoken in an area spanning both sides of the Norwegian-Swedish border around the municipality of Arjeplog on the Swedish side and across the border into Saltdal and Beiarn municipalities in Norway. On the Swedish side, the Pite Saami area is essentially limited to the Pite River drainage above the waterfall at Storforsen, and the sections of the Skellefte River drainage from the town of Arjeplog and farther upriver. The map in Figure 1.3 on the facing page gives a rough idea of the traditional geographic area, which is the light area on the map. It is based on Lagercrantz (1926), Ruong (1943), Manker (1947), Bergsland (1962) and Sammallahti (1998), as well as on my own knowledge gained by discussing family histories with Pite Saami individuals.

My own research indicates that Pite Saami is currently still spoken by a few members of the Luokta-Mavas, Semisjaur-Njarg and Ståkke *samebyar*, as well as by settled Saami families from the same areas. Furthermore there are a few speakers from the Arjeplog municipality who have since moved to other areas outside of Arjeplog municipality, even as far away as southern Sweden. Ethnic Pite Saami individuals from Norway have indicated to me that the last Pite Saami speakers on the Norwegian side died several generations ago.

---

⁶ Manker (1947: 473) includes a map of all Swedish *samebyar* as a fold-out, and a map of these three Pite Saami *samebyar*.

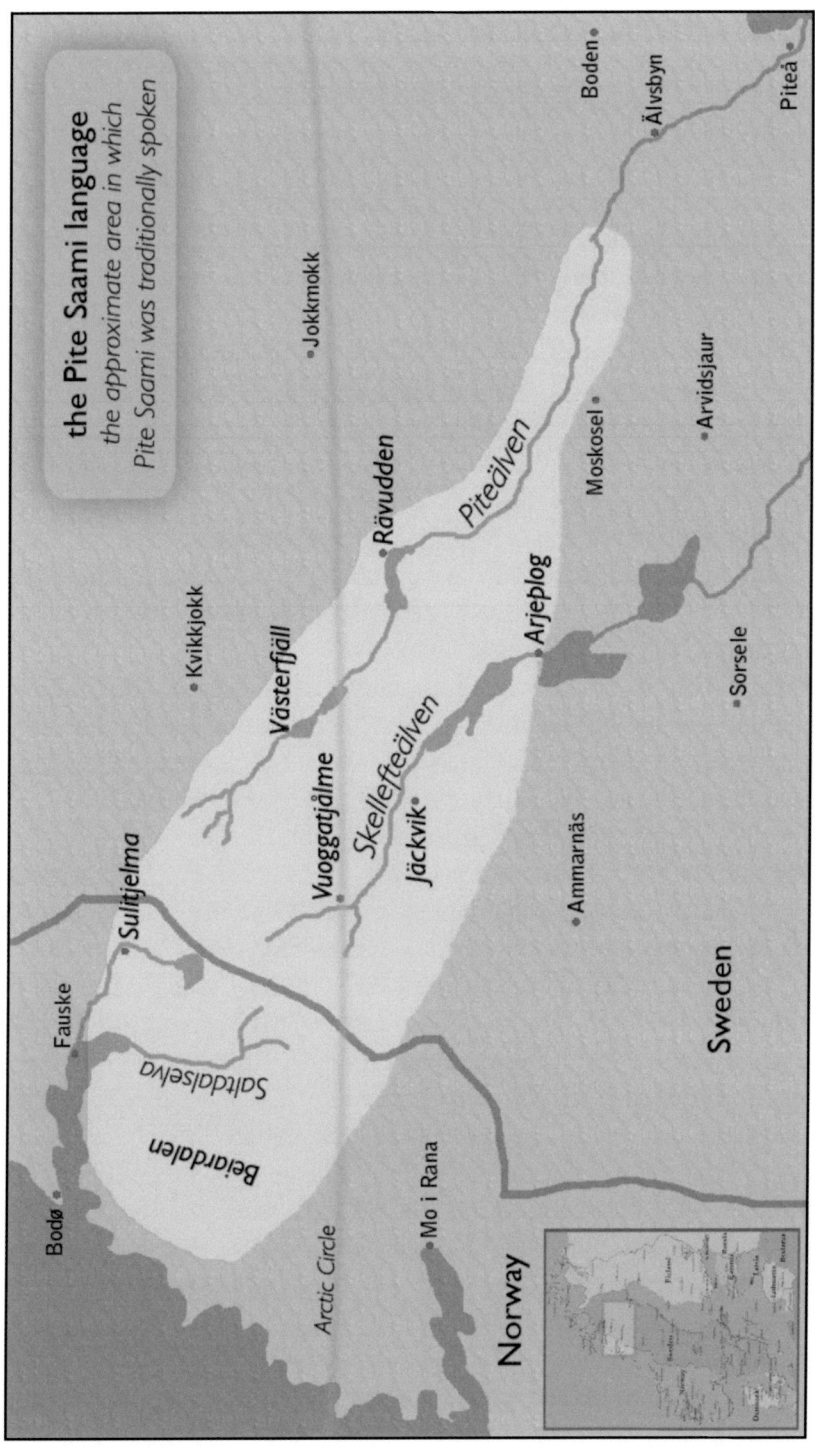

Figure 1.3: An approximate map of the territory in which the Pite Saami language was traditionally spoken

1 Introduction

1.1.4 The state of the Pite Saami language

Traditionally, most Pite Saami families lived either as semi-nomadic reindeer herders or as sedentary farmers, fishers and hunters. Despite having always been in contact, these two groups lived very different lifestyles, and spoke Saami in relative isolation from one another. While reindeer herding Saami have often been a topic of Saami studies, the settled Saami are neglected or even actively prejudiced against for not being 'true' Saami since they do not herd reindeer. The data supporting the present study and gathered as part of the Pite Saami Documentation Project (cf. §1.2.2) originated from both groups.

By the eighteenth century, the Saami peoples had, in general, been converted from animistic polytheism to Christianity, marking the beginning of Saami assimilation to North Germanic culture (cf. Pulkkinen 2005). Strict policies in the mid-nineteenth century sent Pite Saami children to special 'nomad schools' where they were not allowed to speak Saami. Attending these schools also kept them away from their families and from regularly participating in Pite Saami life, while reinforcing the state's drive to exclusively promote Swedish culture and social values (cf. Valijärvi & Wilbur 2011).

Accompanying this shift, traditional realms of Pite Saami experience are slowly being left behind in favor of Swedish ones. With the introduction of modern conveniences, most Pite Saami individuals have moved to permanent dwellings in populated communities, particularly Arjeplog, thereby leaving behind traditional ways of life. Along with this demographic shift, they are also losing the need to carry out traditional occupations using the Pite Saami language. As a result, all Pite Saami speakers today speak Swedish fluently, and indeed use Swedish significantly more often in everyday life (cf. Valijärvi & Wilbur 2011).

A gradual reverse in political and social policies in Sweden over the last decades led initially to the acceptance and then to the active promotion of multiculturalism, particularly concerning the Saami people. This has helped to positively change attitudes towards Pite Saami identity. However, concerning the Pite Saami language and many traditional cultural realms, this change seems inadequate for revitalization. For instance, the Swedish government's minority language law from 2010 only applies the blanket term *samiska* ('the Saami language'), and, in doing so, completely disregards the reality that there are five different Saami languages in Sweden. Even within *Sápmi*, Pite Saami is threatened by larger Saami languages, in particular by North Saami, which has an active speech community of around 30,000 speakers, regular television, radio, print and internet resources, and first-language instruction in public school (cf. Salminen 2007: 209–211). The robust status of North Saami in addition to the lack of an officially recognized Pite Saami orthography allow local government agencies to conveniently support North Saami alone in fulfilling the language law's requirements; any positive effects on the Pite Saami language are essentially negated.

According to my own data collected from Pite Saami individuals during fieldwork, there are around 30 speakers left,[7] of around 2000 ethnic Pite Saami individuals (Krauss 1997: 24). With one exception, all speakers are older than 50. Based on my own observations, all speakers are fluent in the Swedish language, even if many of them did not learn Swedish until they began school. Indeed, Swedish dominates everyday life for most speakers today, particularly for those who do not work in reindeer husbandry, and for those not living in the traditional Pite Saami area. Only a few households (less than five) use Pite Saami on a regular basis at home or in family situations, and these are still involved in reindeer husbandry. In public realms, the language is rarely used today. For a more detailed description and analysis of the situation the language is currently in, see Valijärvi & Wilbur (2011).

1.2 Linguistic documentation of Pite Saami

The Pite Saami language has been the subject of academic research in the past; cf. Halász (1896), Lagercrantz (1926), Ruong (1943) and Lehtiranta (1992). This extant body of research was consulted in coming to terms with Pite Saami linguistic structures in creating the present description. However, in fulfilling the goal of describing the Pite Saami language as it is spoken in the early 21st century, the Pite Saami Documentation Project corpus, collected from 2008 through 2013, is the main source of data. With this in mind, I consider this a corpus-based description, as opposed to a literature-based description, which would have attempted to incorporate these previous works to a much greater extent. Indeed, everything not specifically cited as coming from another source is based on my own analysis of the corpus. The current description will hopefully be seen as a supplement to previous work on Pite Saami, and together with previous studies, can facilitate exploring language change as exemplified by a severely endangered language.

In the following sections, previous studies on Pite Saami are summarized in §1.2.1. The current corpus and the documentation involved in creating it are described in §1.2.2. Then §1.2.3 provides a short guide to using this description.

---

[7] Cf. Salminen (2007: 221), who claims there are only 10 speakers, while the English abstract in Lehtiranta (1992) erroneously claims that the Pite Saami language is "now extinct."

1.2.1 Previous studies

In the late 19th century the Hungarian scholar Ignácz Halász studied Pite Saami, and wrote several studies in Hungarian on the language. *Lule- és Pite-lappmarki nyelvmutatvéanyok és szótár*[8] (Halász 1885) contains the Gospel of Matthew in Lule Saami, and a combined Lule Saami/Pite Saami wordlist with translations in Hungarian and German. *Népköltési gyüjtemény: a Pite Lappmark Arjepluogi egyházkerületéböl*[9] (Halász 1893) consists of a significant text collection of short Pite Saami texts, transcribed using the traditional Finno-Ugrian transcription. Each text is translated as a whole into Hungarian. The majority of the texts are traditional narratives, and a few poems and songs are also transcribed and translated. *Pite lappmarki szótár és nyelvtan*[10] (Halász 1896) includes morphological paradigms and a Pite Saami wordlist with translations into Hungarian and German.

Sprachlehre des Westlappischen nach der Mundart von Arjeplog[11] (Lagercrantz 1926) is a grammar in German. It is based on three months of fieldwork during which Lagercrantz consulted three Pite Saami individuals who had settled in the Beiarn district in Norway but who were originally from the Arjeplog municipality. The book covers semantically driven descriptions of clause structures, a limited description of morphology, and an extended analysis of the phonological system, based on phonetic acoustic experiments.

Lappische Verbalableitung dargestellt auf Grundlage des Pitelappischen[12] (Ruong 1943) is the dissertation of Israel Ruong, who later became professor of Saami languages and culture at Uppsala universitet. Ruong's native language was Pite Saami; his dissertation, an elaborate categorization of Pite Saami verb derivations, is his only study specifically dealing with the Pite Saami language.

Arjeploginsaamen äänne- ja taivutusopin pääpiirteet[13] (Lehtiranta 1992) is a Finnish-language description of Pite Saami phonology and inflectional patterns, and is based on recordings, publications and archived materials on Pite Saami from 1950 and earlier. Some paradigms can be found at the end of the book, as well as several Pite Saami texts with phonetic and orthographic transcriptions, as well as Finnish translations. The phonetic transcriptions are presented in the transcription standard used in Finno-Ugrian studies.

---

[8] 'Linguistic samples and a wordlist from Lule and Pite Saami territory'.
[9] 'Collection of traditional verses from the bishopric of Arjeplog in Pite Saami territory'.
[10] 'Wordlist and grammatical description from Pite Saami territory'.
[11] 'A grammar of West Saami based on the Arjeplog dialect'.
[12] 'Saami verbal derivation as illustrated by Pite Saami'.
[13] 'The fundamentals of Arjeplog Saami phonology and inflection'.

Note that these studies deal with Pite Saami as it was spoken before 1950. Finno-Ugristian studies have traditionally dealt with historical-comparative studies, and have not always been concerned with the synchronic state of Saami languages. Indeed, the distance some scholars keep from the synchronic situation is highlighted by the erroneous claim by Lehtiranta that Pite Saami is "now extinct" (Lehtiranta 1992: English abstract). Consequently, the present study is the first extensive description of the Pite Saami language in English and for a general linguistic audience.

Since the present study is intended to be a synchronic description of the Pite Saami language as used in the early 21st century and reflected by the Pite Saami Documentation Project corpus, the previous work mentioned above have played an indirect but important role in its creation. However, these works were referred to in detail particularly when the data from the corpus were not substantial enough to allow relatively certain conclusions to be drawn. Data based at least partly on sources other than the documentation corpus are clearly marked as such in this description. Specifically, the sections in Lagercrantz (1926) concerning phrasal and sentence-level syntactic phenomena in Part A '*Ausdruckslehre*' (pp. 19–99) were informative, while Part B '*Formenlehre*' (pp. 103-141), the paradigms throughout Halász (1896) as well as the paradigms in the appendix to Lehtiranta (1992: 150–166) were consulted regarding morphology. In writing Chapter 10 on derivational morphology, Ruong's thesis (particularly Chapters 6 through 40, which present his data) provided valuable insights into the variety and complexity of Pite Saami derivation from both morphological and semantic perspectives.

In addition to the academic linguistic studies mentioned above, a number of other texts exist concerning the Pite Saami language and its people. Valijärvi & Wilbur (2011) describe the current state of the Pite Saami language from the point of view of sociology of language. Sjaggo (2010) deals with the etymology of a selection of Pite Saami place names along the river Piteälven in the Arjeplog municipality. A large number of Pite Saami *vuole*[14] (songs in the Saami singing tradition of *yoik*) were recorded in the first half of the 20th century. These can be found transcribed in a number of works: Tirén (1942) includes 139 transcriptions of Pite Saami melodies and lyrics, with German translations; Grundström & Väisänen (1958) have 93 songs by Jonas Eriksson Steggo in the form of transcribed melodies and lyrics, with translations in Swedish and German; Grundström & Smedeby (1963) provide 73 songs by a variety of Pite Saami individuals in the form of transcribed melodies and lyrics, also with translations in Swedish

---

[14] This is nominative plural; the nominative singular form is *vuolle*.

1 Introduction

and German. Wickman (1964) discusses a short Pite Saami text from a recording done in 1939 by Israel Ruong; the text is presented in three transcription standards (Finno-Ugrian close phonetic standard, the author's own phonemic transcription, and a modified North Saami orthography) and includes an English translation. Lars Rensund's books (1982, 1986) detail personal recollections by the author, himself a Pite Saami, and are interspersed with sentences and occasionally entire narratives in Pite Saami. Bylund (1956) provides an in-depth study of the colonization of Pite Saami territory by Swedish settlers up to the middle of the 19th century. No educational materials, bible translations or other common texts exist in the Pite Saami language. With the exception of the works by Lars Rensund, most Pite Saami speakers today are not aware of any of the works mentioned above.

1.2.2 The Pite Saami Documentation Project corpus

The data forming the basis of the present study were collected as a part of the Pite Saami Documentation Project. This description is a direct result of that project, the main goal of which is the linguistic documentation of the Pite Saami language. The project has so far resulted in audio and video recordings documenting current language usage and grammatical structures and includes an archived corpus comprising 29,208 transcribed and translated Pite Saami words (as of early March 2014; cf. the Appendix for a list of recordings). From June 2008 until July 2011, the project was carried out by Joshua Wilbur at the Nordeuropa-Institut at Humboldt-Universität zu Berlin, with support from the Endangered Languages Documentation Programme (ELDP; a part of the Hans Rausing Endangered Languages Project, with financial support from the Arcadia foundation and hosted by the School for Oriental and African Studies (SOAS) at the University of London). A continuation of the project is underway in 2013 and 2014 at Albert-Ludwigs-Universität Freiburg thanks to generous continued funding from ELDP.

Current trends in documentary linguistics were taken into account.[15] Himmelmann's proposal that "a language documentation is a lasting multipurpose record of a language" (Himmelmann 2006: 1) is a defining motivation behind the project. Accordingly, the resulting documentation consists of a documentation corpus of a variety of linguistic genres, including Pite Saami situations potentially of interest to non-linguistic disciplines and to members of the Pite Saami

---

[15] Cf. Bird & Simons (2003), Gippert et al. (2006), Woodbury (2011), Austin & Sallabank (2011), Grenoble & Furbee (2010), the book series *Language Documentation and Description*, among others.

1.2 Linguistic documentation of Pite Saami

language community themselves, as well as the present description. Initial results have been archived at five archives at international, national, regional and local levels:

- *The Endangered Languages Archive* (ELAR) at the School for Oriental and African Studies in London;

- *The Language Archive* at the Max Planck Institute for Psycholinguistics in Nijmegen;

- *Dialekt-, ortnamns och folkminnesarkivet i Umeå*[16] (DAUM) in Umeå, Sweden;

- *Ájtte: Svenskt Fjäll- och Samemuseum*[17] in Jokkmokk, Sweden;

- *Silvermuseet*[18] in Arjeplog, Sweden.

Working with multiple archiving sites as well as having all data in a digital format help ensure accessibility to and longevity of the data.

Access to the materials is available via the archives (in some cases, this is possible via the world wide web). Ideally, an archive should provide interested parties with access to archived materials, while respecting the privacy and the wishes of recording participants as necessary; with this in mind, access rights to the data related to any given session reflect the wishes of speakers involved in a specific session concerning availability to the linguistics and other scientific communities, the Pite Saami and greater Saami communities, and other individuals and groups in general. Furthermore, as part of a scientific endeavor, the claims made in this book about Pite Saami linguistic structures should be reproducible; with this in mind, the original data are available to the academic community via the Language Archive at the Max Planck Institute for Psycholinguistics in Nijmegen, the Netherlands; see §1.2.3.2 for more details on accessing the archive.

1.2.2.1 Collection methods

Data were collected and recordings were transcribed during a total of 23 months at the field site in and around Arjeplog, Sweden, with the invaluable assistance

---

[16] 'The Department of Dialectology, Onomastics and Folklore Research in Umeå'.
[17] 'Ájtte: the Swedish Mountain and Saami Museum'; *ájtte* is the Lule Saami word for a traditional Saami storage shed.
[18] 'The Silver Museum'.

1 Introduction

of a number of Pite Saami speakers. They were compensated for their time and effort with a modest consultant honorarium.

The documentation corpus consists of more than 55 hours of recordings covering a variety of genres; cf. the Appendix for a list of recordings, including an indication of genre and medium. As the morphological structure of Pite Saami words is quite complex, it was necessary to rely on elicitation techniques to gather a sufficient number of word forms for a wide variety of lexemes as a basis for morphological analyses. As a result, the majority of recordings (approximately 45 hours) consist of elicitation sessions intended to gather specific details concerning the structure of the language. These were often conducted using Swedish as a metalanguage, but Pite Saami was used whenever efficient and useful, and more frequently in recordings made later in the project. A variety of elicitation methods were used. To a large extent, elicitation sessions were conducted as translational interviews (particularly in early recordings to collect initial wordlists) and sentence completion (using both Swedish and Pite Saami triggers, mostly to complete morphology paradigms). However, other methods were used as well, such as vocabulary card ordering tasks to test syntactic structures, and tasks using toy blocks to gather data on spatial relations. Many non-elicitation linguistic situations were also recorded, covering genres such as conversations, explanations, narrations, performances, as well as songs and readings; in the current documentation corpus, such recordings comprise approximately 17,700 transcribed words. A few written texts were also collected to supplement recordings.

Each collection of materials[19] in the corpus corresponds to a recorded linguistic event. Each collection has a unique name based on the pattern:

pitYYMMDDabc

(pit = Pite Saami, YYMMDD = abbreviated date of recording with a two-digit year, abc = further disambiguation as needed). Recordings done for the project from 2012 onwards use the ISO 639-3 code *sje* as a prefix for session names instead of *pit*, and a four-digit year; e.g., sje20121014b. All digital files related to a certain collection are named based on this pattern.

In almost all cases, the following recording equipment, standards and software were used for documentation. A small number of deviations exist, and are indicated in the archived metadata for the relevant sessions.

---

[19] Note that the archive at the Max Planck Institute for Psycholinguistics in Nijmegen, the Netherlands, refers to the entire collection of files concerning a single recording as a 'session', not a 'collection'.

1.2 Linguistic documentation of Pite Saami

Video: a Panasonic NV-GS500EG-S video camera using miniDV cassettes in short play (SP) mode, using a wide-angle lens attachment and a tripod. In most cases, a RØDE SVM stereo video microphone was mounted on the camera for audio in place of using the built-in microphone.

Audio: an Edirol R-09 digital audio recorder set to record 16-bit WAV format at 44.1 kHz. A variety of microphones was used, depending on the specific recording situation; these included a RØDE SVM stereo video microphone, a Sennheiser lapel microphone connected to a Sennheiser EW 112-p G2 wireless set and a Sennheiser MKE 300 shotgun microphone.

Still images: a Canon IXUS 80IS digital photo camera was used to take digital photographs to supplement documentation. Images are in JPEG format.

Editing/Computing: video/audio recordings were transferred to a Macintosh MacBook Pro for further editing, as necessary. Video was edited using Final Cut Express and Final Cut Pro software. Audio was archived in the original quality, while video was compressed to MPEG-2 or MPEG-4 format.

Transcribing/annotating: the multimedia annotation program ELAN[20] was used to transcribe and annotate recordings. Annotation/transcription files are archived in both ELAN format and in plain text format.

Initial transcriptions of recordings were completed with the help of native speaker assistants.[21] Transcriptions in the corpus are written in various versions of the Pite Saami orthography under development by the wordlist project *Insamling av pitesamiska ord* (cf. §1.2.3.4), but have been standardized according to the principles explained in §1.2.3.4 when cited in this book. All transcribed words are provided with annotations in the form of at least a translation into English or Swedish or as morpheme-by-morpheme glosses. Such glosses can serve as the sole translation of a transcribed word or utterance, particularly for data from transcribed elicitation sessions. Both glosses and free translations into English and/or Swedish may be provided, especially in non-elicited text genres. Relevant notes or commentary may also exist as annotations.

Metadata were collected in a database using the FileMaker Pro program, then exported to XML and plain text formats for archiving. Information collected concerns participants, the recording situation, location, equipment used and a summary of the contents of the recording, among other things.

Any given collection consists minimally of the following set of digital files:

- audio recording in WAV format (16-bit, 44 kHz)

---

[20] ELAN is free software developed by the Technical Group of the Max Planck Institute for Psycholinguistics (see www.lat-mpi.eu/tools/elan/).

[21] I am particularly indebted to Elsy Rankvist for her invaluable transcription assistance.

13

1 Introduction

- transcription/annotation file in ELAN and in plain text format
- metadata concerning the session in XML and plain text formats
- metadata concerning the entire collection in XML

In addition to the above files, collections may also include the following files:

- video recording in MPEG-2 or MPEG-4 format
- digital images in JPEG format
- other supplementary files

The transcription/annotation files are divided into numbered, utterance-based units and include at least a transcription of any Pite Saami language usage. A specific utterance can be referred to using the collection/session name and the utterance number. The Pite Saami original is translated into Swedish and/or English, and provided with linguistic glosses. Other comments are included as well, whenever deemed relevant or useful. Finally, in cases with code-switching, the language being used in a certain utterance, or part thereof, is indicated. Tiers in all ELAN files are organized hierarchically based on the template in Figure 1.4 for each speaking participant in a recording, plus a 'notes' tier for general comments. A list of all recordings in the corpus can be found in the Appendix on page 261, including brief descriptions of content and an indication of the number of Pite Saami words transcribed and translated per recording.

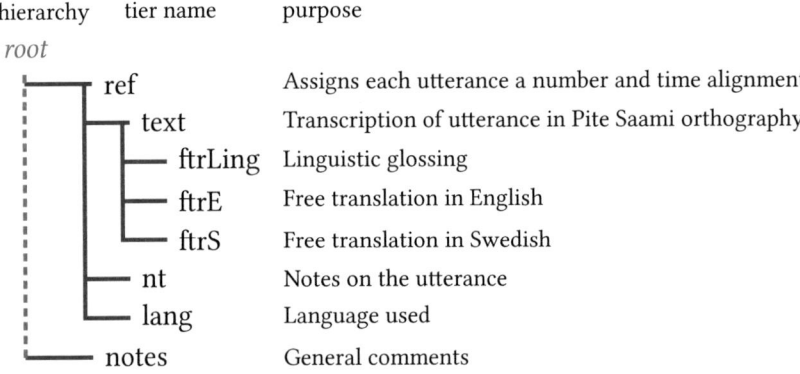

Figure 1.4: ELAN tier hierarchy used in the documentation corpus

1.2.3 Using this description

This description of the grammar and the accompanying documentation corpus are together intended to outline the structural features of the Pite Saami language and provide an empirical foundation for claims made in the present work. In addition, the documentation should give interested individuals (linguists, Saami individuals, etc.) the opportunity to explore other aspects of the language as well. Finally, it should also secure a record of the language as spoken by those Pite Saami individuals who likely comprise the last generations of speakers for future generations of ethnic Pite Saami individuals.

The following sections are meant to assist in utilizing both the description and the accompanying documentation corpus. The first section (§1.2.3.1) deals with accountability and verifiability, while the second section (§1.2.3.2) provides brief instructions on how to access data from the corpus. Then, §1.2.3.3 illustrates how examples from the corpus are presented. Finally, §1.2.3.4 covers orthographic considerations and includes a list of phonemes and the graphemes used to represent these. A list of symbols and abbreviations used in the present work is provided starting on page xiii.

1.2.3.1 Accountability and verifiability

Data in the present study are cited with a bracketed reference to the collection name followed by the specific utterance number or timecode within a recording. This should allow the reader to easily find the evidence cited and make his/her own judgement about the conclusions made. References to specific recordings marked with '*e*' after the closing bracket indicate that the presented utterance was attained during an elicitation session. For instance, the reference

[pit090930a.239]*e*

refers to utterance number *239* on recording *pit090930a*, and indicates that this example is from an elicitation session.

In order to verify, scrutinize or otherwise review the actual primary data on which the present study is based, the data can be accessed via one of the archives listed in §1.2.2. Specific instructions are provided in the following section.

1.2.3.2 Accessing archived materials

The archivists at the IMDI archive located at the Max Planck Institute for Psycholinguistics in Nijmegen, the Netherlands, have kindly agreed to host the Pite

1 Introduction

Saami Documentation Project spoken language corpus. For those interested in accessing the data in connection with the present description, I recommend using this archive. Pite Saami materials are available via the on-line IMDI-browser at http://corpus1.mpi.nl/ds/imdi_browser/ under the hierarchical node: Endangered Languages/Donated Corpora/Pan-Saami Language Archive/Pite.

1.2.3.3 Explaining examples

Examples from the corpus are numbered consecutively for easy reference, and consist of several lines of text. The spoken text is presented in italics in the initial line in the orthographic standard, followed by interpretive information in the form of a morpheme-by-morpheme breakdown in the second line and English glosses in the third line. Finally, the last line contains a free translation in English and a reference to the source recording in the corpus; this reference includes either the number of the specific utterance or its initial time code.[22] Examples are formatted as shown in Figure 1.5.

(no.) *Pite Saami original text*
       Pite Saami text with morpheme boundari-es
       Morpheme-by-morpheme glossing
       'free English translation'   [source]

Figure 1.5: Template used in examples of utterances

In Chapter 2 on prosody and Chapter 3 on segmental phonology, many examples of individual words are provided to illustrate phonological aspects of Pite Saami. In most cases, the phonological representation and phonetic realization (both using IPA standards) and the orthographic representation (based on the current working version) are included, as well as a gloss and a reference to the source recording, as summarized in Figure 1.6 on the next page. In such examples, the phonemic representation also indicates any linear morpheme boundaries. The source recording for these words indicates the recording name and utterance number or time code in most cases. However, when only a four-digit number is present (e.g., [0457]), this indicates that the original recording is not from the documentation corpus, but from the Wordlist Project (cf. §1.2.3.4). The number refers to the record number of the word in the Wordlist Project's lexical

---

[22] A source recording reference followed by '*e*' indicates that the example shown was from elicited data; cf. §1.2.3.1.

1.2 Linguistic documentation of Pite Saami

```
(no.)   /phonem-ic/        orthography                        [source]
        [phonetic]         'gloss'
```

Figure 1.6: Template used in examples for individual words

database, as collected by the members of the Wordlist Project. The database and recordings of the individual lexical items are archived at the IMDI archive located at the Max Planck Institute for Psycholinguistics in Nijmegen, the Netherlands (cf. §1.2.3.2). Some examples in Chapter 10 on derivational morphology are also from this lexical database, and are marked in the same way.

1.2.3.4 Orthographic considerations

At the time of writing, Pite Saami does not have an officially recognized orthography. In the past, adapted versions of the Swedish orthographic standards[23] and Lule Saami orthographies[24] have been used to write Pite Saami for a non-technical, non-linguistic audience. However, from 2008 through 2011, *Arjeplogs sameförening* (the local Saami association in Arjeplog) received funding to complete a lexicographic project called *Insamling av pitesamiska ord*,[25] (cf. Bengtsson et al. 2011) and hereinafter referred to simply as 'the Wordlist Project'. One of the outcomes of the Wordlist Project was a working orthography for Pite Saami. I have attempted to adopt this working orthographic standard in writing Pite Saami data in this description and the transcriptions provided in the accompanying documentation. This orthography uses the Swedish alphabet and many Swedish sound-to-grapheme correspondences, but also resembles to some extent Lule Saami orthographic systems, particularly the most recent one as found in Korhonen (2005). To help understand the orthography, the correlations between sounds and graphemes are discussed here and listed in Table 1.1 starting on page 19 for consonants, and in Table 1.2 on page 22 for vowels. Chapter 3 describes the segmental phonology represented by these graphemes in detail. An orthography proposal for the Pite Saami language, including a more thorough description of these rules, is currently being put together by the members of the

---

[23] Cf. Lars Rensund's books (1982; 1986).

[24] E.g., at literacy courses for Pite Saami individuals held in Arjeplog occasionally during the last decade and sponsored by the Swedish Saami Parliament.

[25] This translates roughly as "collecting Pite Saami words". A working version of the resulting lexical database is currently available online at: http://saami.uni-freiburg.de/psdp/pite-lex/. The database as well as recordings of individual entries are available at the IMDI archive located at the Max Planck Institute for Psycholinguistics in Nijmegen, the Netherlands (cf. §1.2.3.2).

1 Introduction

Wordlist Project and the Pite Saami Documentation Project, and is scheduled to be published, together with the Wordlist Project's wordlist, in late 2014 with funding from Arjeplog municipality (cf. Wilbur forthcoming 2014).

It is important to note that the standards used in this book are based on a *working* orthography, i.e., it is still subject to inconsistencies and potentially to further refinement. Moreover, the following description and the implementation of the orthography is based on my interpretation of the recurring patterns used by the Wordlist Project in developing the orthography proposal mentioned above. While I generally use the spellings found in the Wordlist Project's wordlist, some deviations may be found in this description and the accompanying transcriptions; these can be due to a variety of factors such as changes to the wordlist as it was developed, deviating analyses on my own behalf, or simple inconsistencies in spelling (a natural occurrence in the development of an orthography) in the source. However, I alone am ultimately responsible for the orthographic choices in the present work.

The unaspirated singleton plosive phonemes are normally represented by the graphemes <b>, <d> and <g>, except as a single word-final consonant, in which case <p>, <t> and <k> are used; this is illustrated for the alveolar plosive phoneme /t/ in (2) through (4).

(2)   /taːlːve/   *dállve*   'winter'

(3)   /pɔtav/   *bådav*   'come (1SG.PRS)'

(4)   /pɔʰtet/   *båhtet*   'come (INF)'

The affricate phonemes are represented by the digraphs <ts> and <tj>; this is illustrated in (5) and (6).

(5)   /tsigːet/   *tsigget*   'set up'

(6)   /almatʃ/   *almatj*   'person'

In general, geminate consonants are written by doubling the relevant grapheme, as illustrated in (7) through (9).

(7)   /kɔtːet/   *gåddet*   'kill'

(8)   /kaːfːa/   *káffa*   'coffee'

(9)   /maŋːel/   *maŋŋel*   'after'

However, geminate segments represented by digraphs, such as <sj> for /ʃ/ or <tj> for /tʃ/ are written by doubling the initial grapheme, as in (10) through (12).

(10) /pɔʃ:o/ *båssjo* 'kitchen'

(11) /maɲ:e/ *mannje* 'daughter-in-law'

(12) /kɔtʃ:ɔt/ *gåttjåt* 'urinate'

Preaspiration is represented by <h> when the preaspirated segment is the initial segment in the consonant center (cf. §2.2.2.4), as in (13) and (14).

(13) /pɔʰtet/ *båhtet* 'come'

(14) /aːʰtʃ:e/ *áhttje* 'father'

If a preaspirated segment is preceded by a sonorant consonant segment, then the preaspiration itself is not marked by a grapheme of its own, as in (15) through (17).

(15) /mur:ʰko/ *murrko* 'fog'

(16) /kum:ʰpe/ *gummpe* 'wolf'

(17) /vu͡an:ʰtsa/ *vuanntsa* 'hen'

For plosives, the preaspiration is evident nonetheless because the corresponding plain segments are spelled differently, using <b, d, g>. However, the current working version of the orthography does not provide a way to distinguish between preaspirated affricates preceded by a sonorant segment, e.g., (17), and plain affricates preceded by a sonorant segment.

In spoken Pite Saami, when the copular and auxiliary verb *lä* is preceded by a word ending in an open syllable, it is often encliticized as *l* on that preceding word. To reflect this in the orthography, *lä* is then written as *'l* immediately following the preceding word, as in (18) and (19).

(18) *gunne lä dån* → *gunne'l dån* 'Where are you?'

(19) *dállke lä bivval* → *dállke'l bivval* 'The weather is warm.'

1 Introduction

Table 1.1: Consonant phonemes and their corresponding graphemes/multigraphs in the working version of the Pite Saami orthography

phoneme (IPA)	grapheme or graphemes	context
p	b	default grapheme
	p	word-finally; first C in a C-cluster
ʰp	hp	default digraph
	p	after sonorant C in C-center
pː	bb	default digraph
	pp	first C in a C-cluster
ʰpː	hpp	default trigraph
t	d	default grapheme
	t	word-finally; first C in a C-cluster
ʰt	ht	default digraph
	t	after sonorant C in C-center
tː	dd	default digraph
	tt	first C in a C-cluster
ʰtː	htt	default trigraph
k	g	default grapheme
	k	word-finally; first C in a C-cluster
ʰk	hk	default digraph
	k	after sonorant C in C-center
kː	gg	default digraph
	kk	first C in a C-cluster
ʰkː	hkk	default trigraph
ts	ts	default digraph
ʰts	hts	default trigraph
	ts	after sonorant C in C-center
tsː	dts	default trigraph
ʰtsː	htts	default tetragraph
tʃ	tj	default digraph
ʰtʃ	htj	default trigraph
	tj	after sonorant C in C-center
tʃː	dtj	default trigraph
ʰtʃː	httj	default tetragraph

Table 1.1: Consonant phonemes and their corresponding graphemes/multigraphs in the working version of the Pite Saami orthography *(continued)*

phoneme (IPA)	grapheme or graphemes	context
f	*f*	default grapheme
fː	*ff*	default digraph
v	*v*	default grapheme
vː	*vv*	default digraph
s	*s*	default grapheme
sː	*ss*	default digraph
ʃ	*sj*	default digraph
ʃː	*ssj*	default trigraph
h	*h*	default grapheme
m	*m*	default grapheme
mː	*mm*	default digraph
n	*n*	default grapheme
nː	*nn*	default digraph
ɲ	*nj*	default grapheme
ɲː	*nnj*	default trigraph
ŋ	*ŋ*	default grapheme
ŋː	*ŋŋ*	default digraph
r	*r*	default grapheme
rː	*rr*	default digraph
l	*l*	default grapheme
lː	*ll*	default digraph
j	*j*	default grapheme
jː	*jj*	default digraph

1 Introduction

Table 1.2: Vowel phonemes and their corresponding graphemes/digraphs in the working-version of the Pite Saami orthography

phoneme (IPA)	grapheme or graphemes	context
aː	á	default grapheme
a	a	default grapheme
ɛ	ä	default grapheme
e	e	default grapheme
	ie	in V1
i	i	default grapheme
u	u	default grapheme
o	o	default grapheme
	uo	in V1
ɔ	å	default grapheme
u͡a	ua	default digraph
	uä	allophone (umlaut)

1.3 Typological profile

Pite Saami is a Western Saami language in the Saamic branch of the Uralic language family. It is currently spoken by around thirty speakers in and around the Arjeplog municipality in Swedish Lapland. (Cf. §1.1 for more details on the current state of the language.)

With the exception of a limited number of grammatical items, Pite Saami words consist minimally of one trochaic foot. All non-final odd syllables are stressed, with the initial syllable being most prominent. (Cf. Chapter 2.)

There are 43 consonant phonemes and 9 vowel phonemes. With the exception of the glottal fricative /h/, there is a length distinction for all consonants (singleton and geminate pairs). There are both voiceless and preaspirated plosive and affricate phonemes. Geminates and preaspirated segments are restricted to foot-medial position. Vowel length is only distinctive in open front position (/a/ and /aː/). (Cf. Chapter 3.)

Linear morphology in Pite Saami is exclusively suffixing. However, grammatical categories are often expressed non-linearly as well. This can take the form of foot-internal consonant alternations, umlaut in the first vowel of the initial foot, and regressive vowel harmony between both vowels of a foot.

1.3 Typological profile

Nouns inflect for number and nine cases. Verbs inflect for person, number, tense and mood. Adjectives come in sets of attributive and predicative forms that are not regularly derivable from one another; attributive adjectives do not inflect, while predicative adjectives inflect for number. Number distinctions are limited to singular and plural for nouns, non-personal pronouns and predicative adjectives, but also exhibit a dual category in pronouns and in verb agreement morphology. (Cf. §4.1 for a brief introduction to Pite Saami morphology; details on inflectional morphology can be found throughout Chapters 5 through 9.)

There are seven word classes (verbs, nominals, adjectivals, adverbs, postpositions, conjunctions and interjections); these can be distinguished by syntactic criteria as well as their behavior concerning inflectional morphology. Nouns, verbs, adjectives and adverbs can be derived using linear and/or non-linear morphological processes. (Cf. §4.2 for an overview of the various word forms; Chapter 5 on nouns; Chapter 6 on pronouns; Chapter 7 on adjectivals; Chapter 8 on verbs; Chapter 9 on the other word classes; Chapter 10 provides some examples for derivational morphology.)

Nominal, adjectival, adverbial and postpositional phrases and the verb complex constitute the main components of Pite Saami clauses, and are covered in Chapter 11.

Pite Saami has nominative/accusative argument alignment. Basic clauses consist minimally of a single finite verb form and potentially further non-finite verb forms, as well as any arguments, complements and adjuncts. Copular clauses require the fully inflected copular verb. Negation is expressed by the fully inflected verb of negation in combination with a special non-finite form of the negated lexical verb. Polar interrogatives can be identified by a question marker, but this is exceptionally rare in current Pite Saami usage. Clause-level possession can be expressed using a transitive verb with the possessor as the subject and the possessum as the object, or using a copular phrase with the possessum as the subject and the possessor in an oblique case. Relativization uses a relative pronoun introducing a relative clause with a fully inflected finite verb; the relative pronoun is not restricted in the syntactic role it has in the relative clause. Constituent order is not determined syntactically, but by information structure. (Chapters 12 through 14 deal with clause-level syntax.)

The Pite Saami language exhibits a number of features which are potentially remarkable from a general typological point of view, even if most of these features are not particularly unusual among the Saami languages. A selection of such features and the sections that deal with these are listed in Table 1.3 on the next page.

1 Introduction

Table 1.3: A selection of potentially interesting features in Pite Saami from a typological perspective

feature	section
utterance-final voicelessness	§2.3.2
preaspirated phonemes	§3.1.1.1
phonemic length distinction for all consonants	§3.1.1.2
morphological categories commonly expressed via stem alternations	§4.1.2
three-way number distinction in personal pronouns and verb agreement	§6.1, §8.1.1
irregular distinction between attributive and predicative adjectives	§7.3
suppletion in the lexeme for 'small'	§7.6
potential mood in verbal inflection	§8.1.3.2
negation expressed by a finite negation verb	§8.2.3
predicative possession expressed by either locative or 'have'-verb	§13.1.4
no regular distinction between polar interrogatives and declaratives	§13.2.2

2 Prosody

This description of the phonology of Pite Saami begins with a discussion of prosodic structures before the segmental phonology is described. This choice of ordering is motivated by the important role that prosodic positions play in the distribution of phonemes (as well as in morphophonology). It is useful to first understand the prosodic structure of Pite Saami words before looking at their segmental composition here, and later to better understand morphophonology.

While there are a number of monosyllabic functional words, all Pite Saami lexical forms and many functional words are minimally bisyllabic. The first two sections (§2.1 and §2.2) describe the prosodic structures of these two groups of words. Then, utterance-level prosodic phenomena are dealt with in §2.3.

2.1 Monosyllabic word structure

While the majority of Pite Saami words are polysyllabic, a small set of functional words are monosyllabic. This set includes, for instance, some interjections, conjunctions and pronouns. These monosyllabic words consist of at least one vowel[1] and one consonant. This consonant can be in either onset or coda position; it is also possible for both consonant positions to be filled. Consonant clusters are licensed in coda position as well. The possible segmental structure templates for monosyllabic words are listed with examples in Table 2.1 on the following page.

2.2 Multisyllabic word structure

All lexical forms and a large number of functional words in Pite Saami are minimally bisyllabic. The smallest prosodic segmental structure attested for polysyllabic words is

$$VCV$$

---

[1] All vowel phonemes except /ua̯/ are attested in monosyllabic words.

Table 2.1: Segmental templates for monosyllabic words

template	examples IPA	orth.	gloss
VC	aj	aj	'also'
	ij	ij	'isn't' (NEG\3SG.PRS)
CV	tɛ	dä	'then'
	lɛ	lä	'is' (be\3SG.PRS)
	jo	juo	'already'
CVC	jus	jus	'if'
	taːt	dát	'that' (NOM.SG)
	men	men	'but'
	vaɲ	vanj	'really'
CVCC	kujt	gujt	'definitely'
	mejt	mejd	'what' (ACC.PL)
CVCCC	taːjst	dájst	'from these' (DEM-PROX-ELAT.PL)

but larger words are both possible and common, and expand upon this minimal foundation; examples are provided throughout the following discussion. Due to a number of phenomena, it is sensible to posit a phonological domain, which, in following basic principles of phonology and the prosodic hierarchy (cf. e.g., Dixon 2010: 280–283, Selkirk 1980, Hayes 1989, Nespor & Vogel 1986), I will refer to as a foot. A Pite Saami foot is trochaic (counting from left to right) and essentially bisyllabic. Multisyllabic words with an odd number of syllables thus have a final (unstressed) syllable which falls outside of the last foot. Whether such a final syllable should belong to the preceding foot or not is a theoretical question which will not be addressed here, but it should be noted that the segments in such syllables are subject to highly restrictive phonotactics compared to those clearly located within a trochaic foot.[2] Evidence for the foot as a domain can be found in prosodic (intonation, cf. §2.2.1; minimal size restrictions as described here), phonological (segmental restrictions, cf. Chapter 3) and morphophonological (stem alternations and vowel harmony, cf. §4.1.2) phenomena.

2.2.1 Word stress

The initial syllable (cf. §2.2.3 on syllabification) of a Pite Saami foot always receives main stress. All other foot-initial syllables receive secondary stress. If

---

[2] Cf. §3.2.1 on the phonotactics of vowel phonemes.

2.2 Multisyllabic word structure

a final syllable is odd, it does not receive any stress. As a result, the patterns of stressed and unstressed syllables presented in Figure 2.1 are attested in Pite Saami; Table 2.2 provides some examples for the syllabic structure of words with up to five syllables.

ˈσσ
ˈσσσ
ˈσσˌσσ
ˈσσˌσσσ
ˈσσˌσσˌσσ
ˈσσˌσσˌσσσ

Figure 2.1: Trochaic rhythmic patterns in Pite Saami; here, σ stands for a syllable

Table 2.2: Four common syllable structure patterns

pattern	example		gloss
ˈσσ	/ˈko.le/	*guole*	fish\NOM.PL
ˈσσσ	/ˈbet.na.ka/	*bednag-a*	dog-NOM.PL
ˈσσˌσσ	/ˈsaːlp.maˌkirː.je/	*sálbma-girrje*	psalm-book\NOM.SG
ˈσσˌσσσ	/ˈkuh.kaˌjol.ki.kijt/	*guhka-juolgi-gi-jd*	long-leg-NMLZ-ACC.PL

Note that some recent borrowings from Swedish deviate from these structures by having an initial unstressed syllable, as they do in Swedish. For instance, the example in (1) is from Swedish *departement*.

(1) /deˈparteˌmɛnːta/ *departemännta* [3583]
 [deˈparteˌmɛnːta] 'department\NOM.SG'

The acoustic correlates for stress seem to be intensity and pitch. Note that vowel length does not play a role in stress. Indeed, there are words with a short first vowel and a long second vowel that receive stress on the first syllable, as in the two examples in (2) and (3).

(2) /ˈanaː/ *aná* [pit101208.246]
 [ˈanaː] 'have\2SG.PRS'

(3) /ˈkolaː-tʃ/ *guolátj* [pit110413a.067]
 [ˈku͡ɔlaːtʃ] 'fish-DIM'

2 Prosody

However, more detailed analyses is required to fully describe the acoustic-phonetic behavior of word-level stress, including the difference between primary and secondary stress.

2.2.2 Relevant prosodic domains

Due to systematic restrictions on the distribution of a number of segments and consonant clusters as well as to the prosodic domains of morphophonological processes, it is useful to name and describe various prosodic positions for polysyllabic words. The domains themselves are described below, while the relevant phonological restrictions and morphophonological processes are described in the pertinent sections on consonant phonemes (§3.1), vowel phonemes (§3.2) and morphophonology (§4.1.2). Only a very limited number of recent loan words do not adhere to this structure. The schema in Figure 2.2 shows these prosodic positions, and they are described further below. In the schema, only segments represented by bold capital letters are obligatory.

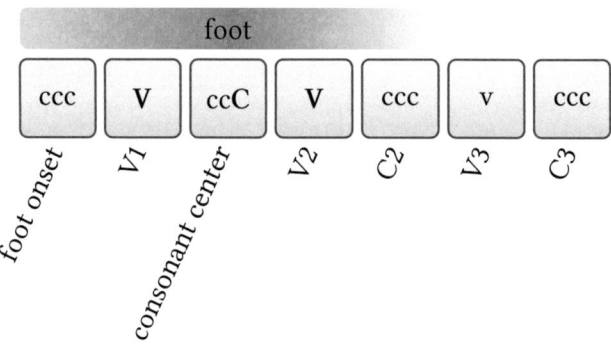

Figure 2.2: Illustration of prosodic domains for segments and the foot; segments represented by C and V are obligatory, while c and v are not.

Note that Table 2.3 on page 31 provides examples of how a word's segments fill these positions; it may be useful to refer to this to better understand these prosodic domains.

2.2.2.1 Foot

A foot in Pite Saami is a prosodic unit consisting of a stressed syllable and the following unstressed syllable, and is thus trochaic. Every multi-syllabic Pite Saami word consists of at least one foot.

2.2.2.2 Foot onset

Foot onset position is the first consonant or consonant cluster of a foot. It is not obligatorily filled. In Saamic linguistics, this has typically been referred to as the 'initium' (cf. Sammallahti 1998: 39).

2.2.2.3 V1

V1 is the first vowel of a foot, and is the peak of the stress-carrying syllable for the foot. It can be long or short, and can be a monophthong or a diphthong. The vowel in the final V1 position[3] of a word is the location for umlaut and ablaut/j-harmony (cf. §4.1.2.2 and §4.1.2.3). In Saamic linguistics, this has been referred to as the 'vowel center' (cf. Sammallahti 1998: 39).

2.2.2.4 The consonant center

The consonant center is the consonant or consonants that follow V1 (the initial vowel) and precede V2 (the second vowel), and essentially form the core of a foot. Every foot has a consonant center. The final consonant segment of the consonant center is the onset of the second syllable due to syllabification (cf. §2.2.3). The final consonant center of a word is the location for consonant gradation. The term 'consonant center' is commonly used in Saami linguistics (cf. Sammallahti 1998: 39).

2.2.2.5 V2

V2 is the second vowel of a foot. It never carries stress. Every foot has a vowel in this position. With the exception of the diphthong phoneme /u͡a/, all vowel phonemes are attested here. In Saamic linguistics, this has been referred to as the 'latus' (cf. Sammallahti 1998: 39).

2.2.2.6 C2

C2 is the consonant or consonants following V2. It is not obligatorily filled. If it is followed by a V3, then its final segment is resyllabified as the onset of the following syllable. In Saamic linguistics, this has also been referred to as the 'consonant margin' (cf. Sammallahti 1998: 39).

---

[3] Only words of four or more syllables can have more than one V1 position.

2.2.2.7 V3

V3 is the unstressed vowel of any syllable following the final foot of a polysyllabic word form, and is thus the last syllable nucleus of a word (when present). Only a limited set of vowel phonemes can occur in this position. If the V3 position is filled, then there is always a consonant margin as well. In Saamic linguistics, this has been referred to as the 'vowel margin' (cf. Sammallahti 1998: 39).

2.2.2.8 C3

C3 is a consonant or one of a limited set of consonant clusters (cf. §3.1.2.2) following V3 of a polysyllabic word, and is thus always word-final (when present). It is not obligatorily filled. If the C3 position is filled, then there is always a vowel in V3 and a consonant margin as well. In Saamic linguistics, this has been referred to as the 'finis' (cf. Sammallahti 1998: 39).

2.2.2.9 Discussion and examples

Table 2.3 on the next page provides several examples for Pite Saami polysyllabic words and how their segments fill the prosodic domains described above. Note that there are always segments in V1, the consonant center and V2, forming a sort of 'minimal core.' Only the final foot of a word can be followed by a single, odd syllable with V3 and potentially C3 segments.

Similarly, only the final foot of a word is subject to morphophonological phenomena (cf. §4.1.2). For instance, *sálbmagirrje* 'book of psalms, hymnal' is a compound consisting of *sálbma* 'psalm' and *girrje* 'book'. It consists of two feet: *sálbma-* and *-girrje*. It is not possible to add another syllable (e.g., via suffixation) between these two feet because they belong to the same compound noun. Furthermore, the inflected form for ACC.SG is *sálbmagirjev*, in which consonant gradation (weakening of *rr* to *r*) is only triggered in the second foot, even though the first foot undergoes gradation (weakening of the cluster /lpm/ to /lm/) in non-compound environments, cf. *sálmav* 'psalm-ACC.SG'. This is illustrated by the word forms in Table 2.4 on the facing page.

2.2.3 Syllabification

The distribution of vowel phonemes between consonant phoneme slots patterns clearly, particularly with respect to intonation and the distribution of vowel phonemes. This, along with the sonority sequencing principle (cf. e.g., Selkirk 1984), indicates that vowels are the nuclei of Pite Saami syllables. However, the location

2.2 Multisyllabic word structure

Table 2.3: Examples showing how the segments of Pite Saami words fill prosodic domains

IPA	foot onset	V1	C-center	V2	C2	V3	C3	gloss
ane		a	n	e				have\SG.IMP
pena	p	e	n	a				dog\NOM.SG
atne-t		a	tn	e	t			have-INF
kolːe	k	o	lː	e				fish\NOM.SG
kolːaː-j	k	o	lː	aː	j			fish-ILL.SG
vaːjpmo	v	aː	jpm	o				heart\NOM.SG
lu̯akːta-j	l	u̯a	kːt	a	j			bay-ILL.SG
ʃɲerːa	ʃɲ	e	rː	a				rat\NOM.SG
uvːata		u	vː	a	t	a		kiss\2SG.PRS
puʰtsu-jta	p	u	ʰts	u	jt	a		reindeer-ILL.PL
saːkasta-v	s	aː	k	a	st	a	v	say-1SG.PRS
petnaki-st	p	e	tn	a	k	i	st	dog-ELAT.SG

minimal core: V1 C-center V2

Table 2.4: Examples showing how the scope of consonant gradation is limited to the final foot of a word

NOM.SG	ACC.SG	gloss
sálbma	*sálmav*	'psalm'
girrje	*girjev*	'book'
sálbmagirrje	*sálbmagirjev*	'hymnal'
	*sálmagirjev	

of syllable boundaries is not as easy to determine; in fact, syllable boundaries are not highly relevant in Pite Saami prosody.

Because the consonant center has by far the widest variety of consonants and consonant combinations of any of the consonant positions, it is best to consider this position first. Although the consonant center spans the preceding and following syllabic nuclei, there is no solid phonotactic or phonological evidence for where the syllable boundary is located inside the consonant center. Table 2.5 on the next page lists the possible syllabification patterns for the consonant center.

Maximizing onsets, the patterns V.CCCV, VC.CCV and V.CCV would create

2 Prosody

Table 2.5: Logically possible syllabification patterns for the consonant center

C-center segment count	possible patterns
one C	V.CV VC.V
two Cs	V.CCV VC.CV VCC.V
three Cs	V.CCCV VC.CCV VCC.CV VCCC.V

highly unusual onsets (such as /vkŋ/, /pm/ or /vɲ/) unattested in any other onset positions. Similarly, trying to maximize codas, the patterns VCCC.V and VCC.V would also result in highly unusual codas (such as /vkŋ/ or /vɲ/) unattested in any other coda positions. While the pattern VCC.CV would also create some otherwise unattested codas (such as /vt/ or /rk/), these are phonologically similar to attested word-final codas such as /st/ or /jk/ (also fricative+plosive and oral-sonorant+plosive, respectively). The patterns VC.CV, V.CV and VC.V result in onsets and codas which are not unusual. However, keeping in mind the far greater diversity of single consonant phonemes licensed in word-initial onset position compared to word-final coda position, syllabification favoring singleton onset consonants results in onsets and codas which most resemble word-initial onsets and word-final codas. Note that even then, onsets and codas in positions other than the consonant center form subsets of the possibilities in consonant center position (with the exception of a few non-native word-onset clusters). It is therefore most plausible that syllables are assigned a single consonant segment as an onset in syllabification. The examples in (4) through (9) show some results of this syllabification for a variety of consonant constellations in the consonant center.

(4) /ana:/   aná   [6278]
      [a.na:]   'have\2SG.PRS'

(5) /atne-t/   adnet   [0006]
      [atˑnet]   'have-INF'

(6) /lokta/   luokta   [pit080702b.54m38s]
      [lo͡okʰ.ta]   'bay\NOM.PL'

(7) /kisto-tʃ/   gistotj   [6048]
      [kis.totʃ]   'box-DIM'

2.2 Multisyllabic word structure

(8) /parka-v/   *bargav*   [6241]
      [par.kaʋ]   'work-1SG.PRS'

(9) /tʃaːjpma-t/   *tjájbmat*   [pit100323a.001]
      [tʃaːjpˋ.matʰ]   'laugh-INF'

This syllabification preference for a single onset segment can be applied to syllable boundaries outside of the consonant center, as shown in (10) and (11).

(10) /saːkasti-t/   *ságastit*   [1480]
      [saː.kas.titʰ]   'speak-INF'

(11) /ɛvu-jna/   *ävujna*   [4372]
      [ɛ.vuj.na]   'happiness-COM.SG'

When the consonant center consists of a geminate phoneme (cf. §3.1.1.2), there is no phonological test which indicates where the syllable boundary is located; indeed, this syllable boundary is likely not relevant in Pite Saami phonology. With this in mind, a symbolic syllable boundary is postulated somewhere within a phonological geminate; this divides the geminate symbolically into two component parts and results in syllables conforming to a syllable template with a singleton in the onset. In the examples in (12) through (15), this symbolic boundary is placed in the middle of the geminate.

(12) /pɔtːɔ/   *båddå*   [0231]
      [pɔtˋ.tɔ]   'while\NOM.SG'

(13) /namːa/   *namma*   [3433]
      [nam.ma]   'name\NOM.SG'

(14) /naːʰpːe/   *náhppe*   [pit080621.54m38s]
      [naːhpˋ.pe]   'milking.cup\NOM.SG'

(15) /aːʰtʃːe/   *áhttje*   [0016]
      [aːhtˋ.tʃe]   'father\NOM.SG'

If a geminate precedes another consonant segment in the consonant cluster, the syllabification border is after the geminate, as in (16):

(16) /pisːte/   *bisste*   [0190]
      [pisː.te]   'spoon\NOM.SG'

2 Prosody

When the final consonant in the consonant center is preaspirated, there is again no test for the location of a syllable boundary, as with geminates. With this in mind, a symbolic boundary is posited between the realization of preaspiration (cf. §3.1.1.1) and the rest of the preaspirated segment, which results in syllables conforming to a syllable template with a simgleton in the onset. The examples in (17) and (18) show a preaspirated plosive and affricate, respectively, with a syllable boundary indicated between the glottal fricative (preaspiration) and the stop or affricate component.

(17) /tɔʰpe/ *dåhpe* [0416]
[tɔh.pe] 'house\NOM.SG'

(18) /keʰtʃe/ *gehtje* [0594]
[keh.tʃe] 'end\NOM.SG'

The same is the case when a geminate precedes a preaspirated segment, as in the example in (19).

(19) /kirːʰko/ *girrko* [0640]
[kir̥r.ko] 'church\NOM.SG'

Note, however, as pointed out above, the actual position of syllable boundaries in Pite Saami does not seem to be relevant in other areas of prosody. For this reason, the consonant center is a preferable prosodic domain to consider when describing prosody and phonotactics, and thus is referred to regularly in the following descriptions.

2.2.4 A note on syllables and feet

With the above description on stress in polysyllabic word structure in mind, it should become clear that syllables are only relevant for bearing word stress and creating feet, while feet form a relevant unit on several levels (prosodic, phonological, morphophonological). As a result, it could be more useful to rephrase the 'bisyllabic minimal word structure' as 'obligatory footedness' for Pite Saami lexical items and many functional words. Furthermore, the choice of the term 'foot' to describe this minimal size requirement may not be ideal because the edges of the Pite Saami foot are quite irrelevant to morphophonological processes. Instead, the *V1+Consonant-Center+V2* core is a vital domain for morphophonology, while segments at the edges are not relevant. Perhaps a better descriptive term would be 'minimal core'.

2.3 Utterance-level prosody

2.3.1 Intonation in utterances

While the following observations are of a preliminary nature, and a more thorough study must be left for future investigation, the relative intensity of stressed syllables in declarative utterances in Pite Saami tends to decrease towards the end of the utterance, with the final stressed lexical item, and particularly the final syllable, being realized with noticeably lower intensity than the beginning syllables. As an example, the waveform and intensity trace for the utterance glossed in (20) are provided in Figure 2.3.

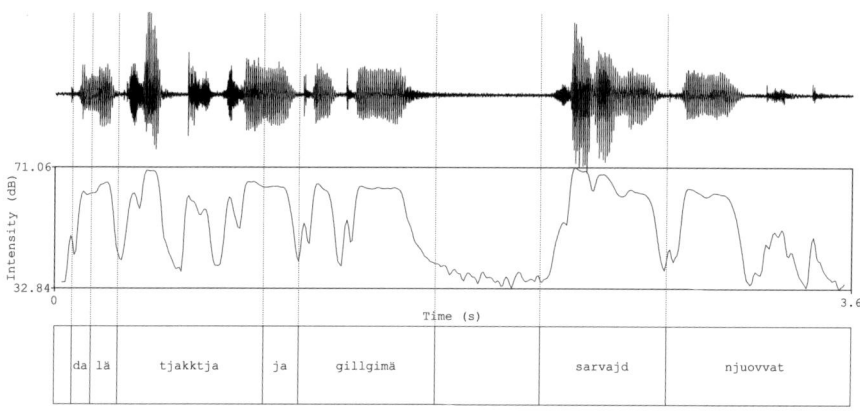

Figure 2.3: Waveform and intensity trace illustrating the drop in intensity at the end of an utterance

(20) da   lä   tjakktja   ja   gillgijmä   sarvajd
      da   lä   tjakktja   ja   gillgi-jmä   sarva-jd
      then be\3SG.PRS autumn\NOM.SG and will-1PL.PST reindeer.bull-ACC.PL
      njuovvat
      njuovva-t
      slaughter-INF
      'It is autumn and we will slaughter the reindeer bulls.'   [pit090826.003]

Here, the initial syllable nucleus of the first lexical item in the sentence *tjakttja* has an intensity of 69.7 dB. The other lexical items hover between 63.5 dB and 70.3

2 Prosody

dB. The final lexical item *njuovvat* begins at 64 dB on the initial syllable nucleus, and drops abruptly to 50 dB on the final syllable nucleus.

2.3.2 Utterance-final weakening

The final two or three syllables of a declarative utterance in Pite Saami can be weakened as a way to mark the end of an utterance.[4] This weakening is typically realized by completely devoicing the final one, two or three syllables, often to the point that these are essentially whispered. Alternatively, this can be realized as creaky voice instead of voicelessness. For instance, in the example utterance depicted in the waveform in Figure 2.4 and transcribed in (21), devoicing occurs in the final lexical word *giesev* 'summer', which contains the last two syllables of the utterance.

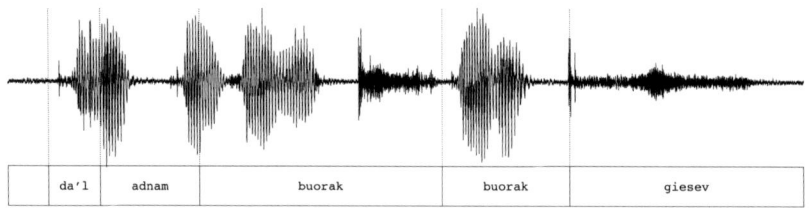

Figure 2.4: Waveform illustrating utterance-final weakening

(21) da'l   adnam   buorak, buorak giesev
      t-a=l   atha-m   pṏɔrakʰ pṏɔrak k͡ɟe̥sę-v̥
      DEM-3PL.NOM=be\3PL.PRS have-PRF good good   summer-ACC.SG
      'They have had a good summer.'   [pit090826.012]

The lack of energy in the waveform corresponding to *giesev* shows clearly that the word is weakened significantly compared to the rest of the utterance. Note that even the vowels are completely devoiced.

It is not clear what triggers this devoicing, and future study, particularly looking at the possibility of it being a turn marker in discourse, is needed.

---

[4] *Arjeplogsmål*, the local Swedish dialect, features a similar phenomenon.

3 Segmental phonology

Pite Saami has 43 consonant phonemes and 9 vowel phonemes. In the present chapter, the first section (§3.1) deals with consonants phonemes, their allophonic variation, and consonant clusters. The second section (§3.2) covers vowel phonemes, their allophonic variation, and schwa-epenthesis.

3.1 Consonants

The consonant phoneme inventory of Pite Saami can be found in Figure 3.1. There are plain and preaspirated phonemes for all plosive and affricate positions, and geminate and singleton pairs for all categories. Preaspirated, geminate and preaspirated geminate phonemes are restricted to the consonant center position.

	bilabial	labiodental	alveolar	post-alveolar	palatal	velar	glottal
plosive	p ʰp p: ʰp:		t ʰt t: ʰt:			k ʰk k: ʰk:	
affricate			ts ʰts ts: ʰts:	tʃ ʰtʃ tʃ: ʰtʃ:			
fricative		f f: v v:	s s:	ʃ ʃ:			h
nasal	m m:		n n:		ɲ ɲ:	ŋ ŋ:	
trill			r r:				
approx.			l l:		j j:		

Figure 3.1: Consonant phoneme inventory

A description of the consonant phonemes and the distribution of their relevant allophones can be found in §3.1.1 for each mode of articulation. This is followed by a discussion of consonant clusters. For the sake of clarity, the term *postaspiration* will be used here to refer to what is commonly referred to simply as *aspiration*; this decision also emphasizes the contrast to *preaspiration*, which is, in fact, more relevant for Pite Saami than postaspiration.

3.1.1 Consonant phonemes and allophonic variations

After a brief note on preaspiration in the following section (§3.1.1.1) and a discussion of gemination in §3.1.1.2, the consonant phonemes and their allophones are

3 Segmental phonology

described in the remaining sections (§3.1.1.3 through §3.1.1.7). They are grouped based on manner of articulation.

3.1.1.1 Preaspiration

In Pite Saami, preaspirated[1] phonemes only occur in consonant center position. While preaspirated phonemes can be plosives or affricates, the phenomenon that goes along with them is essentially the same. The period of aspiration, i.e., the voicelessness preceding the formation of the oral closure, is realized in different ways and depends on the preceding segment. If the preceding segment is a voiced continuant consonant, then the final part of that segment is devoiced.

While a minimal contrast between a voiceless obstruent preceding a preaspirated consonant phoneme and a voiceless obstruent preceding a plain counterpart phoneme (e.g., /st/ vs. /sʰt/) is theoretically possible, this cannot be detected because such a consonant cannot be devoiced as it is already voiceless (e.g., /st/→[st] and /sʰt/→[st]). When following a high front vowel /i/, preaspiration is realized as a voiceless palatal fricative [ç]. In all other cases, preaspiration is a voiceless glottal fricative [h]. This is summarized in Table 3.1.

Table 3.1: The phonetic realizations of preaspiration

preceding segment	realization of preaspiration	example
voiced consonant	end devoicing of voiced consonant	/mʰp/→ [m̥mp]
front high vowel /i/	voiceless palatal fricative [ç]	/iʰp/→ [içp]
other vowels	voiceless glottal fricative [h]	/aʰp/→ [ahp]

3.1.1.2 Geminates

The occurrence of geminate consonants is restricted to the consonant center. As illustrated in Table 3.1 on the preceding page, only the glottal fricative /h/ does

---

[1] As is hopefully evident from this discussion on preaspiration, the term 'preaspiration' is not entirely accurate from a phonetic-acoustic point of view since the acoustic correlate of this phenomenon is not actually aspiration in all cases. Nonetheless, there are several reasons to select this term: 1. in the majority of cases, the acoustic correlate is in fact preaspiration, 2. this phonemic phenomenon is often referred to as preaspiration in the literature on other Saami languages (cf. e.g., Sammallahti 1998: 54–55 or Feist 2010: 57,67), and 3. preaspiration can be reconstructed for the half-long and long Proto-Saami plosive and affricate phonemes (cf. Sammallahti 1998: 54) that became the current Pite Saami preaspirated phonemes.

not have a comparable geminate phoneme. Geminate segments are realized with a longer overall duration than the corresponding singleton phonemes. This observation is based not only on speakers' observations that such sounds are 'longer', but also on my own observations and analyses, including an acoustic-phonetic comparison of duration in geminate phonemes; cf. §3.1.1.3.5 for a detailed comparison non-voiced plosive durations in the consonant center.

For plosives and affricates, only one stop closure is formed, and the overall duration of the stop closure is longer than the duration of a corresponding single consonant. Some examples are provided in (1) through (5).

(1) /tap:en/   *dabben*   [3672]
    [tap:en]   'DEM\INESS.SG'

(2) /pat:e/   *badde*   [pit080701b.082]
    [pat:e]   'ribbon\NOM.SG'

(3) /pɛk:a/   *bägga*   [pit080702b.067]
    [pɛk:a]   'wind\NOM.SG'

(4) /va:ts:e-t/   *vádtset*   [2049]
    [va:t:setʰ]   'go-INF'

(5) /tʃitʃ:e/   *tjidtje*   [3618]
    [tʃit:ʃe]   'mother\NOM.SG'

Preaspirated plosive and affricate geminates also exist. In such cases, the duration of both the preaspiration phase and the following stop closure are longer than in the corresponding preaspirated single consonants. Some examples are found in (6) through (9).

(6) /tʃɛʰp:e/   *tjähppe*   [pit090930b.077]
    [tʃɛhp:e]   'clever\PRED.SG'

(7) /ma:ʰt:e-t/   *máhttet*   [pit080926.03m21s]
    [ma:ht:etʰ]   'can-INF'

(8) /ma:ʰts:a-j/   *máhttsaj*   [6613]
    [ma:ht:saj]   'turn.around-3SG.PST'

(9) /a:ʰtʃ:e/   *áhttje*   [0016]
    [a:ht:ʃe]   'father\NOM.SG'

3 Segmental phonology

For all other consonants, the overall duration of a geminate is longer than for the corresponding singleton consonant. Examples of such geminates are provided in (10) through (20).

(10) /taːfːo/   *dáffo*   [2367]
      [taːfːo]   'area\NOM.SG'

(11) /raːvːe/   *rávve*   [1366]
      [raːvːe]   'peace\NOM.SG'

(12) /ɔsːe/   *åsse*   [2269]
      [ɔsːe]   'part\NOM.SG'

(13) /ɔʃːe/   *åssje*   [2270]
      [ɔʃːe]   'horsetail\NOM.SG'

(14) /ɲamːa/   *njamma*   [pit080701b.005a]
      [ɲamːa]   'suck\3SG.PRS'

(15) /pinːa/   *binna*   [2446]
      [pinːa]   'little.bit\NOM.SG'

(16) /maɲːe/   *mannje*   [pit080621.74m04s]
      [maɲːe]   'daughter.in.law\NOM.SG'

(17) /maŋːel/   *maŋŋel*   [pit080924.529]
      [maŋːel]   'after'

(18) /kɔrːoti-t/   *gårrodit*   [4693]
      [kɔrːotɪtʰ]   'ice.over-INF'

(19) /tɔlːɔ/   *dållå*   [0421]
      [tɔlːɔ]   'fire\NOM.SG'

(20) /paːjːa-t/   *bájjat*   [3439]
      [paːjːatʰ]   'let-INF'

Due mostly to the nature of morphophonemic stem alternations, there are numerous minimal pairs differing only in the presence of a singleton versus a geminate consonant; cf. §4.1.2.1 on consonant gradation for examples.

It is also possible to have geminate fricative or sonorant phonemes, as described above, followed by a plosive or affricate phoneme, as illustrated by the examples in (21) through (24).

3.1 Consonants

(21) /pɛvːte/ *bävvde* [0289]
 [pɛvːte] 'table\NOM.SG'

(22) /lusːpe/ *lusspe* [1077]
 [lusːpe] 'rapids\NOM.SG'

(23) /kalːka/ *gallga* [6626]
 [kalːka] 'will\3SG.PRS'

(24) /kaːrːʰtʃe/ *gárrtje* [0554]
 [kaːr̥tʃe] 'tight\PRED.SG'

A series of two identical consonant phonemes can arise at the internal stem boundary of a compound. In such cases, the resulting duration can be longer than for a single plosive, but is not necessarily so, as the two phonemes are often realized as a singleton, as in (25).

(25) /tʃepot+taːkːte/ *tjiebotdákkte*² [3771]
 [tʃiepotaːkʰte] 'cervical.vertebra\NOM.SG'

Due to the morpheme boundary separating such segments, it is clear that this is not a case of a geminate phoneme, even if the realization may resemble that of a geminate.

3.1.1.3 Plosives

The plosive series in Pite Saami consists of the phonemes and their phonetic realizations shown in Table 3.2 on the next page. The distribution of the allophones will be discussed here. As all three relevant places of articulation behave in much the same way, the various manners of articulation for each place will be treated together.

3.1.1.3.1 Voiceless singleton plosives The segments /p t k/ are bilabial, alveolar and velar (respectively) voiceless singleton plosive phonemes. The voiceless singleton plosives can occur in all prosodic consonant positions and are subject to allophonic variation, depending on the prosodic environment. In syllable-onset position, a plain (unaspirated) voiceless plosive [p t k] is produced, as seen in examples (26) through (32).

---

² The word *tjiebotdákkte* literally means 'throat-bone', cf. *tjiebot* 'throat' and *dákkte* 'bone'.

3 Segmental phonology

Table 3.2: Plosive phonemes and their realizations

/p/	:	[p] [pʰ] [p̚]
/pː/	:	[pː]
/ʰp/	:	[hp] [̥p] [çp]
/ʰpː/	:	[hpː]
/t/	:	[t] [tʰ] [t̚]
/tː/	:	[tː]
/ʰt/	:	[ht] [̥t] [çt]
/ʰtː/	:	[htː]
/k/	:	[k] [kʰ] [k̚]
/kː/	:	[kː]
/ʰk/	:	[hk] [̥k] [çk]
/ʰkː/	:	[ʰkː]

(26) /pena/   *bena*   [pit090926.057]
      [p͡iena]   'dog\NOM.SG'

(27) /saːvːa-pa/   *sávvabah*   [pit100323a.060]
      [saːʋːapaʰ]   'wish-3DU.PRS'

(28) /tɔj/   *dåj*   [pit100323a.014]
      [tɔj]   '2SG.NOM'

(29) /vosta/   *vuosta*   [pit080917c.09m47s]
      [ʋu͡ɔsta]   'cheese\NOM.PL'

(30) /koptok/   *gåbdåk*   [pit091001.035]
      [kopʰtokʰ]   'wide\PRED.SG'

(31) /juka-v/   *jugav*   [pit100323a.115]
      [jʊkaʋ]   'drink-1SG.PRS'

(32) /pora-kit/   *buoragit*   [pit100323a.213]
      [pu͡ɔrakɪtʰ]   'good-ADVZ'

The plain voiceless singleton pronunciations [p t k] are also found in consonant clusters in word-onset position, an environment usually found in recent and older loan words from (North) Germanic, as in examples (33) and (34).

(33) /trotnik/   *drodnik*³   [0377]
      [trotʼnikʰ]   'queen\NOM.SG'

(34) /klaːsːa/   *glássa*⁴   [0529]
      [klaːsːa]   'ice.cream\NOM.SG'

The voiceless singleton plosive phonemes are postaspirated word-finally[5] as [pʰ tʰ kʰ], as in examples (35) through (37). This is also the case across an internal compound boundary, as in (38).[6]

(35) /orːo-p/   *årrop*   [pit100323a.158]
      [orːopʰ]   'be-1PL.PRS'

(36) /pora-kit/   *buoragit*   [pit100323a.213]
      [pu͡ɔrakɪtʰ]   'good-ADVZ'

(37) /iktok/   *iktuk*   [pit100323a.169]
      [ikʰtokʰ]   'alone'

(38) /pɔktʃanit+kɔsːɔs/   *båktjanitgåssås*   [5993]
      [pɔkʰtʃanitʰkɔsːɔs]   'whooping.cough\NOM.SG'

When preceding a non-homorganic plosive or affricate, a short aspiration occurs between the two segments, as in (39) here, and in (37) and (38) above.

(39) /vopta/   *vuopta*   [pit080701b.092]
      [ʋu͡ɔpʰta]   'hair\NOM.PL'

For all three plosive singleton phonemes, the closure is not released when a homorganic consonant follows; they are then realized as [p̚ t̚ k̚]. Word-internally, this situation is only found in the consonant center and with a homorganic sonorant, as shown in examples (40) through (43).

(40) /vaːjpmo/   *vájbmo*   [pit080701b.115]
      [ʋaːjp̚mo]   'heart\NOM.SG'

---

[3] From Swedish *drottning*.
[4] From Swedish *glass* (<French *glace*).
[5] Note, however, that speakers from the northern parts of Pite Saami territory tend to voice the voiceless plosives phonemes as [b d g] in word-final position.
[6] The word *båktjanitgåssås* in (38) refers to the whooping cough, and is a compound composed of *båktjanit* 'to suffocate' and *gåssås* 'cough'.

3 Segmental phonology

(41) /etni-t/   *ednit*   [pit100323a.251]
   [etʰɪtʰ]   'have-2DU.IMP'

(42) /jekŋa/   *jegŋa*   [pit080702b.070]
   [jekŋa]   'ice\NOM.SG'

(43) /votja/   *vuodja*   [pit080926.01m15s]
   [vo͡ɔtʲa]   'butter\NOM.SG'

3.1.1.3.2 Voiceless geminate plosives The segments /pː tː kː/ are bilabial, alveolar and velar (respectively) geminate plosive phonemes. They are very restricted in their distribution as they only occur in the consonant center and never occur word-initially or word-finally. Examples for the geminate plosive phonemes can be found in examples (44) through (46).

(44) /topːen/   *dobben*   [3581]
   [topːen]   'yonder'

(45) /patːe/   *badde*   [pit090930a.215]
   [patːe]   'ribbon\NOM.SG'

(46) /pɛkːa/   *bägga*   [pit080621.77m27s]
   [pɛkːa]   'wind\NOM.SG'

When preceding a non-homorganic plosive or affricate, a short aspiration occurs between the two segments, as in (47).

(47) /lu̯akːta/   *luakkta*   [pit080917c.03m51s]
   [lo͡ak:ʰta]   'bay\NOM.SG'

3.1.1.3.3 Preaspirated singleton plosives The segments /ʰp ʰt ʰk/ are preaspirated bilabial, alveolar and velar (respectively) singleton plosive phonemes. They are only licensed as the sole consonant or the final consonant segment in the consonant center. The phonetic realization of preaspiration depends on the preceding phoneme, as described in §3.1.1.1. Examples can be found in (48) through (52).

(48) /naːʰpe/   *náhpe*   [pit080621.55m16s]
   [naːhpe]   'milking.cup\NOM.PL'

(49) /tɔʰpe/   *dåhpe*   [pit100310b.083]
   [tɔhpe]   'house\NOM.SG'

3.1 Consonants

(50) /nurːʰtas/   *nurrtas*   [pit081011.177]
      [nur̥tas]   'towards.the.north'

(51) /kijʰto-v/   *gijtov*   [pit080621.11m45s]
      [kijjto̥ʋ]   'thanks-ACC.SG'

(52) /tiʰke/   *dihke*   [2359]
      [tiçke]   'louse\NOM.SG'

3.1.1.3.4 Preaspirated geminate plosives   The plosive segments /ʰpː ʰtː ʰkː/ are preaspirated bilabial, alveolar and velar (respectively) geminate phonemes. They are only licensed as the sole consonant in the consonant center. Examples can be found in (53) through (55); cf. §3.1.1.1 on allophonic variation in preaspiration.

(53) /tʃɛʰpːe/   *tjähppe*   [pit090930b.077]
      [tʃɛhpːe]   'clever\PRED.SG'

(54) /naːʰpːe/   *náhppe*   [pit080621.54m38s]
      [naːhpːe]   'milking.cup\NOM.SG'

(55) /maːʰtːe-t/   *máhttet*   [pit080926.03m21s]
      [maːhtːetʰ]   'can-INF'

3.1.1.3.5 Comparison of non-voiced plosive durations in the consonant center
While a thorough study of length phenomena in Pite Saami is beyond the scope of the current study, it is worth noting the actual duration which the various plosive phonemes are realized with in the consonant center. Specifically, a plain geminate plosive and a singleton preaspirated plosive have approximately the same duration for the period of stop closure (around 300ms), and are at least 100ms longer than plain singleton plosives and 100ms shorter than a preaspirated geminate plosive. In this respect, plain geminate plosives and preaspirated singleton phonemes seem to group together concerning stop closure duration. Table 3.3 on the following page shows some (near) minimal sets and duration measurements as a comparison. However, this alignment seems to be irrelevant phonologically.

3.1.1.4 Affricates

The affricate series in Pite Saami consists of the phones and their phonetic realizations shown in Table 3.4 on the next page. As affricates, they begin as a plosive

3 Segmental phonology

Table 3.3: Minimal sets or near minimal sets for comparison of stop closure durations (in milliseconds) for plain and preaspirated singletons and geminates

	plain single /p/ 145-150ms short	plain geminate /p:/ 320-340ms	preasp. single /ʰp/ 280-340ms medium	preasp. geminate /ʰp:/ 460-490ms long
set 1	[tɔpe] 150ms house\GEN.SG [pit100310b]	[tup:en] 320ms outside [3581]	[tɔhpe] 340ms house\NOM.SG [pit100310b]	[tɔhp:o] 490ms sheath\NOM.SG [3627]
set 2	[na:perti-t] 145ms drill-INF [3378]	[nup:e] 340ms other [1317]	[na:hpe] 280ms milking.bowl\NOM.PL [pit080917a]	[na:hp:e] 460ms milking.bowl\NOM.SG [pit080917a]

stop, which is then released into a sibilant fricative. These are described on the following pages.

Table 3.4: Affricate phonemes and their realizations

/ts/	:	[ts]
/ts:/	:	[t:s]
/ʰts/	:	[hts] [̥ts] [çts]
/ʰts:/	:	[ht:s]
/tʃ/	:	[tʃ]
/tʃ:/	:	[t:ʃ]
/ʰtʃ/	:	[htʃ] [̥tʃ] [çtʃ]
/ʰtʃ:/	:	[ht:ʃ]

3.1.1.4.1 Plain singleton affricates The segments /ts tʃ/ are unvoiced alveolar and postalveolar (respectively) singleton affricate phonemes. Both can occur in syllable onset position. Examples can be found in (56) through (59).

(56) /tsis:a-t/   *tsissat*   [3700]
       [tsis:atʰ]   'pee-INF'

(57) /pɔtsoj/   båtsoj   [0263]
     [pɔtsoj]   'reindeer\NOM.SG'

(58) /tʃaːtse-v/   tjátsev   [1861]
     [tʃaːtsev]   'water-GEN.SG'

(59) /pɔtʃesti-t/   båtjestit   [0262]
     [pɔtʃestitʰ]   'wring-INF'

The postalveolar affricate /tʃ/ can also occur in word-final[7] position, frequently as the diminutive suffix -tj, as in (60).

(60) /petnaka-tʃ/   bednagatj   [5717]
     [petʰakatʃ]   'dog-DIM\NOM.SG'

3.1.1.4.2 Plain geminate affricates The segments /tsː tʃː/ are unvoiced alveolar and postalveolar (respectively) geminate affricate phonemes. As with all other geminates, the affricate geminates only occur in the consonant center. The duration of the stop closure is longer in geminate affricates compared to their singleton affricate counterparts, while the duration of the fricative element is not relevant. Examples can be found in (61) and (62).

(61) /vaːtsːe-t/   vádtset   [2049]
     [vaːtːsetʰ]   'go-INF'

(62) /tʃitʃːe/   tjidtje   [3618]
     [tʃitːʃe]   'mother\NOM.SG'

3.1.1.4.3 Preaspirated singleton affricates The segments /ʰts ʰtʃ/ are preaspirated alveolar and postalveolar (respectively) singleton affricate phonemes. Just as with the preaspirated plosives, the preaspirated affricates only occur as the sole consonant or the final consonant in the consonant center. The phonetic realization of preaspiration depends on the preceding phoneme, as described in §3.1.1.1. Examples can be found in (63) through (65).

(63) /puʰtsu/   buhtsu   [pit110413b.085]
     [puhtsu]   'reindeer\NOM.PL'

---

[7] There is one particle *guts* with the alveolar affricate in final position, but it is not clear what this is or whether it is /ts/ or /tts/ in the consonant center (it is spelled inconsistently, as well). Noticeably, it is monosyllabic, and could be an abbreviated form of a typical bisyllabic word which has been lexicalized in its rapid-speech form, in which case it was historically in word-medial position.

3 Segmental phonology

(64) /pɔʰtʃe-t/   *båhtjet*   [0239]
      [pɔhtʃetʰ]   'milk-INF'

(65) /vu͡a:nːʰtsa/   *vuanntsa*   [2140]
      [vu͡an̥ntsa]   'hen\NOM.SG'

3.1.1.4.4 Preaspirated geminate affricates The segments /ʰtsː ʰtʃː/ are preaspirated alveolar and postalveolar (respectively) geminate affricate phonemes. Just as with the preaspirated geminate plosives, the preaspirated geminate affricates only occur in the consonant center. The duration of the preaspiration and stop closure is longer in geminate affricates compared to their singleton affricate counterparts, while the duration of the fricative element is not phonologically relevant. Examples can be found in (66) and (67).

(66) /maːʰtsːa-j/   *máhttsaj*   [6613]
      [maːhtːsaj]   'turn.around-3SG.PST'

(67) /aːʰtʃːe/   *áhttje*   [pit110415.19m16s]
      [aːhtːʃe]   'father\NOM.SG'

3.1.1.5 Fricatives

The fricative series in Pite Saami consists of the phonemes and their phonetic realizations shown in Table 3.5 on the facing page.

3.1.1.5.1 Singleton fricative consonants The segments /f v s ʃ h/ are singleton labiodental (unvoiced and voiced), alveolar, post-alveolar and glottal fricatives, all of which are attested in syllable onset and word-internal coda position. Some examples are provided in (68) through (75).

(68) /taːfo-st/   *dáfost*   [6803]
      [taːfostʰ]   'area-ELAT.SG'

(69) /viva-v/   *vivav*   [pit110415.08m08s]
      [vivɑʊ]   'son.in.law-ACC.SG'

(70) /saːkasti-t/   *ságastit*   [1480]
      [saːkastɪtʰ]   'speak-INF'

(71) /kese-n/   *giesen*   [pit100310b.019]
      [ki͡esen]   'summer-INESS.SG'

3.1 Consonants

Table 3.5: Fricative phonemes and their realizations

/f/	:	[f]
/fː/	:	[fː]
/v/	:	[v] [vʋ] [ʋ]
/vː/	:	[vː] [vʋː] [ʋː]
/s/	:	[s]
/sː/	:	[sː]
/ʃ/	:	[ʃ]
/ʃː/	:	[ʃː]
/h/	:	[h]

(72) /ʃulːo/   *sjullo*   [1598]
      [ʃulːo]   'ugly'

(73) /uʃuta-v/   *usjudav*   [6815]
      [uʃutaʋ]   'think-1SG.PRS'

(74) /hɔlːɔ-t/   *hållåt*   [0856]
      [hɔlːotʰ]   'say-INF'

(75) /pahaː/   *bahá*   [0101]
      [pahaː]   'evil\NOM.SG'

The phonemes /v s/ can also occur in word-final position, as in examples (76) and (77).

(76) /kaːlaːv/   *gáláv*   [4332]
      [kaːlɑːv]   'ford\NOM.SG'

(77) /nevres/   *nievres*   [5101]
      [ni̯evres]   'bad'

For some speakers from the north-eastern parts of Pite Saami territory, /ʃ/ is also possible word-finally because the diminutive suffix is sometimes /-ʃ/(instead of /-tʃ/); however there are not enough data in the corpus to determine when the diminutive suffix is /-ʃ/.

Two of these phonemes require further explanation. First of all, the labiodental voiced fricative /v/ is often realized as a labiodental approximant [ʋ] when

3 Segmental phonology

following an open front vowel /a/ or /a:/, as illustrated by examples (69) and (73) above.[8] In this case, the open front vowel is realized as an open back vowel [ɑ]. Furthermore, /v/ is frequently realized as either [ʋ] or as a voiced labial-velar approximant [w] in word-initial position as well, particularly in the Pite Saami dialects along the Pite River to the north. However, the [ʋ] pronunciation seems to be in free variation with a fricative [v] sound. This is illustrated by the example in (78).

(78)   /vuas:ta/   [wũãs:ta]~   *vuassta*   [pit110517b2.038]
                    [vũãs:ta]   'cheese\NOM.SG'   [pit080917c.9m42s]

Secondly, a glottal fricative [h] as the sole consonant in word-final position is possible, but it seems to be limited to certain morphological conditions in contemporary Pite Saami, and only realized by some speakers, and then inconsistently. However, some of the literature describing older stages of Pite Saami[9] indicates that at a previous stage of the language, a word-final /h/ was obligatory when it had morphological status. Two examples for this variation can be seen in (79) and (80).

(79)   /parka/   [parka]~   *barga*   [pit101208.032]
                    [parkah]   'work\CONNEG'   [pit101208.029]

(80)   /kola:-tʃ-a/ [kŏɔ̃la:tʃa]~ *guolatja*   [pit110413a.077]
                    [kŏɔ̃la:tʃah] 'fish-DIM-GEN.SG' [pit110413a.079]

3.1.1.5.2 Geminate fricative consonants The segments /f: v: s: ʃ:/ are geminate labiodental (unvoiced and voiced), alveolar and post-alveolar fricatives. As with all geminate phonemes, these fricatives only occur in consonant center position. The unvoiced labiodental geminate /f:/ is rather uncommon and unique in this series in that it never occurs as part of a consonant cluster. Note that, unlike the singleton fricative series, there is no glottal geminate fricative phoneme /h:/. Some examples are provided in (81) through (85).

---

[8] This fact is even evident in some Swedish place name spellings which use the more open vowel-like spelling <au> instead of the fricative spelling <av>, such as in *Båtsjaur*, a small community near Arjeplog whose name is likely based on the (Pite) Saami words *båtsoj* 'reindeer' and *jávvre* 'lake'.

[9] Cf. the paradigms in Lehtiranta (1992: 150–159) indicate that there is an *-h* suffix for NOM.PL, GEN.SG, CONNEG and 2SG.PRS, among others. Note that Lehtiranta (1992) describes Pite Saami up through 1950, but not after that. Also note that Lagercrantz (1926: 104,120) does not include any such suffix in these morphosyntactic contexts.

(81) /taːfːo/   dáffo   [2367]
[taːfːo]   'area\NOM.SG'

(82) /raːfːe/   ráffe   [2713]
[raːfːe]   'rapids\NOM.SG'

(83) /raːvːe/   rávve   [1366]
[raːvːe]   'peace\NOM.SG'

(84) /ɔsːe/   åsse   [2269]
[ɔsːe]   'part\NOM.SG'

(85) /ɔʃːe/   åssje   [2270]
[ɔʃːe]   'horsetail\NOM.SG'

3.1.1.5.3 Fricatives and preaspiration When the voiced fricative phoneme /v/ precedes a preaspirated segment, it becomes devoiced towards the end of its realization as [vv̥].[10] The near minimal pair illustrated by the examples in (86) and (87) shows a voiced fricative preceding a plain and a preaspirated plosive, respectively.

(86) /naːvːte/   návvde   [6042]
[naːvːte]   'predator\NOM.SG'

(87) /naːvʰtɛ/   návte   [1252]
[naːvv̥tɛ]   'like this'

Evidence for a preaspirated segment following the other fricatives is impossible to ascertain due to their inherent voicelessness.

3.1.1.5.4 Dialect variation and the historical voiced dental fricative A number of Pite Saami lexemes historically featured a voiced dental fricative *ð in Proto-Saamic. These items are subject to variation in the corresponding synchronic phoneme across Pite Saami territory. Specifically, Proto-Saamic *ð can correspond to a singleton or geminate alveolar voiceless plosive /t tː/, alveolar trill /r rː/, or voiced dental fricative /ð ðː/; the selection of phoneme varies from speaker to speaker. The alveolar plosives and trills /t tː r rː/ are realized as described in §3.1.1.3 and §3.1.1.7. For speakers with /ð ðː/, these are realized as a

---

[10] Cf. §3.1.1.8 for essentially the same phenomenon in sonorant phonemes.

3 Segmental phonology

voiced dental fricative singleton [ð] or geminate [ð:], respectively.[11] Phonemes subject to this variation are only found in the consonant center. To illustrate this, the phonemic variation in the word for stone, which goes back to Proto-Saamic *keaðᴄē (Sammallahti 1998: 243), is presented in Table 3.6.

Table 3.6: Phonemic variation in the historical voiced dental fricative

variant	phonemic form	phonetic form	gloss
t	/kɛt:ke/	[kɛt:ʰke]	
r	/kɛr:ke/	[kɛr:ke]	'stone\NOM.SG'
ð	/kɛð:ke/	[kɛð:ke]	

Generally speaking, the phoneme /t/ is found on the northern side and the phoneme /r/ on the southern side, although the borders are not absolutely clear. The phoneme /ð/ is least common, and seems to only be found in the speech of the eldest speakers. Speakers are quite aware of this variation. In the current working version of the Pite Saami orthography, the grapheme <r> has been chosen to represent all three variants (thus the word for stone is spelled *gärrge*), although spellings using the grapheme <d> or even <ð> may be used as well.

Other lexemes subject to this variation include (here in the orthographic representations): *åddet/ årret/ åððet* 'sleep', *åddå/ årrå/ åððå* 'new' and *gidda/ girra/ gidda* 'spring (season)'.

3.1.1.6 Nasals

The nasal series in Pite Saami consists of the phones and their phonetic realizations shown in Table 3.7 on the next page. The distribution of the allophones will be discussed here, as well as in §3.1.1.8 concerning the devoiced allophones.

3.1.1.6.1 Singleton nasal consonants The segments /m n ɲ ŋ/ are singleton bilabial, alveolar, palatal and velar nasal consonant phonemes. They can be found in onset and coda positions, with the exception of the velar nasal, which cannot

---

[11] The phonological system of the few speakers who have the voiced dental fricatives /ð ð:/ actually has two more phonemes than the systems of speakers with /t t:/ or /r r:/, as these latter four phonemes are already present in the phonology of all speakers. Note that, because /ð/ is very uncommon and not a feature that all speakers share, it is not included in the consonant inventory presented in Table 3.1 on page 37.

Table 3.7: Nasal phonemes and their realizations

/m/	:	[m] [mm̥]
/mː/	:	[mː] [mm̥ː]
/n/	:	[n] [nn̥]
/nː/	:	[nː] [nn̥ː]
/ɲ/	:	[ɲ] [ɲɲ̥]
/ɲː/	:	[ɲː] [ɲɲ̥ː]
/ŋ/	:	[ŋ] [ŋŋ̥]
/ŋː/	:	[ŋː] [ŋŋ̥ː]

appear word-initially[12] and is only attested once word-finally (shown in example (98)). Note that the devoiced allophones are triggered by a following preaspirated phoneme (cf. §3.1.1.8). Some examples for singleton nasal phonemes in various positions within words can be found in (88) through (98).

(88) /mɔn/   mån   [pit100323a.004]
     [mɔn]   '1SG.NOM'

(89) /ɔro-jmen/   årojmen   [pit100323a.181]
     [ɔrojmən]   'reside-1DU.PST'

(90) /pɔrːɔ-m/   bårråm   [pit100323a.103]
     [pɔrːɔm]   'eat-PRF'

(91) /ɲimki-t/   njimgit   [1287]
     [ɲɪmkitʰ]   'glue-INF'

(92) /nɛjːta/   näjjda   [pit110415.06m31s]
     [nɛ̥jːta]   'girl\NOM.SG'

(93) /pɛrtna/   bärdna   [pit080926.01m19s]
     [pɛr̥tʰa]   'bear\NOM.SG'

(94) /ɲitʃːe/   njidtje   [pit080701b.114]
     [ɲitʃːe]   'breast\NOM.SG'

---

[12] A phonotactic restriction barring a phonemic velar nasal in word-initial position is a common trait for languages spoken in Europe and western Asia (cf. Anderson 2013).

3 Segmental phonology

(95) /maɲe/   *manje*   [pit080621.74m26s]
       [maɲe]   'daughter.in.law\NOM.PL'

(96) /vaɲ/   *vanj*   [pit090702.035]
       [vaɲ]   'really'

(97) /jekŋa/   *jegŋa*   [pit080702b.070]
       [jĩekŋa]   'ice\NOM.SG'

(98) /mudiŋ/   *mudiŋ*   [pit080708_Session02.026]
       [mudiŋ]   'sometimes'

3.1.1.6.2 Geminate nasal consonants The segments /mː nː ɲː ŋː/ are geminate bilabial, alveolar, palatal and velar nasal consonant phonemes. As is the case for all other geminate phonemes, their distribution is restricted to the consonant center. Note that the devoiced allophones are triggered by a following preaspirated phoneme (cf. §3.1.1.8). Some examples with the geminate nasal phonemes can be found in (99) through (104).

(99) /ɲamːa/   *njamma*   [pit080701b.01m38s]
       [ɲamːa]   'suck\3SG.PRS'

(100) /pinːa/   *binna*   [2446]
       [pinːa]   'little.bit\NOM.SG'

(101) /maɲːe/   *mannje*   [pit080621.74m05s]
       [maɲːe]   'daughter.in.law\NOM.SG'

(102) /maŋːel/   *maŋŋel*   [pit080924.529]
       [maŋːel]   'after'

(103) /kumːʰpe/   *gummpe*   [0671]
       [kumm̥pe]   'wolf\NOM.SG'

(104) /parːʰka-t/   *barrgat*   [pit101208.005]
       [parr̥katʰ]   'work-INF'

3.1.1.7 Oral sonorants

Pite Saami has three oral sonorant phonemes; because their behavior is very similar, they will be described together in the rest of this section. Their phonetic realizations are shown in Table 3.8 on the facing page, as well as in §3.1.1.8 concerning the devoiced allophones.

Table 3.8: Oral sonorant phonemes and their realizations

/r/	:	[r] [r̥] [ɾ]
/r:/	:	[r:] [r̥:]
/l/	:	[l] [l̥]
/l:/	:	[l:] [l̥:]
/j/	:	[j] [j̥]
/j:/	:	[j:] [j̥:]

3.1.1.7.1 Singleton trill consonant The segment /r/ is a singleton alveolar trill. It can occur in syllable onset and coda positions. In rapid speech, it is often realized as an alveolar tap [ɾ], particularly intervocalically. Some examples are found in (105) through (108). It becomes devoiced [r̥] towards the end of its realization when preceding a preaspirated phoneme. Word-finally, it is also optionally completely devoiced as [r̥].

(105) /raːʃːo/   rássjo   [1385]
      [raːʃːo]   'rain\NOM.SG'

(106) /kɔrɔ/   gårå   [0768]
      [kɔrɔ]   'bad'

(107) /ɛrʰpo-jn/   ärpojn   [6794]
      [ɛr̥pojn]   'wire-COM.SG'

(108) /felpar/   fielbar   [0473]
      [felpar]   'snowdrift\NOM.SG'

3.1.1.7.2 Geminate trill consonant The segment /r:/ is a geminate alveolar trill. It only occurs in the consonant center. It becomes devoiced [r̥:] towards the end of its realization when preceding a preaspirated phoneme. Examples can be found in (109) and (110).

(109) /kɔr:oti-t/   gårrodit   [4693]
      [kɔr:otɪtʰ]   'ice.over-INF'

(110) /paːrʰko/   bárrko   [0147]
      [paːr̥:ko]   'bark\NOM.SG'

3 Segmental phonology

3.1.1.7.3 Singleton lateral approximant The segment /l/ is a lateral approximant. It can occur in syllable onset and coda positions. It becomes devoiced [l̥] towards the end of its realization when preceding a preaspirated phoneme. Some examples are found in (111) through (115).

(111) /lɔkev/   lågev   [2313]
       [lɔkev]   'ten'

(112) /pala/   bala   [6332]
       [pala]   'become.scared\2SG.PRS'

(113) /kalka-v/   galgav   [6627]
       [kalkɑʊ]   'will-1SG.PRS'

(114) /ɔlol/   ålol   [2257]
       [ɔlol]   'jaw\NOM.SG'

(115) /salʰpek/   salpek   [4773]
       [sal̥pekʰ]   'antler.tool\NOM.SG'

3.1.1.7.4 Geminate lateral approximant The segment /lː/ is a geminate lateral approximant. It only occurs in the consonant center, and it becomes devoiced [lː̥] towards the end of its realization when preceding a preaspirated phoneme. This phoneme is found in the examples in (116) and (117).

(116) /tɔlː ɔ/   dållå   [0421]
       [tɔlː ɔ]   'fire\NOM.SG'

(117) /ilːʰtʃak/   iltjak   [0894]
       [il̥ːtʃakʰ]   'stubborn'

3.1.1.7.5 Singleton central approximant The segment /j/ is a central approximant phoneme. It can occur in syllable onset and coda positions. It becomes devoiced [j̥] towards the end of its realization when preceding a preaspirated phoneme. Some examples are found in (118) through (122).

(118) /jekŋa/   jegŋa   [0922]
       [j͡iekŋa]   'ice\NOM.SG'

(119) /aːja/   ája   [2685]
       [aːja]   'spring\NOM.SG'

(120) /tijstak/   *dijstak*   [pit081017.00m57s]
       [tijstakʰ]   'Tuesday\NOM.SG'

(121) /aːjʰte-n/   *ájten*   [pit100310b.100]
       [aːjj̥ten]   'shed-INESS.SG'

(122) /aːjːʰtaː-j/   *ájjtáj*   [6676]
       [aːjj̥ːtaːj]   'shed-ILL.SG'

3.1.1.7.6 Geminate central approximant The segment /jː/ is a geminate central approximant. It only occurs in the consonant center, and becomes devoiced [jj̥ː] towards the end of its realization when preceding a preaspirated phoneme. Examples are found in (123) as well as (122) above.

(123) /paːjːa-t/   *bájjat*   [3439]
       [paːjːatʰ]   'let-INF'

3.1.1.8 Sonorants and preaspiration

All sonorant phonemes become devoiced towards the end of their realization when preceding a preaspirated plosive or affricate.[13] Since preaspiration is limited to the consonant center, this devoicing is (with the exception of word-final devoiced /r/) also limited to the consonant center. Some near minimal pairs are listed in (124) through (131).

(124) /parːko/   *barrgo*   [0146]
       [parːko]   'job\NOM.SG'

(125) /paːrːʰko/   *bárrko*   [0147]
       [paːrr̥ːko]   'bark\NOM.SG'

(126) /kaːmːpal/   *gámbal*   [2493]
       [kaːmːpal]   'old'

(127) /kumːʰpe/   *gummpe*   [0671]
       [kumm̥ːpe]   'wolf\NOM.SG'

(128) /riŋːko/   *riŋngo*   [2326]
       [rɪŋːko]   'lasso.ring\NOM.SG'

---

[13] Cf. §3.1.1.5.3 for essentially the same phenomenon in voiced fricative phonemes.

3 Segmental phonology

(129) /ruŋːʰka/   *ruŋŋka*   [1428]
       [ruŋŋ̥ːka]   'raven\NOM.SG'

(130) /aːjto/   *ájdo*   [0023]
       [aːjto]   'path.in.snow\NOM.PL'

(131) /aːjʰte/   *ájte*   [6677]
       [aːjj̥te]   'shed\NOM.PL'

These examples all show a sonorant preceding a preaspirated plosive; note that a preaspirated affricate triggers the same devoicing in the preceding sonorant.

3.1.2 Consonant clusters

In Pite Saami, it is frequently the case that up to three consonants can occur consecutively, particularly in the consonant center. Because syllabification does not cross word boundaries, consonant clusters in word-initial and word-final position are necessarily tautosyllabic. However, word-internally, syllabification of the final consonant as a syllable onset (cf. §2.2.3 on syllabification) creates a syllable boundary within a group of consecutive consonants. There are two ways of approaching such word-internal consecutive consonant groups: on the one hand, one can consider the syllable boundary to be a significant fissure dividing such a consonant grouping into two units, and then only study any tautosyllabic consonant clusters that result. On the other hand, one can disregard any syllable boundaries, and thus treat any consonant groupings, even those spanning a syllable boundary (heterosyllabic consonant clusters), as a unit. In determining whether syllable boundaries are a meaningful part of Pite Saami phonotactics, a discussion of the inventories for both tautosyllabic and heterosyllabic consonant clusters is provided below.

In the following, tautosyllabic consonant clusters will be described first, before moving on to heterosyllabic consonant groupings. Note that this does not include consecutive consonants which arise in compounding at an internal root-boundary.

3.1.2.1 Consonant clusters in syllable onset position

In syllable onset position, 21 CCs and 2 CCCs are attested, as listed in Table 3.9 and Table 3.10 on the next page; all are in word-initial position.[14] Words with an

---

[14] This is because syllabification results in onsets consisting of a single consonant word-internally; thus tautosyllabic consonant clusters can only occur in word-initial onset position.

onset cluster tend to be of either unknown or of Germanic origin, which helps explain why eleven of the word-initial CCs and both of the CCCs would not be attested in word-internal onsets even if syllabification allowed tautosyllabic consonant clusters word-internally.

Table 3.9: Bipartite consonant clusters in syllable onset position

C_1		C_2	attested CCs
plosive	+	sonorant	pr, pl, tr, kn, kr, kl
sibilant	+	obstruent	sp, st, sk, sv, ʃk, ʃv
fricative	+	sonorant	fr, fl, sm, sn, sɲ, sl, ʃm, ʃɲ, ʃl

Table 3.10: Tripartite consonant clusters in syllable onset position

C_1		C_2		C_3	attested CCCs
s	+	plosive	+	r	str, skr

3.1.2.2 Consonant clusters in syllable coda position

Because syllabification results in syllable onsets of a single consonant segment (cf. §2.2.3), only the coda of the initial syllable can host tautosyllabic consonant clusters in the consonant center. An inventory of these CCs is provided in Table 3.11.

Table 3.11: Tautosyllabic CC clusters in the consonant center (all in coda position)

C_1		C_2	attested CCs
fricative	+	plosive	vt, vk
oral sonorant	+	plosive	rp, lp, jp, rt, lt, jt, rk, lk

Syllable codas in word-final position are more restrictive, as only three CCs and one CCC are frequently found in this position, while four other CCs are found in a very limited set of words; the attested clusters in word-final syllable codas are listed in Table 3.12 on the next page. The regularly occurring word-final

3 Segmental phonology

coda clusters are quite common suffixes.[15] The clusters /rt rm lm jk/ are limited to a single, seemingly native lexical item each, but there are not enough data at this point to make any further conclusions.

Table 3.12: Word-final consonant clusters

type	attested
CCs	st, jt, lt (*rare:* rt, rm, lm, jk)
CCC	jst

3.1.2.3 Heterosyllabic consonant clusters in the consonant center

The inventories of tautosyllabic consonant clusters in various word positions detailed above are lacking any regularity concerning position within syllable structure (onset or coda). In other words, the sets of coda clusters licensed word-internally only overlap with the coda clusters licensed word-finally to a very limited extent. Specifically, only the clusters /jt lt rt/ are attested both word-internally and word-finally, while all the other clusters are unique to either word-internal or to word-final position. Furthermore, the relatively large number of word-initial consonant clusters, but complete lack of consonant clusters in other syllable-onset positions word-internally is also asymmetrical. These facts indicate that perhaps a different approach to explaining the data would be more fruitful.

Keeping the above in mind, as well as the exceptional role that the consonant center plays in morphophonology (consonant gradation, cf. §4.1.2.1) and phonotactics (geminates, preaspiration, overall length), an inventory of the possible heterosyllabic consonant clusters, e.g., disregarding syllable boundaries, that occur in the consonant center as a unit proves more insightful in describing Pite Saami phonology.

In addition to the 21 geminate consonants that can occur alone in the consonant center, there are a total of 213 heterosyllabic CCs attested in the consonant center. Table 3.13 on the facing page lists the 197 heterosyllabic CCs with either two singleton consonants or a geminate consonant and a singleton consonant.

---

[15] The suffixes -*st* ELAT.SG, -*jst* ELAT.SG, -*jt* ACC.PL form an integral part of any noun paradigm. The suffix -*lt* is limited to a handful of directional particles and may be an old case suffix. It should also be noted that Pite Saami speakers from the northern side of Pite Saami territory use -*s* and -*js* for elative case marking.

3.1 Consonants

Table 3.13: Heterosyllabic consonant clusters in the consonant center

C_1	C_2	possible clusters
plosive +	plosive	pt, p:t, pk, p:k, tk, t:k, kt, k:t
	affricate	pts, p:ts, pʧ, p:ʧ, kts, k:ts, kʧ, k:ʧ
	fricative	ps, p:s, tv, t:v, ks, k:s, kʃ, k:ʃ
	nasal	pm, p:m, pn, p:n, pɲ, p:ɲ, tm, t:m, tn, t:n, tɲ, t:ɲ, kŋ, k:ŋ
	oral sonorant	pr, p:r, pl, p:l, pj, p:j, tj, t:j, kl, k:l
fricative +	plosive	vt, v:t, vʰt, v:ʰt, vk, v:k, vʰk, v:ʰk, sp, s:p, st, s:t, sk, s:k, ʃk, ʃ:k
	affricate	vts, v:ts, vʰts, v:ʰts, vʧ, v:ʧ, vʰʧ, v:ʰʧ
	fricative	vs, v:s, vʃ, v:ʃ
	nasal	fn, f:n, vn, vɲ, vŋ, sm, s:m, sn, s:n, sŋ, ʃm
	oral sonorant	vr, v:r, vl, v:l, vj, v:j
nasal +	plosive	mp, m:p, mʰp, m:ʰp, mk, m:k, mʰk, m:ʰk, nt, nnt, nʰt, n:ʰt, nʰk, n:ʰk, ɲk, ŋk, ŋ:k, ŋʰk, ŋ:ʰk
	fricative	ms, m:s, mʃ, m:ʃ
oral sonorant +	plosive	rp, r:p, rʰp, r:ʰp, rt, r:t, rʰt, r:ʰt, rk, r:k, rʰk, r:ʰk, lp, l:p, lʰp, l:ʰp, lt, l:t, lʰt, l:ʰt, lk, l:k, lʰk, l:ʰk, jp, j:p, jʰp, j:ʰp, jt, j:t, jʰt, j:ʰt, jk, j:k, jʰk, j:ʰk
	affricate	rʰts, r:ʰts, rʰʧ, r:ʰʧ, lʰʧ, l:ʰʧ, jʰts, j:ʰts
	fricative	rf, r:f, rv, r:v, rs, r:s, rʃ, r:ʃ, lf, l:f, lv, l:v, ls, l:s, jv, j:v, js, j:s
	nasal	lm, ln, lɲ, lŋ, rm, rn, rŋ, jm, jn, jŋ
	oral sonorant	rj, r:j, lj, l:j, jr, j:r, jl, j:l

Most combinations of various natural classes are found; however, it is striking that a nasal as the first element can only have an obstruent as the second element. It is also noteworthy that a single oral sonorant plus a nasal is attested, but no double oral sonorant plus a nasal.

Turning to heterosyllabic consonant clusters with three members (tripartite CCs), there are 16 attested in the consonant center; these clusters are listed in Table 3.14 on the next page. The heterosyllabic consonant clusters in the first two rows of this table are fairly common, and correspond paradigmatically to consonant clusters lacking the plosive but with only the fricative and sonorant (see above on heterosyllabic CCs and §4.1.2.1 on consonant gradation). The other three tripartite consonant clusters /jst mst rtm/ are only attested in one or two

3 Segmental phonology

Table 3.14: Tripartite consonant clusters in the consonant center

C_1	C_2	C_3	possible CCCs
fricative +	plosive +	sonorant	vtn, vtɲ, vkŋ
sonorant +	plosive +	sonorant	rpm, lpm, jpm, rtn, ltn, jtn, rtɲ, ltɲ, rkŋ, lkŋ
other limited CCCs			jst, mst, rtm

words each,[16] and there are not enough data to reach any further conclusions at this point.

Due to the morphophonological process of consonant gradation, which features paradigmatic stem allomorphy characterized by quantitative alternations in the consonant center in many cases (cf. §4.1.2.1), almost all of the heterosyllabic CCs can be grouped into short~long pairs, e.g., /pt~pːt/ or /jʰts~jːʰts/. There are only 16 heterosyllabic CCs which do not seem to have a corresponding quantitative partner; for reasons explained below, it is useful to divide these into the two groups listed in (132):

(132) Group A: /vn vɲ vŋ lm ln lɲ lŋ rm rn rŋ jm jn jɲ/
Group B: /sŋ ʃm ɲk/

Members of the first and larger group all have a corresponding morphophonemic partner, but this corresponding partner is a consonant cluster consisting of three consonant segments, and differs qualitatively as well. Specifically, tripartite CCs consisting of /v l r j/ followed by a plosive+sonorant pair correspond to Group A (those lacking the plosive element of the relevant tripartite CC); these pairings are listed in Table 3.15 on the facing page.

The remaining heterosyllabic CCs /sŋ ʃm ɲk/(Group B) seem to lack a quantitative partner. It is likely that the corresponding long CCs /sːŋ ʃːm ɲːk/ would be acceptable since CCs with very similar phonemic structures in quantitative pairs exist. However, a lack of data at this point prevents this from being ascertained for certain.

It is worth noting that the only consonant cluster which occurs in a word-medial position other than the consonant center is /st/ from the suffix -st-, a derivational morpheme which derives a verb, e.g., *basestit* 'to fry quickly' (cf. *basset* 'to fry').[17]

---

[16] Recent loan words from Swedish may also contain tripartite CCs not found elsewhere in Pite Saami, e.g., *kɔnstɔ* 'art' <Swedish *konst*.

[17] Cf. §10.2.2 for more on this verbalizer.

Table 3.15: Quantitative and qualitative CC~CCC pairs

CC	~	CCC	CC	~	CCC
vn	:	vtn	lm	:	lpm
vɲ	:	vtɲ	ln	:	ltn
vŋ	:	vkŋ	lɲ	:	ltɲ
rm	:	rpm	lŋ	:	lkŋ
rn	:	rtn	jm	:	jpm
rŋ	:	rkŋ	jn	:	jtn

Ultimately, this massive inventory of consonants and consonant clusters in the middle of words can only really make sense when one understands the extent to which morphology is expressed in this position, as becomes clear in Chapters 4 through 10.

3.2 Vowels

Pite Saami has eight monophthong vowel phonemes and one diphthong vowel phoneme. These are listed in Figure 3.2, with the monophthongs in the vowel chart on the left, and the diphthong on the right.

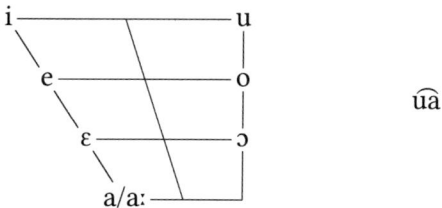

Figure 3.2: Vowel phoneme inventory

A discussion of these phonemes and the distribution of the relevant allophones follows. Note that there is a short open front vowel /a/ and a long open front vowel /aː/; for the latter case, length is marked with a triangular colon <aː> in phonemic transcription, as according to IPA standards, and with an acute accent <á> when represented in orthography.

The monophthong phonemes /a aː ɛ i u ɔ/ are realized as monophthongs in all cases. The monophthong phonemes /e/ and /o/ are realized as slight diphthongs

3 Segmental phonology

in V1 position, namely as [i͡e] and [u͡o], respectively. They can be very short in duration. There is a relatively minimal difference between the beginning and ending positions of each of the [i͡e] and [u͡o] phones in the oral cavity, a closeness which is even reflected in inconsistencies in the working version of the Pite Saami orthography: both <e> and <ie> are used for /e/, and <o> and <uo> for /o/.

The diphthong phoneme /u͡a/ is restricted to V1 position. Due to vowel harmony, /u͡a/ can be realized as [o͡ɛ] or [o͡a], and needs not be particularly long in duration.

Note that farther north within the Pite Saami language territory, monophthong phonemes are often realized as slight diphthongs. This is closer to Lule Saami within the Saami dialect continuum; indeed, many Lule Saami monophthong vowel phonemes are realized as slight diphthongs (cf., e.g., Spiik 1989: 11).

Because there is no significant difference in behavior between monophthongs and diphthongs which would justify treating them separately, all nine vowel phonemes are dealt with together in the following section.

3.2.1 Vowel phonemes and allophonic variations

The following sections describe the Pite Saami vowel phonemes and their allophonic realizations in the three vowel positions V1, V2 and V3. Table 3.16 on the facing page summarizes the distribution of the vowel phonemes in these three prosodic vowel slots. All vowel phonemes are licensed in V1, and all except /ɛ/ and /u͡a/ occur in V2.[18] However, V3 position is the most restrictive and allows only /i ɛ a u/. This distribution reflects the fact that V1 is the most prosodically relevant slot, and V3 the least significant.

3.2.1.1 Close front high vowel

The segment /i/ is a close front high vowel. In V1 position, it is not realized with a very narrow oral cavity, but closer to [ɪ], while in V2 and V3 position it is even less close and essentially [ɪ], and tends to be shorter in duration. When a palatal approximant /j/ immediately follows, this triggers a slight raising of /i/ so that it is closer to [i]. Some examples are found in (133) through (136).

(133)   /kartʃeti-t/   *gartjedit*   [0555]
        [kartʃetɪtʰ]   'decrease-INF'

---

[18] The phoneme /ɛ/ only occurs in a limited phonological context in V2 of grammatical words, and is therefore in parentheses in Table 3.16.; cf. §3.2.1.3.

Table 3.16: Distribution of vowel phonemes in the three prosodic vowel slots

vowel	V1	V2	V3
i	+	+	+
e	+	+	-
ɛ	+	(-)	+
a	+	+	+
aː	+	+	-
ɔ	+	+	-
o	+	+	-
u	+	+	+
u͡a	+	-	-

(134) /jimki-t/   jimkit   [2775]
       [jimkɪtʰ]   'blink-INF'

(135) /li-jin/   lijin   [4114]
       [lijɪn]   'be-3PL.PST'

(136) /tʃilmi-jt/   tjilmijt   [1877]
       [tʃilmijt]   'eye-ACC.PL'

3.2.1.2 Close-mid front vowel

The segment /e/ is a close-mid front vowel. In V1 position, it is realized as a slight diphthong [i͡e], while in V2 position it is normally a monophthong [e]. It is not attested in V3 position.[19] Some examples are found in (137) through (139).

(137) /eːo/   ello   [0449]
       [i͡eːo]   'reindeer.herd\NOM.SG'

(138) /reʰpe-ha/   rehpeha   [2790]
       [ri͡ehpeha]   'red.fox-NOM.PL'

(139) /kole/   guole   [pit110413a.002]
       [ku͡ole]   'fish\NOM.PL'

---

[19] Note that, in the current working orthography, the V3 position can contain the grapheme <e>, but this is in fact the phoneme /i/ realized as [ɪ].

3 Segmental phonology

3.2.1.3 Open-mid front vowel

The segment /ɛ/ is a open-mid front vowel. It normally occurs in V1 position. Examples can be found in (140) and (141).

(140) /pɛk:a/ *bägga* [2302]
[pɛk:a] 'wind\NOM.SG'

(141) /rɛʃ:me/ *rässjme* [2754]
[rɛʃ:me] 'ice.fishing.line\NOM.SG'

The phoneme /ɛ/ can also be found in V2 position, but this is limited to grammatical words and it is never followed by a final consonant.[20] In such cases, /ɛ/ is realized slightly more open than when in V1 position. Examples can be found in (142) through (145).

(142) /kɔn:ɛ/ *gånne* [0759]
[kɔn:ɛ] 'where'

(143) /aʰtɛ/ *ahte* [0014]
[ahtɛ] 'in.order.to'

(144) /ta:lɛ/ *dále* [2303]
[ta:lɛ] 'now'

(145) /sin:ɛ/ *sinne* [pit080702b.144]
[sɪn:ɛ] 'inside'

In a few recent loan words from Swedish which are originally French or Latin loans words in Swedish that have retained their second syllable stress, /ɛ/ can occur as the vowel of the second syllable. However, as this is the stressed syllable in such cases, it is, from a prosodic perspective, still in the V1 position of a normal Pite Saami trochaic foot. Two examples are provided in (146) and (147).

(146) /adrɛs:a/ *adrässa* [2683]
[adrɛs:a] 'address\NOM.SG'

(147) /profɛs:or/ *profässor* [4268]
[profɛs:or] 'professor\NOM.SG'

---

[20] The current working Pite Saami orthography is rather inconsistent with the spelling of the /ɛ/ phoneme. In V1 position, it is spelled with <ä>, while in V2 (in grammatical words) it is spelled <e>.

3.2 Vowels

Due to the verbal suffixes *-jmä* '1PL.PST' and *-jdä* '2PL.PST', verbs with a bisyllabic stem in these forms thus feature /ɛ/ in the third and final syllable, as in (148) and (149). Note also that the current working orthography inconsistently spells /ɛ/ as <e> or <ä> in these suffixes.

(148) /juga-jmɛ/   *jugajmä*   [pit100323a.138]
 [jʊkajmɛ]   'drink-1PL.PST'

(149) /åro-jtɛ/   *årojdä*   [pit100323a.223]
 [ɔrojtɛʰ]   'reside-2PL.PST'

Otherwise, /ɛ/ is unattested in V3 position.

3.2.1.4 Short open front vowel

The segment /a/ is an open front vowel of short duration. It can occur in V1, V2 and V3 positions. When preceding /v/, such as before the suffix *-v* ACC.SG or *-v* 1SG.PRS, /a/ is usually pronounced more to the back towards [ɑ].[21] Examples can be found in (150) through (153).

(150) /sita-v/   *sidav*   [pit080926.03m14s]
 [sitɑʋ]   'want-1SG.PRS'

(151) /pala/   *bala*   [6332]
 [pala]   'become.scared\2SG.PRS'

(152) /kola-tʃ/   *guolatj*   [pit110413a.150]
 [kʊ̃olatʃ]   'testicle-DIM\NOM.SG'

(153) /saːkasta/   *ságasta*   [pit101208.228]
 [saːkasta]   'say\2SG.PRS'

3.2.1.5 Long open front vowel

The segment /aː/ is an open front vowel of long quantity. It can occur in V1 and V2 positions. When preceding a /v/, such as before the suffix *-v* ACC.SG or *-v* 1SG.PRS, /a/ is usually pronounced more to the back towards [ɑ].[22] Examples can be found in (154) through (158).

---

[21] Simultaneously, /v/ is optionally but frequently pronounced as [ʋ] when following /a/ or /aː/; cf. §3.1.1.5.1.

[22] See previous footnote.

(154) /paːla/   *bála*   [6314]
[paːla]   'dig\2SG.PRS'

(155) /kolaː-tʃ/   *guolátj*   [pit110413a.066]
[ko͡olaːtʃ]   'fish-DIM\NOM.SG'

(156) /maːnːaː/   *mánná*   [1129]
[maːnːaː]   'child\NOM.SG'

(157) /anaː-v/   *anáv*   [pit101208.263]
[anaːv]   'have-1SG.PRS'

(158) /kaːlaːv/   *gáláv*   [4332]
[kaːlɑːʊ]   'ford\NOM.SG'

3.2.1.6 Open-mid back vowel

The segment /ɔ/ is a open-mid back vowel. It can occur in V1 or V2 position. However, if it is in V2 position, then V1 is also /ɔ/. Examples can be found in (159) through (163).

(159) /ɔktse/   *åktse*   [2823]
[ɔkʰtse]   'nine'

(160) /pɔtːɲe/   *båddnje*   [0230]
[pɔtːɲe]   'husband\NOM.SG'

(161) /pɔjʰtot/   *båjtot*   [0242]
[pɔjjtotʰ]   'wrong'

(162) /pɔjːʰtʃɔ/   *båjjtjå*   [2569]
[pɔjjːtʃɔ]   'boy\NOM.SG'

(163) /jɔkɔ-tʃ/   *jågåtj*   [3435]
[jɔkɔtʃ]   'stream-DIM\NOM.SG'

3.2.1.7 Close-mid back vowel

The segment /o/ is a close-mid back vowel. In V1 position, it is realized as a slight diphthong [o͡o], while in V2 position it is the monophthong [o]. It is not attested in V3 position. Some examples are found in (164) through (167).

3.2 Vowels

(164) /poːre/ *buorre* [0213]
 [pu͡oːre] 'good'

(165) /kolːe/ *guolle* [pit110413a.003]
 [ku͡olːe] 'fish\NOM.SG'

(166) /vaːjpmo/ *vájbmo* [pit080701b.115]
 [vaːjp̚mo] 'heart\NOM.SG'

(167) /aːnoti-p/ *ánodip* [6301]
 [aːnotɪpʰ] 'request-1PL.PRS'

3.2.1.8 Close back vowel

The segment /u/ is a close back vowel. In V1 position, it is not realized with a completely narrow oral cavity, while in V2 and V3 positions it is even less close and essentially [ʊ], and tends to be shorter in duration. Some examples are found in (168) through (173).

(168) /jukːsa/ *jukksa* [0934]
 [jukːsa] 'ski.binding\NOM.SG'

(169) /murːʰko/ *murrko* [pit080702b.065]
 [murr̥ːko] 'fog\NOM.SG'

(170) /puʰtsu/ *buhtsu* [pit110413b.088]
 [puhtsʊ] 'reindeer\GEN.SG'

(171) /tsiptsu-t/ *tsibtsut* [5712]
 [tsipʰtsʊtʰ] 'pinch-INF'

(172) /ɲalːka-jmus/ *njallgajmus* [4462]
 [ɲalʲkajmʊs] 'tasty-SUPERL'

(173) /sulːu-tʃ/ *sullutj* [5148]
 [sulːʊtʃ] 'island-DIM\NOM.SG'

3.2.1.9 Close back to open front vowel

The segment /u͡a/ is a diphthong which begins as a close but slightly centralized back vowel and opens to an open front vowel [ʊ͡a] in most cases. However, the

3 Segmental phonology

vowel in V2 position can trigger vowel harmony that slightly closes the end position of the oral closure so that it is realized as [u͡ɛ],[23] but the triggering vowels vary between Pite Saami dialects. For southern dialects, only a close /i/ or close-mid vowel /e/ in V2 position can trigger this harmony. In northern dialects, an open front /a/ in V2 position[24] also triggers this vowel harmony. A few cognate pairs are provided in Table 3.17.

Table 3.17: Examples of allophony for the diphthong /u͡a/

allophone	phonemic	phonetic		orthography	gloss
[u͡a]	ku͡al:to	ku͡al:to		gualldo	'snow.flurry\NOM.SG'
	tʃu͡ar:vo-t	tʃu͡ar:votʰ		tjuarrvot	'call.out-INF'
[u͡ɛ]	ju͡atke-t	ju͡ɛtʰketʰ		juätkit	'extend-INF'
	pu͡aj:te	pu͡ɛj:te		buäjjde	'fat\NOM.SG'
		northern	southern		
[u͡ɛ]~[u͡a]	lu͡ak:ta	lu͡ɛkt:a	lu͡akt:a	luakkta	'bay\NOM.SG'
	vu͡asta	vu͡ɛsta	vu͡asta	vuasta	'cheese\NOM.SG'

Note that this vowel harmony is triggered by a purely phonological context, as opposed to the vowel harmony described in §4.1.2.3 in the chapter on morphology, which is triggered morphologically.

3.2.2 Epenthetic schwa

In a small number of Pite Saami words, a vowel is inserted between two non-homorganic consonants in the consonant center position. This centralized vowel is exceptionally short in duration, and is transcribed here with a superscript schwa [ᵊ]. Waveforms for the two examples provided in (174) and (175) are found in Figure 3.3 on the facing page.

(174) /rip:re/   *ribbre*   [1403]
       [ripᵊre]   'liver\NOM.SG'

(175) /ɲa:lka/   *njálga*   [1277]
       [ɲa:lᵊkah]   'candy\NOM.PL'

---

[23] Despite the orthography being quite phonemic rather than phonetic, these two allophones of /u͡a/ are reflected in spelling: [u͡a] is spelled <ua> and [u͡ɛ] is spelled <uä>.

[24] There are not enough data at this time to know whether a long /a:/ also triggers this in northern dialects.

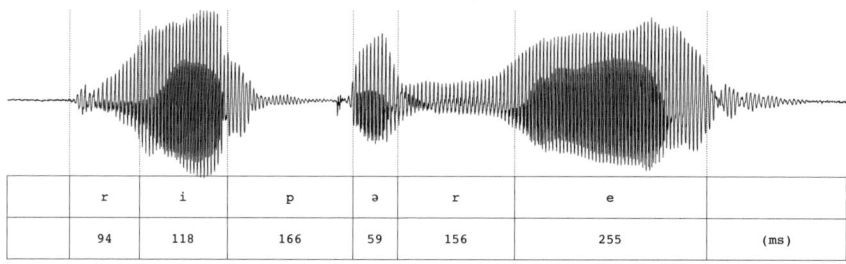

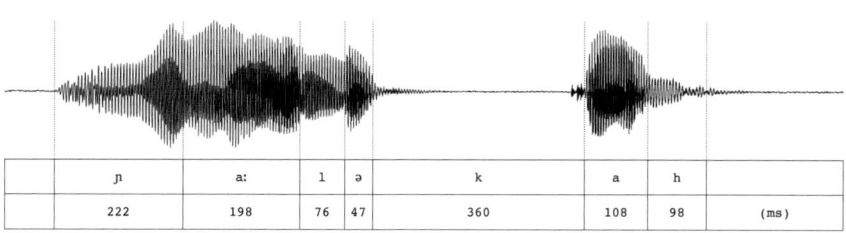

Figure 3.3: Waveforms of two words (*ribbre* 'liver' and *njálga* 'candy') with an epenthetic schwa, including segmental durations

In both cases, the epenthetic schwa is clearly linked to more energy, and it stands out from the surrounding consonants. These waveforms also make visible the shorter duration of the epenthetic schwa (59ms and 47ms, respectively) compared to the other vowels (the shortest of which is 108ms).

Speakers are rarely conscious of this vowel, and it is not reflected in the orthography. In neighboring Lule Saami, a similar epenthetic vowel exists and is predictable based on the prosodic and phonological structure of a word (cf. Spiik 1989: 14–15). It therefore seems likely that this epenthetic schwa is not phonemic in Pite Saami either. However, more data are needed to confirm this and thoroughly describe its distribution. The fact that this epenthetic vowel seems to be significantly more prevalent in northern Pite Saami dialects complicates the situation further. The examples in (176) through (178) provide dialectal variants, with the more southern variant first (lacking the epenthetic vowel), and the more northern variant second (with the epenthetic schwa).

(176)   /spa:j·ta/   [spa:jj̥:ta] ~   *spájta*   [1711]
                    [spa:jᵊta]   'fast'   [pit110518a.3m22s]

3 Segmental phonology

(177) /ɲalːke/ [ɲalːke]~ *njallge* [pit091001.087]
 [ɲalᵊkːe] 'tasty' [pit081111.2m59s]

(178) /t͡ʃuavːt͡ʃa/ [t͡ʃu̯aʊːt͡ʃa]~ *tjuavvtja* [1954]
 [t͡ʃu̯ɔʊᵊt͡ʃa] 'whitefish\NOM.SG' [pit0906_Ahka-
 javvre_a.168]

4 Morphological patterns and word classes

Morphology plays an essential role in Pite Saami, a highly synthetic language. Based on morphological patterning and in addition to syntactic criteria, seven word classes can be posited. §4.1 first provides an introduction to morphological phenomena in Pite Saami, before §4.2 summarizes the word classes.

4.1 Overview of morphology

A number of inflectional categories exist in Pite Saami; Table 4.1 provides a summary of inflectional categories relevant for each sub-category of the relevant word classes.

Table 4.1: Inflectional categories for pertinent word classes and sub-categories of word classes

word class/sub-category	inflectional categories
verbs	
• finite forms	person, tense, mood
• non-finite forms	aspect, connegation, etc.
nominals	
• nouns	case, number
• interrogative, relative pronouns	case, number
• personal, reflexive pronouns	case, number, person
• demonstrative pronouns	case, number, distance
adjectivals	
• attributive adjectives	comparative, superlative
• predicative adjectives	comparative, superlative, number

Derivational morphology is commonly used to create nouns, verbs, and, to a lesser extent, adjectives and adverbs. Both derivational and inflectional morphology manifest themselves linearly (by suffixing) or non-linearly, via consonant gradation, umlaut and/or vowel harmony. More often than not, linear and non-linear morphological phenomena are combined.

The present section only provides an overview of these various morphological phenomena, and is divided into §4.1.1 on linear morphology and §4.1.2 on non-linear morphological processes. Because morphological behavior varies between the word classes, it is described in more detail individually in the relevant word class chapters.

4.1.1 Linear morphology

Concerning linearly separable morphology, Pite Saami is an exclusively suffixing language. Both inflectional and derivational suffixes exist. According to the general linear morphological structure of Pite Saami words, derivational suffixes attach to a root before inflectional suffixes occur on the resulting stem, as illustrated in (1).

(1) [lexical root + derivational morphemes + inflectional morphemes]$_{word}$

4.1.2 Non-linear morphology (morphophonology)

There are three ways in which non-linear morphology can be expressed in Pite Saami:

- stem consonant alternations (consonant gradation)
- stem vowel alternations in V1 position (umlaut)
- regressive vowel harmony in V1 and V2 vowels

These are triggered by a word's position within an inflectional paradigm, or in derivation. All inflectional non-linear morphology is restricted to the final foot of a given word, while derivational non-linear morphology can also occur in a non-ultimate foot. Non-linear processes may apply simultaneously. The following sections describe these phenomena in more detail: §4.1.2.1 for consonant gradation, §4.1.2.2 for umlaut and §4.1.2.3 for vowel harmony.[1]

---

[1] Cf. Korhonen (1969) for historical explanations of these morphophonological processes in Saami.

4.1.2.1 Consonant gradation

The term *consonant gradation*[2] refers to regular alternations of the consonant phonemes in the consonant center of the final foot of a word.[3]

All consonant phonemes in the consonant center are included in the present classification of such alternations. These alternations come in pairs of stem allomorphs that differ quantitatively and/or qualitatively. Alternations can be between a preaspirated and the corresponding non-aspirated consonant (^{h}x-x), a geminate consonant and the corresponding singleton consonant (x:-x), a geminate+singleton and the corresponding singleton+singleton (x:y-xy), two singletons and only the latter singleton (xy-y), and three singletons and only the initial and final singleton (xyz-xz).[4]

These patterns and the attested alternations are provided in Table 4.2 on the following page. The term *strong grade* (abbreviated 'str') is used to refer to the form with preaspiration, a geminate or more consonant segments than the corresponding form. Likewise, the term *weak grade* (abbreviated 'wk') refers to the form lacking a preaspirated or geminate consonant, or having fewer consonant segments, respectively. To facilitate reading Table 4.2, the attested alternations for each pattern are organized by alternations with a non-aspirated element first, followed by patterns with at least one preaspirated element. Furthermore, the individual lists of alternations are organized by mode of articulation and by the order set forth in the consonant phoneme inventory in Table 3.1 on page 37. Some examples illustrating this can be found below.

The minimal pair in (2) shows a consonant gradation alternation /^{h}p-p/, which corresponds to the pattern ^{h}x-x.

(2) /dɔ^{h}pe/ /dɔpe/ [pit100324]
  dåhpe dåbe
  house\NOM.SG house\GEN.SG

---

[2] This term is quite common in Saami linguistics, e.g., in Feist (2010), although it is also known as 'grade alternation', e.g., in Sammallahti (1998). As much of the literature on Saami linguistics is in languages other than English, it may be useful to provide some translations of the term 'consonant gradation': German: *Stufenwechsel*, Swedish: *stadieväxling*, Finnish: *astevaihtelu*, Hungarian: *fokváltakozás* and Russian: *чередование ступеней*.

[3] Cf. §2.2.2 on prosodic positions, including the foot and the consonant center.

[4] There are certainly other ways to classify these alternations in the consonant center as well. For instance, one could disregard any consonant phonemes that are present in both alternations (then x:-x and x:y-xy would be the same type), or consider the x:-x and ^{h}x:-x patterns in Table 4.2 to be the same type as simply a case of alternating consonant phonemes. However, the patterns in the present classification demonstrate the regularity of patterning between phonological features (such as geminate vs. singleton).

4 Morphological patterns and word classes

Table 4.2: Consonant center gradation patterns

strong	↔	weak	attested alternations
ʰx	↔	x	ʰp-p, ʰt-t, ʰk-k, ʰts-ts, ʰtʃ-tʃ
x:	↔	x	f:-f, v:-v, s:-s, ʃ:-ʃ, m:-m, n:-n, ɲ:-ɲ, r:-r, l:-l, j:-j
			ʰp:-ʰp, ʰt:-ʰt, ʰk:-ʰk, ʰtʃ:-ʰtʃ, ʰts:-ʰts
x:y	↔	xy	p:t-pt, p:k-pk, p:ts-pts, p:tʃ-ptʃ, p:s-ps, p:m-pm, p:n-pn,
			p:ɲ-pɲ, p:r-pr, p:l-pl, p:j-pj, t:k-tk, t:m-tm, t:n-tn, t:ɲ-tɲ,
			k:t-kt, k:tʃ-ktʃ, k:ts-kts, k:s-ks, k:ʃ-kʃ, k:ŋ-kŋ, k:l-kl,
			f:t-ft, f:n-n, v:t-vt, v:k-vk, v:ts-vts, v:tʃ-vtʃ, v:s-vs, v:ʃ-vʃ,
			v:r-vr, v:l-vl, v:j-vj, s:p-sp, s:t-st, s:k-sk, s:m-sm, s:n-sn,
			ʃ:k-ʃk,
			m:s-ms, m:ʃ-mʃ, n:t-nt, ŋ:k-ŋk
			r:p-rp, r:t-rt, r:k-rk, r:ts-rts, r:f-rf, r:s-rs, r:ʃ-rʃ, r:f-rf,
			r:v-rv, r:j-rj, l:p-lp, l:t-lt, l:k-lk, l:f-lf, l:v-lv, l:s-ls, l:j-lj,
			j:p-jp, j:t-jt, j:k-jk, j:s-js, j:f-jf, j:v-jv, j:r-jr, j:l-jl
			m:ʰp-mʰp, m:ʰk-mʰk, n:ʰt-nʰt, n:ʰts-nʰts, ŋ:ʰk-ŋʰk,
			r:ʰp-rʰp, r:ʰt-rʰt, r:ʰk-rʰk, r:ʰtʃ-rʰtʃ, r:ʰts-rʰts, l:ʰp-lʰp, l:ʰt-lʰt,
			l:ʰk-lʰk, l:ʰts-lʰts, l:ʰtʃ-lʰtʃ, j:ʰt-jʰt, j:ʰk-jʰk, j:ʰtʃ-jʰtʃ, j:ʰts-jʰts
xy	↔	y	pm-m, pɲ-ɲ, tn-n, tɲ-ɲ, tj-j, kŋ-ŋ
xyz	↔	xz	vtn-vn, vtɲ-vɲ, rpm-rm, rtn-rn, rtj-rj, lpm-lm, ltn-ln,
			ltɲ-lɲ, jpm-jm, jtn-jn

The minimal pairs in (3) and (4) are examples of consonant gradation patterns which differ in a geminate-singleton alternation. The consonant gradation alternations illustrated are /v:-v/ and /r:k-rk/, respectively, and correspond to the patterns x:-x and x:y-xy.

(3) /sa:v:a/   /sa:va/   [pit100323a]
    sávva   sáva
    wish\3SG.PRS wish\2SG.PRS

(4) /pɛr:ko/   /perko/   [pit090926]
    bärrgo   biergo
    meat\NOM.SG   meat\NOM.PL

The minimal pairs in (5) and (6) are examples of consonant gradation patterns in which a phoneme present in the first form is absent in the second form. The

4.1 Overview of morphology

consonant gradation alternations illustrated here are /tn-n/ and /jpm-jm/, respectively, and correspond to the patterns xy-y and xyz-xz.

(5) /atna/ /ana/ [pit101208]
 adna ana
 have\3SG.PRS have\2SG.PRS

(6) /va:jpmo/ /va:jmo/ [pit110413a]
 vájbmo vájmo
 heart\NOM.SG heart\NOM.PL

As may be inferred from the examples above, paradigmatic alternations between NOM.SG and NOM.PL forms for nouns, or between 2SG.PRS and 3SG.PRS forms for verbs are often a good source of minimal pairs concerning consonant gradation alternations, and are a useful way to determine consonant gradation patterns.

Note that the geminate plosives and affricates /p: t: k: ts: tʃ:/ are lacking in Table 4.2 on the facing page for the pattern x:-x, although alternations such as p:-p could be expected. However, due to a lack of sufficient data and some conflicting data in the corpus, it is not entirely clear what the current status is for consonant gradation in words with a consonant center consisting solely of a geminate plosive or affricate. The fact that Pite Saami lacks consonant gradation in a limited number of contexts is one of the main differences to Lule Saami to the north, which does not lack consonant gradation, and Ume Saami to the south, which features consonant gradation even less frequently (cf. Sammallahti 1998: 21–23). The example in (7) illustrates a word clearly lacking consonant gradation in the corpus data, here with the geminate velar plosive /k:/.

(7) /va:k:e/ /va:k:e/ (*/va:ke/) [pit110522]
 vágge vágge
 valley\NOM.SG valley\NOM.PL

Corpus data also indicate that variation within the Pite Saami area complicates things. For instance, the adjective *tjábbe* 'beautiful' undergoes consonant gradation in the speech of speakers from the northern parts of Arjeplog, but does not for southern speakers, as illustrated in (8). For northern speakers, the gradation is realized as an alternation in voicing, and not length.

(8) /tʃa:p:a/ /tʃa:p:e/ /tʃa:b:e/ [pit110522, sje20131017]
  southern northern
 tjábba tjábbe
 beautiful\ATTR beautiful\PRED

77

4 Morphological patterns and word classes

This being the case, some speakers from farther north may have further voiced plosive phonemes /b: d: g:/ that only occur in consonant gradation alternations with the corresponding unvoiced phonemes /p: t: k:/. However, it is not clear based on the corpus data how widespread this feature is, or if it also affects geminate affricates.

Finally, it is not clear from the corpus data what the status of the phonological contexts lacking consonant gradation mentioned in Sammallahti (1998: 21) (working from a historical perspective and with older data) is. Further research is needed to complete the picture, and variation within Pite Saami and possible effects of language attrition should also be taken into consideration.

4.1.2.2 Umlaut

The term *umlaut* refers to regular allomorphic alternations of the vowels in the V1 position of a stem.[5] The two umlaut patterns attested in the corpus are listed in Table 4.3.

Table 4.3: The two attested umlaut patterns

IPA			orthography		
ɛ	↔	e	ä	↔	ie
u͡a	↔	o	ua/uä	↔	uo

These umlaut alternations are qualitative and not quantitative. These alternations are not triggered by the phonological environment, but instead morphologically. The allomorph /ɛ/ in the first pattern is found in the same paradigmatic slots for each inflectional class as /u͡a/[6] in the second pattern, just as the allomorphs /e/ and /o/ also correspond to the same paradigmatic slots. Word forms for *bägge* 'wind' in (9) and for *buälldet* 'burn' in (10) provide examples of the two umlaut patterns.

(9)   /bɛg:a/   /beg:a/   [pit080621]
       bägga   biegga
       wind\NOM.SG   wind\NOM.PL

---

[5] Cf. §2.2.2 on prosodic positions, including V1 position.
[6] Note that /u͡a/ has an allomorph [u͡ɛ] triggered by purely phonological vowel harmony; cf. §3.2.1.9.

(10) /pua̯ːlta/   /polta/   [pit101208]
     buallda   *buolda*
     ignite\3SG.PRS ignite\2SG.PRS

For lexemes subject to consonant gradation, forms featuring /ɛ/ or /u͡a/ are typically in the strong grade, while forms with /e/ or /o/ are normally in the weak grade; cf. the word forms in example (10).

4.1.2.3 Vowel harmony

The term *vowel harmony* (abbreviated 'VH') here refers to non-adjacent regressive phonological assimilation concerning the place of articulation of the V1 vowel of a stem in the context of certain V2 vowels.[7] Specifically, mid-high or high front vowels in V2 position in specific paradigmatic slots trigger raising of the vowel in V1 position. Because the paradigmatic slots that trigger vowel harmony differ between word classes and inflectional classes, and do not apply across the board, vowel harmony is not a purely phonological process, but morphophonological. Furthermore, the results of harmony on the same underlying vowel are inconsistent, and may be due to a word's membership is certain morphological classes concerning vowel harmony. However, future research must be conducted to come to a more thorough conclusion on this.

Verbs and nouns can be subject to vowel harmony, but the assimilation patterns vary both between these word classes and within them. Table 4.4 on the following page summarizes the various patterns and the word classes that they are attested in based on the current corpus.

The morphological categories that trigger vowel harmony also vary. This is the case not only between nouns and verbs (as these have different inflectional categories), but also between inflectional classes for verbs. These categories are presented in Table 4.5 on the next page.

Some examples for vowel harmony are provided here. In (11), an example is shown of vowel harmony in the Class Ie noun *guolle* 'fish', as it alternates between /o/ in the V1 vowel of the NOM.SG form, and /u/ in the NOM.PL form.

(11) /kole/   /kulij/   [pit110413a]
     guole   *guli-j*
     fish\NOM.PL fish-GEN.PL

In (12), an example of vowel harmony in the class II verb *bassat* 'wash' is provided. Here, a vowel harmony alternation between /a/ in the V1 vowel of the

---

[7] Cf. §2.2.2 on prosodic positions, including V1 and V2 positions.

79

4 *Morphological patterns and word classes*

Table 4.4: Vowel harmony assimilation patterns and the word classes these are found in

VH pattern			nouns	verbs
ɛ/e	→	i	✓	✓
u͡a/o	→	u	✓	✓
aː	→	ɛ	✓	✓
ɔ	→	u	✓	✓
a	→	ɛ	✓	
a	→	i		✓
aː	→	i		✓
a	→	e		✓

Table 4.5: Paradigm slots that trigger vowel harmony

word class	inflectional class	forms triggering VH
nouns	class Ie	GEN.PL, ACC.PL, ILL.PL, INESS.PL, ELAT.PL, COM.SG, COM.PL
verbs	class II	1DU.PRS, 3PL.PRS, 1SG.PST, 2SG.PST, 3PL.PST, PL.IMP
	class III	1DU.PRS, 3PL.PRS, 1SG.PST, 2SG.PST, 3SG.PST, 1DU.PST, 2DU.PST, 3DU.PST, 1PL.PST, 2PL.PST, 3PL.PST, PL.IMP

2SG.PRS form, and /i/ in the 2SG.PST form is evident (in addition to a consonant gradation alternation).

(12) /pasa/ /bisːe/ [pit101208]
 basa *bisse*
 wash\2SG.PRS wash\2SG.PST

Finally, (13) shows an example of vowel harmony in the class III verb *buälldet* 'burn'. Here, a vowel harmony alternation between /o/ in the V1 vowel of the 2SG.PRS form, and /u/ in the 2SG.PST form is evident (in addition to a consonant gradation alternation).

(13)   /polta/   /pulːte/   [pit101208]
       buolda   bullde
       ignite\2SG.PRS ignite\2SG.PST

See §5.3.1.2 for more details on vowel harmony in nouns, and §8.4.2.1 in verbs. Note that, for nouns, vowel harmony is also referred to as '*j*-suffix vowel harmony'.

4.2 Overview of word classes

By characterizing the morphological and syntactic behavior of words in Pite Saami, and grouping such words based on that behavior, a total of seven word classes can be distinguished. These can be divided into two general categories containing generally *open* word classes and *closed* word classes, and are listed in Table 4.6. The specific syntactic criteria and inflectional categories defining these are summarized in Table 4.7 on the next page.

Table 4.6: Pite Saami word classes and the corresponding chapter/section

open word classes	Ch./Sec.	closed word classes	Sec.
nominals		adpositions	§9.2
nouns	Ch. 5	conjunctions	§9.3
pronouns	Ch. 6	interjections	§9.4
adjectivals			
adjectives	Ch. 7		
numerals	§7.9		
verbs	Ch. 8		
adverbials	§9.1		

Some word classes consist of two or more subclasses: *nominals* refer to *nouns* and *pronouns* (personal, demonstrative, reflexive, interrogative and relative), and *adjectivals* include both *adjectives* and *numerals*. Note that pronouns and numerals are closed subclasses belonging to open classes.

This categorization is intended to provide a broad starting point for classifying Pite Saami words; details for each word class can be found in the relevant chapters below. Chapter 5 concerns the nominal subclass *nouns*, which provide fairly straightforward examples of the morphophonological complexities involved in Pite Saami inflection and derivation, while the nominal subclass *pronouns* is dealt

Table 4.7: Morphological and syntactic criteria for word classes

word class	inflectional categories	syntactic criteria
nominals	case/number	head of a nominal phrase
adjectivals	number (for predicate adjectives)	head of an adjectival phrase
verbs	tense/mood/person/number, non-finite forms (connegation, aspect)	head of a verb complex
adverbials	none	head of an adverbial phrase
adpositions	none	head of an adpositional phrase
conjunctions	none	connect words, phrases, clauses, texts
interjections	none	independent words at clause-level

with in Chapter 6. Chapter 7 then covers the adjectival subclasses *adjectives* and *numerals*. Following this, Chapter 8 deals with *verbs*. Finally, the remaining small classes (*adverbials, adpositions, conjunctions* and *interjections*) are covered in Chapter 9.

5 Nominals I: Nouns

Nouns in Pite Saami form an open class of words that are formally defined by their ability to head a nominal phrase. As the head of an NP, a noun inflects for case and number. Each nouns consists of a lexical stem followed by an inflectional class marker and a portmanteau suffix indicating case and number, as illustrated in (1).

(1) Σ + class-marker + case/number

Pite Saami noun stems can have up to three allomorphic forms throughout the nominal paradigm due to a complex combination of morphophonological processes. The current chapter first describes the morphological categories number (§5.1) and case (§5.2) in a general way in order to provide a background for the variables discussed in §5.3 on morphological case and number marking. A description of the inflectional class markers and the resulting inflectional classes for nouns is given in §5.4.[1] The final section (§5.5) deals briefly with the possessive suffixes, an infrequent set of archaic suffixes that indicate number and case and signify the possessor of the head noun's referent.

5.1 Number in nouns

Pite Saami nouns inflect for singular and plural in all grammatical cases except the essive and possibly the abessive case. Dual is not a relevant category for nouns, despite being an integral category in verb morphology and for some pronoun classes. Number is expressed along with case by portmanteau suffixes, stem alternations, or a combination of both. §5.3 on number and case marking treats this in more detail.

There is no formal distinction between count and mass nouns in Pite Saami, as illustrated by the example in (2), in which the words for 'flour', 'sugar' and 'food' are all inflected for plural.

---

[1] Cf. §10.1 for derivational morphology creating nouns.

(2) dán   ájten   inimä   jáfojd   ja
    d-á-n   ájte-n   ini-mä   jáfo-jd   ja
    DEM-PROX-INESS.SG shed-INESS.SG have-1PL.PST flour-ACC.PL and

    suhkurijd   ja   gárvojd   ja   iehtjá biebmojd
    suhkuri-jd   ja   gárvo-jd   ja   iehtjá biebmo-jd
    sugar-ACC.PL and clothing-ACC.PL and other food-ACC.PL
    'In this shed we had flour and sugar and clothing and other food.'
                                                              [pit100310b.100-104]

When the singular form is used, a noun's referent is either generic, as illustrated by both nouns in (3), or it refers to a single unit, as the noun *ájten* 'shed' in example (2) above.

(3) men vuästa,   del   káfan   njallge
    men vuästa   del   káfa-n   njallge
    but cheese\NOM.SG definitely coffee-INESS.SG tasty
    'But cheese, (it's) definitely tasty in coffee.'   [pit080924.139]

5.2 The nominal case system

Pite Saami has nine cases: nominative, genitive, accusative, illative, inessive, elative, comitative, abessive, and essive.[2] Nouns inflect for these cases, in addition to number, via portmanteau suffixes, stem alternations, or a combination of both. A general description of the cases is provided here. Note that the case system is valid for pronouns (also a subclass of nominals) as well, but not for adjectives and numerals. Case is expressed along with number by portmanteau suffixes, stem alternations, or a combination of both. §5.3 on treats this in more detail.

5.2.1 Nominative case

In addition to being used as the citation form, most commonly in singular, nominative case (NOM) marks the grammatical subject of a verbal clause (typically the most agent-like argument for transitive verbs) as in (4) and (5).

(4) dä   stuor sarves   båhta
    dä   stuor sarves   båhta
    then big   moose\NOM.SG   come\3SG.PRS
    'Then a big moose arrives.'   [pit090702.319]

---

[2] The terminology chosen here for the nine cases reflects the names used traditionally in Uralic studies.

(5) ja dä dáhka almatj dålåv
    ja dä dáhka almatj dålå-v
    and then make\3SG.PRS person\NOM.SG fire-ACC.SG
    'And then one makes a fire.' [pit100404.102]

The possessed noun in a possessive copular clause (cf. §13.1.4) is also in the nominative case, as in (6).

(6) muvne lä bijjla
    muvne lä bijjla
    1SG.INESS be\3SG.PRS car\NOM.SG
    'I have a car.' (lit.: 'at-me is car') [pit080926.01m44s]*e*

5.2.2 Genitive case

The genitive case (GEN), the only adnominal case in Pite Saami, marks the possessor modifying the head of a noun phrase (the possessed noun), as in (7).

(7) gokt lä dan almatja namma
    gokt lä d-a-n almatj-a namma
    how be\3SG.PRS DEM-DIST-GEN.SG person-GEN.SG name\NOM.SG
    majna ságasta?
    ma-jna ságasta
    REL-COM.SG talk\2SG.PRS
    'What is the name of that person who you are talking with?'
    [pit110521b1.040]*e*

Furthermore, the nominal complement in a postpositional phrase occurs in the genitive case, as the noun *gåde* 'hut' in (8).

(8) gåde sinne suovastit
    gåde sinne suovasti-t
    hut\GEN.SG in smoke-INF
    'to smoke (something) inside a hut' [pit100405a.157]

5.2.3 Accusative case

The accusative case (ACC) marks the object of a transitive verb, as illustrated by the monotransitive clause in (9).

5 Nominals I: Nouns

(9) dä virtiv válldet giehpajd ja ribrev ja
    dä virti-v válde-t giehpa-jd ja ribbre-v ja
    then must-1SG.PRS take-INF lung-ACC.PL and liver-ACC.SG and
    dagarijd   ulgos
    dagari-jd   ulgos
    such-ACC.PL out
    'Then I have to take out the lungs, the liver and such things.'
    [pit080909.103]

In ditransitive clauses, the accusative marks the object referring to the theme while the recipient is marked by the illative, as in (10).

(10) mån   vaddav   gajka buhtsujda   biebmov
     mån   vadda-v   gajka buhtsu-jda biebmo-v
     1SG.NOM give-1SG.PRS all\ILL reindeer-ILL.PL food-ACC.SG
     'I give food to all the reindeer.'
     [pit110413b.137]e

The accusative can also mark nouns functioning as a clause-level temporal adverbial phrase denoting a period of time, as in (11).

(11) jo dan   vuolen udemä   ijav
     jo d-a-n   vuolen ude-mä   ija-v
     yes DEM-DIST-GEN.SG under sleep-1PL.PST night-ACC.SG
     'Yes, and we slept under that for a night.'
     [pit090702.305]

5.2.4 Illative case

The illative case (ILL) marks nouns that are the goal of the action expressed by a verb of motion, as in (12).

(12) muhten båtsoj   ij   både   gärrdáj
     muhten båtsoj   ij   både   gärrdá-j
     some   reindeer\NOM.PL NEG\3PL.PRS come\CONNEG corral-ILL.SG
     'Some reindeer don't come into the corral.'
     [pit080909.007]

In addition, the illative case marks nouns that refer to the addressee of communication, as in (13), and the recipient of 'giving' actions, as in (14).

(13) muv   áhttje   hålloj   såmes raddnáj...
     muv   áhttje   hållo-j   såmes raddná-j
     1SG.GEN father\NOM.SG say-3SG.PST some friend-ILL.SG
     'My father said to some friend...'
     [pit090702.505]

(14) vadde   Jåssjåj   aj
    vadde   Jåssjå-j   aj
    give\SG.IMP Josh-ILL.SG also
    'Give (one) to Josh, too!'   [pit090519.033]

Finally, familial relations can also be expressed using an illative construction. In such cases, the 'ego' of the family relation is in the illative, as in (15).

(15) dån   lä   eddno   munje
    dån   lä   eddno   munje
    2SG.NOM be\2SG.PRS maternal.uncle\NOM.SG 1SG.ILL
    'You are my maternal uncle.' (lit.: you are maternal uncle to me)
                                                  [pit110413b.035]e

In this example, the illative nominal is a pronoun, but it is plausible that full nouns are possible in this function as well, although there are no such tokens in the corpus.

5.2.5 Inessive case

The inessive case (INESS) marks nouns that function as adjuncts to verbal clauses indicating the location of the event or action, as in (16).

(16) nå,   mav   enabov   dihki   Áhkkabakten?
    nå   ma-v   enabo-v   dihki   Ahkkabakte-n
    well what-ACC.SG more-ACC.SG do\2SG.PST Ahkkabakte-INESS.SG
    'Well, what more did you do in Áhkkabakkte?'   [pit080924.021]

Similarly, as the complement of the copular verb, an inessive noun indicates the location of the subject referent, as in (17).

(17) vággen   Sálvojåhkå'l
    vágge-n   Sálvo-jåhkå=l
    valley-INESS.SG Sálvo-creek\NOM.SG=be\3SG.PRS
    'Sálvo Creek is in the valley.'   [pit100404.007]

The possessor noun in a possessive copular clause (cf. §13.1.4) is also in the inessive case, as in (18).

(18) sámen   lä   bena
    sáme-n   lä   bena
    Saami-INESS.SG be\3SG.PRS dog\NOM.SG
    'The Saami man has a dog.' (lit.: at Saami is dog)   [pit080917a.068]e

5.2.6 Elative case

The elative case (ELAT) marks nouns as the source of an action of transfer, as in (19), as well as the origin, as in (20) and (21).

(19) *váldav tjåjvev ribrist luovas*
válda-v tjåjve-v ribri-st luovas
take-1SG.PRS stomach-ACC.SG liver-ELAT.SG loose
'I loosen the stomach from the liver.' [pit080909.079]

(20) *nå gåsse dija älgijdä Örnvikast vuodjet vadnásav?*
nå gåsse dija älgi-jdä Örnvika-st vuodje-t vadnása-v
well when 2PL.NOM begin-2PL.PST Örnvik-ELAT.SG drive-INF boat-ACC.SG
'Well when did you start taking the boat from Örnvik?' [pit080924.563]

(21) *dån båda Amerigist*
dån båda Amerig-ist
2SG.NOM come\2SG.PRS America-ELAT.SG
'You come from America.' [pit080621.28m02s]e

The elative also marks the addressee of a question (the source of information), as in (22).

(22) *Eddest galgav gatjadit*
Edde-st galga-v gatjadi-t
Edgar-ELAT.SG will-1SG.PRS ask-INF
'I will ask Edgar.' [pit090519.357]

Similarly, in a copular clause, the elative case can mark a noun whose referent is a source of pain, as in (23).

(23) *mån lev åjvest*
mån le-v åjve-st
1SG.NOM be-1SG.PRS head-ELAT.SG
'I have a headache.' (lit.: 'I am from head') [pit110331b.079]e

The noun referring to the material that something consists of or is made of is in the elative case, as in (24) and (25).

(24) *mån iv tuhtje dav färska málest*
mån i-v tuhtje d-a-v färska måle-st
1SG.NOM NEG-1SG.PRS like\CONNEG DEM-DIST-ACC.SG fresh blood-ELAT.SG
'I don't like that (made) of fresh blood.' [pit080924.271]

(25) dá   lä   sasnest   gårroduvum
    d-á   lä   sasne-st   gårro-duvu-m
    DEM-PROX\NOM.PL be\3PL.PRS furless.leather-ELAT.SG sew-PASS-PRF
    'These are sewn out of furless leather.'   [pit080708_Session08.001]

The elative case can be used to mark the agent which carries out the action referred to by a passivized verb, as in (26).

(26) gåhte   lä   tsiggijduvvum   mánájst
    gåhte   lä   tsiggij-duvvu-m   máná-jst
    hut\NOM.SG be\3SG.PRS build-PASS-PRF   child-ELAT.PL
    'The hut has been built by children.'   [pit110518a.28m41s]*e*

In comparative constructions, elative marks a noun whose referent is the standard in the comparison, as in (27).

(27) mån   lev   stuorab   Svienast
    mån   le-v   stuora-b   Sviena-st
    1SG.NOM be-1SG.PRS big-COMP Sven-ELAT.SG
    'I am bigger than Sven.'   [pit110331b.087]*e*

5.2.7 Comitative case

The comitative case (COM) marks nouns referring to someone or something participating in an action together with the agent as in (28), or some other participant, as in (29).

(28) men ådtjo   sáme   gielav   ságastit   duv
    men ådtjo   sáme   giela-v   ságasti-t   duv
    but may\2SG.PST Saami\GEN.SG language-ACC.SG speak-INF 2SG.GEN
    årbenij?
    årbeni-j
    sibling-COM.PL
    'But were you allowed to speak the Saami language with your siblings?'
                                                    [pit080924.366]

(29) válda   káfav   suhkorijn   jala suhkorahta?
    válda   káfa-v   suhkori-jn   jala suhkor-ahta
    take\2SG.PRS coffee-ACC.SG sugar-COM.SG or sugar-ABESS
    'Do you take your coffee with sugar or without sugar?'
                                                    [pit110509b.11m41s]*e*

5 Nominals I: Nouns

The comitative also marks nouns referring to an instrument used to carry out an action, as in (30).

(30)   *del vuodja   bijlajn   Örnvikaj   ja dä   vádnasijn*
        del vuodja   bijla-jn   Örnvika-j   ja dä   vádnasi-jn
        now drive\3SG.PRS car-COM.SG Örnvik-ILL.SG and then boat-COM.SG
        Tjeggelvasa   badjel
        Tjeggelvas-a   badjel
        Tjeggelvas-GEN.SG over
        'Now one drives to Örnvik by car, then by boat over Lake Tjeggelvas.'
                                                                                    [pit080924.471]

When two persons or things are equated with respect to a certain characteristic, the comitative marks the noun whose referent is the standard of comparison, as in (31).

(31)   *Svenna   lä   akta vuoras Ingerijn*
        Svenna   lä   akta vuoras Inger-ijn
        Sven\NOM.SG be\3SG.PRS one old   Inger-COM.SG
        'Sven is as old as Inger.' (lit.: Sven is one age with Inger)   [pit110331b.135]*e*

5.2.8 Abessive case

The referent of a noun marked by the abessive case (ABESS) is lacking or missing, as illustrated by (32)[3] and (33).

(32)   *válda   káfav   suhkorijn   jala suhkorahta?*
        válda   káfa-v   suhkori-jn   jala suhkor-ahta
        take\2SG.PRS coffee-ACC.SG sugar-COM.SG or   sugar-ABESS
        'Do you take your coffee with sugar or without sugar?'
                                                                              [pit110509b.11m41s]*e*

(33)   *dån   lä   vájmodak   dal*
        dån   lä   vájmo-dak   dal
        2SG.NOM be\2SG.PRS heart-ABESS now
        'You are heartless now.'   [pit110413a.226]*e*

Note that nouns in abessive are rare in natural speech, and limited to elicitation sessions in the corpus.[4] While the meaning of nouns in the abessive case is quite

---

[3] This example is also found in (29) above but is repeated here for convenience, as well as to focus on the abessive noun.

[4] The Wordlist Project's wordlist indicates that the word *ájnát* can also be used to express 'without' (entry 4367; cf. §1.2.3.4), but the corpus does not provide any tokens of this.

5.2 The nominal case system

clear, their morphophonological behavior is problematic; see §5.3.3 for more details.

5.2.9 Essive case

The essive case (ESS) generally marks predicative nouns functioning as complements of verbs such as *sjaddat* 'become', as in (34) and (35), and *gåhtjoduvvat* 'be called', as in (36). Note that nouns in the essive case do not inflect for number.

(34) *bednan sjaddav*
 bedna-n sjadda-v
 dog-ESS become-1SG.PRS
 'I become a dog.' [pit110509b.05m49s]*e*

(35) *jegŋa sjaddá tjáhtsen*
 jegŋa sjaddá tjáhtse-n
 ice\NOM.SG become\3SG.PRS water-ESS
 'Ice becomes water.' [pit110331b.160]*e*

(36) *dut såhke vadnásan gåhtjoduvva*
 d-u-t såhke vadnása-n gåhtjo-duvva
 DEM-RMT-NOM.SG birch\NOM.SG boat-ESS call-PASS\3SG.PRS
 'Yonder birch is called a boat.' [pit110509b.14m02s]*e*

Furthermore, the complement of the particle *dugu* 'like' can be in the essive case, as illustrated by the example in (37).

(37) *dat vuodja dugu goullen*
 d-a-t vuodja dugu goulle-n
 DEM-DIST-NOM.SG swim\3SG.PRS like fish-ESS
 'He swims like a fish.' [pit110413a.059]*e*

However, while my main consultant accepted constructions like in (37), her initial response normally consisted of nearly the same construction, only with the noun in nominative case, as in (38).

(38) *vuodja dugu goulle*
 vuodja dugu goulle
 swim\3SG.PRS like fish\NOM.SG
 'He swims like a fish.' [pit110413a.052]*e*

Finally, it should be pointed out that essive is not particularly common in the corpus; tokens for this case are only found in elicitation sessions. In summary,

5 Nominals I: Nouns

there are not enough data to come to any definitive conclusions concerning the status of essive in current Pite Saami usage.

5.3 Number and case marking on nouns

As indicated in the previous sections, Pite Saami nouns inflect for nine cases and two number categories (only the essive and possibly the abessive cases do not inflect for number). While case and number are generally marked by nominal suffixes, they are often supplemented by other morphophonological marking strategies, or even expressed solely by non-linear morphology. These other strategies are:

- consonant alternations in the stem (also known as *consonant gradation*)
- stem-vowel alternations (umlaut)
- vowel harmony

Concerning nouns, the segmental alternations are discussed in detail in §5.3.2, while vowel harmony is presented in §5.4.1.1. First, a short discussion of the nominal suffixes follows here.

5.3.1 Nominal suffixes

Pite Saami has a number of portmanteau suffixes expressing case and number. Only NOM.SG, NOM.PL and GEN.SG are generally not marked by any linear morphology. The nominal suffixes marking case and number are listed in Table 5.1 on the facing page. Note that the status of the abessive suffixes is unclear, including whether they inflect for number, as discussed in §5.3.3. Nouns in essive case do not inflect for number.

In NOM.PL and GEN.SG, the *-h* suffix is optional in Pite Saami (and therefore appears in parentheses in Table 5.1).[5] The COM.SG suffix has two allomorphs: *-jn* and *-jna*, which seem to be in free variation in the corpus, and not determined phonologically.

5.3.1.1 Nominal suffixes and syncretism

Several of the nominal inflectional suffixes, considered by themselves, are homophonous:

---

[5] The paradigms in Lehtiranta (1992: 156–157) also indicate an optional *-h*, while Lagercrantz (1926: 104–105) does not indicate any *-h* at all.

5.3 Number and case marking on nouns

Table 5.1: Nominal case and number suffixes

	SINGULAR	PLURAL
NOM	-	- (~ -h)
GEN	- (~ -h)	-j
ACC	-v	-jt
ILL	-j	-jda
INESS	-n	-jn
ELAT	-st	-jst
COM	-jn(a)	-j
ABESS	-dak, -daga, -gat, -gahta, -ahta	
ESS		-n

- *-j* for ILL.SG, GEN.PL, and COM.PL

- *-jn* for INESS.PL and COM.SG

- *-n* for ESS and INESS.SG

- (optional) *-h* for NOM.PL and GEN.SG[6]

For Class III nouns[7] which do not exhibit any stem allomorphy, the corresponding inflected noun forms within a paradigm are therefore syncretic. Two examples are listed in Table 5.2.

Table 5.2: Syncretic inflectional form sets for Class III nouns without stem allomorphy

ILL.SG/GEN.PL/COM.PL	INESS.PL/COM.SG	ESS/INESS.SG	NOM.PL/GEN.SG	
almatjij	*almatjijn*	*almatjin*	*almatja(h)*	'person'
ålolij	*ålolijn*	*ålolin*	*ålola(h)*	'tool'

However, for nouns which have stem allomorphy (consonant gradation, umlaut and/or *j*-suffix vowel harmony), different stem allomorphs are chosen for ILL.SG than for GEN.PL and COM.PL, for ESS than for INESS.SG, and for NOM.SG than for NOM.PL and GEN.SG.

---

[6] The alternative to the optional *-h* suffix for NOM.PL and GEN.SG forms is no suffix (except for Class III nouns, which are marked by *-Ca*).

[7] Cf. §5.4.3.

5 Nominals I: Nouns

As a result, only the inflected forms for GEN.PL and COM.PL, for INESS.PL and COM.SG (the *-jn* variant of the latter), as well as for NOM.PL and GEN.SG are syncretic in all noun paradigms. Some examples are provided in Table 5.3.

Table 5.3: Syncretic inflectional form pairs valid for all noun classes

NOM.PL/GEN.SG	GEN.PL/COM.PL	INESS.PL/COM.SG	class	
luokta(-h)	*luokta-j*	*luokta-jn*	Ia	'bay'
vajmå(-h)	*vajmå-j*	*vajmå-jn*	Id	'heart'
guole(-h)	*guli-j*	*guli-jn*	Ie	'fish'
vágge(-h)	*väggi-j*	*väggi-jn*	Ie	'valley'
ålma(-h)	*ålma-j*	*ålma-jn*	II	'man'
almatja(-h)	*almatji-j*	*almatji-jn*	IIIa	'person'
bednaga(-h)	*bednagi-j*	*bednagi-jn*	IIIb	'dog'

5.3.1.2 Nominal suffixes with a *-j* component

When looking at the inflectional suffixes, it is noticeable that a number of suffixes contain a *-j* component, as highlighted by Table 5.4. It is tempting to posit a plural marking suffix *-j* because it occurs in GEN.PL, ACC.PL, ILL.PL, INESS.PL, ELAT.PL and COM.PL; however, the ILL.SG suffix *-j* and the COM.SG suffix *-jn(a)* both have a similar *-j* element, but are clearly not plural.

Table 5.4: Nominal case/number suffixes with a *-j-* segment

	SINGULAR	PLURAL
NOM		
GEN		*-j*
ACC		*-jt*
ILL	*-j*	*-jda*
INESS		*-jn*
ELAT		*-jst*
COM	*-jn(a)*	*-j*
ABESS		
ESS		

5.3 Number and case marking on nouns

Furthermore, as illustrated in Table 5.5, the plural cases with a -*j* component in the suffix trigger vowel harmony in stem consonants in Class Ie nouns (cf. §5.4.1.1), but so does the COM.SG suffix, while the ILL.SG suffix does not trigger *j*-suffix

Table 5.5: Nominal case/number suffixes with a -*j*- segment and triggering *j*-suffix vowel harmony

	SINGULAR	PLURAL
NOM		
GEN		✓
ACC		✓
ILL	X	✓
INESS		✓
ELAT		✓
COM	✓	✓
ABESS		
ESS		

vowel harmony (despite being segmentally identical to GEN.PL and COM.PL suffixes). Thus, -*j* suffixes that trigger vowel harmony also fail to align with number marking. As a result, I do not analyze any -*j* suffix as a plural marker, but do point out this nearly pervasive plural pattern.[8]

5.3.2 Non-linear noun morphology

In addition to the suffixes described above, most nouns are also marked for case and number by non-linear stem allomorphy (cf. §4.1.2). Because NOM.SG, NOM.PL and GEN.SG lack suffixes completely,[9] nouns in these three case/number categories can only be marked by non-linear morphology.

To illustrate this, the inflectional paradigm for the noun *bärrgo* 'meat' is provided in Table 5.6 on the next page and described here. Note that, due to /o/ occurring in V2 position in all forms as the inflectional class marker, the stem has two allomorphs: *bärrg*- and *bierg*-.

In summary, the inflectional paradigm for *bärrgo* is characterized by both consonant gradation and umlaut in the stem, and the morphological environment determines which of these allomorphs is selected. As a result, the ACC.PL form

---

[8] Cf. 'eidemic resonance' in Bickel & Nichols (2007: 209–210).
[9] As mentioned in §5.3.1 above, there is an optional -*h* suffix marking NOM.PL and GEN.SG.

5 Nominals I: Nouns

Table 5.6: The inflectional paradigm for the noun *bärrgo* 'meat'

	SINGULAR	PLURAL
NOM	*bärrgo*	*biergo*
GEN	*biergo*	*biergoj*
ACC	*biergov*	*biergojd*
ILL	*bärrgoj*	*biergojda*
INESS	*biergon*	*biergojn*
ELAT	*biergost*	*biergojst*
COM	*biergojn*	*biergo*
ABESS	*biergodak*	*biergodahta*
ESS	*bärrgon*	

biergojd is marked for case/number by the weak *bierg-* stem and the *-jd* suffix simultaneously, and the ILL.SG form *bärrgoj* is marked by the strong *bärrg-* stem and the *-j* suffix. The most obvious evidence that the choice of stem allomorph is morphologically meaningful can be found in a comparison of the NOM.SG form *bärrgo* and the NOM.PL[10] form *biergo*. These forms differ exclusively in the choice of the strong versus the weak stem allomorph and in the choice of umlaut. Thus, the NOM.SG form *bärrgo* is marked for case/number by the fact that the stem is in the strong grade and features the vowel *ä*, while the NOM.PL stem is in the weak grade and features the vowel *ie*.

This pattern of non-linear case/number marking throughout the paradigm for *bärrgo* is illustrated in Table 5.7 on the facing page. Here, two patterns are manifest: the forms for NOM.SG, ILL.SG and ESS show one pattern, while all other case/number combinations exhibit the other pattern. This alignment of stem allomorph selection is more or less prevalent throughout Pite Saami noun paradigms whenever stem allomorphy is a part of a noun's inflectional paradigm. Note, however, that not every noun undergoes consonant gradation and/or umlaut; instead, their presence are determined by the phonological form of a noun. Consonant gradation is described in detail in §4.1.2.1, and umlaut in §4.1.2.2; some examples of nouns with consonant gradation and umlaut alternations are shown in Table 5.8 on the next page and Table 5.9 on page 98, respectively.

---

[10] As the NOM.PL form is always syncretic with the GEN.SG form, a comparison of the latter with the NOM.SG form would be equally insightful.

5.3 Number and case marking on nouns

Table 5.7: Non-linear morphological case/number marking in the paradigm for the noun *bärrgo* 'meat'

	SINGULAR	PLURAL
NOM	ä+str	
GEN		
ACC		
ILL	ä+str	ie+wk
INESS		
ELAT		
COM		
ABESS		
ESS	ä+str	

Table 5.8: Consonant gradation patterns for nouns, with NOM.SG and NOM.PL example pairs

strong	-	weak	NOM.SG		NOM.PL	
ʰx	-	x	/tɔʰpe/ *dåhpe*	-	/tɔpe/ *dåbe*	'house'
xː	-	x	/kolːe/ *guolle*	-	/kole/ *guole*	'fish'
			/naːʰpːe/ *náhppe*	-	/naːʰpe/ *náhpe*	'milking bowl'
xːy	-	xy	/ɲaːrka/ *njárrga*	-	/ɲaːrka/ *njárga*	'cape' (geog.)
xy	-	y	/etno/ *edno*	-	/eno/ *eno*	'river'
xyz	-	xz	/vaːjpmo/ *vájbmo*	-	/vaːjmo/ *vájmo*	'heart'

5.3.3 Problematic case/number marking in abessive case

Unlike the other cases, the behavior of nouns in the abessive case is a bit of an enigma, even if its meaning, which typically translates as 'without', is quite clear (cf. §5.2.8). Indeed, it is difficult to come to any certain conclusions about the rela-

5 Nominals I: Nouns

Table 5.9: Umlaut alternation patterns for nouns, with NOM.SG and NOM.PL example pairs

x - y	NOM.SG	NOM.PL	
ɛ - e	/pɛk:a/	- /pek:a/	'wind'
	bägga	biegga	
u͡a - o	/lu͡ak:ta/	- /lokta/	'bay'
	luakkta	luokta	

tionship between abessive as a case *per se* and the morphophonological marking of nouns in the abessive case. It seems to be rarely used in natural speech, and is only attested in the corpus in elicitation sessions. Even in elicitation sessions, language consultants were often hesitant or uncertain of the word forms they produced, and often produced conflicting forms for a single item. Indeed, the slipperiness of the abessive case is nothing new, as both Lagercrantz (1926) and Lehtiranta (1992) only provide incomplete treatments of abessive.

One potential source of the confusion (even for speakers) is the fact that abessive suffixes are unique in two ways. First, there is significant allomorphy, and, secondly, some of the allomorphs are the only bisyllabic nominal inflection suffixes in Pite Saami. The attested forms are -*dak*, -*daga*, -*gat*, -*gahta* and -*ahta* (cf. examples (32) and (33) on page 90). Furthermore, the weak grade usually accompanies abessive, but sometimes the strong grade does. In some cases of Class Ie nouns, *j*-suffix vowel harmony is triggered, in others it is not. In some cases, number is clearly marked, in other cases, there is no distinction between singular and plural.

As a result, the following sections on inflectional noun classes are only able to provide a limited and preliminary description concerning abessive.

5.4 Inflectional classes for nouns

Nouns in Pite Saami can be grouped into three main inflectional classes, with several subclasses, based on recurring patterns across case/number inflectional paradigms. Each noun is marked by a class suffix[11] which is attached directly after the noun stem and precedes case/number suffixes (cf. Figure 1 on page 83).

---

[11] I am indebted to phonologist and Lule Saami scholar Bruce Morén-Duoljá for inspiring me to consider an approach to the data involving post-stem class marking morphology.

5.4 Inflectional classes for nouns

For the majority of nouns, this suffix consists only of a vowel (in V2 position); however, the class marking suffixes in the less frequent classes II and III deviate from this pattern. The presence of umlaut alternations and/or consonant gradation for a given noun is not dependent on the noun's membership in a specific class, but is determined by whether the phonemes occupying the V1 position and the consonant center of the final foot, respectively, are susceptible to umlaut and/or consonant gradation. Furthermore, some derivational suffixes (such as the diminutive suffix *-tj*) can block consonant gradation and umlaut from happening in the new derived form. Note that membership in a specific noun class does not seem to be semantically motivated.

The following sections present the four inflectional noun classes based on a preliminary analysis of the corpus; it is possible that, with more research, more noun classes may result, or that the present classes may need revision. Because each noun paradigm consists of seventeen inflectional forms, most of the data on which these classes are based come from elicitation sessions, as it is far beyond realistic for a single, non-native-speaker linguist to collect a sufficiently large natural (i.e., un-elicited, spontaneous) spoken language corpus which includes all inflectional forms for a large variety of nouns.

There are two main criteria for positing the different noun classes:

- the allomorphy of the NOM.SG form of a noun stem in relation to the rest of the inflectional paradigm (i.e., consonant gradation, umlaut)

- the regularity of the pattern of vowels occurring between the stem and case/number suffixes (i.e., the class marking suffix)

To illustrate these differences, it is sufficient to look at the class suffix in NOM.SG and the alignment of consonant gradation allomorphs, as summarized in Table 5.10. The header *grade alignment* refers to the choice of stem allomorph in NOM.SG versus NOM.PL whenever consonant gradation is relevant for a specific

Table 5.10: Noun classes and their defining features

class	grade alignment	class suffix in NOM.SG
I	str-wk	-a/á/o/å/e
II	wk-str	-Vj
III	wk-str	-

5 Nominals I: Nouns

noun paradigm: the value 'str-wk' indicates that NOM.SG is marked by the strong grade and NOM.PL by the weak grade, while 'wk-str' is the opposite pattern.

Class I is a sort of default class and is therefore dealt with first in §5.4.1, while classes II and III are described in §5.4.2 and §5.4.3. The final section (§5.4.4) provides a brief summary of the noun classes, including a table listing examples from each class.

5.4.1 Class I

Nouns in Class I are characterized by:

- *str-wk* grade alignment (when relevant)

Class I nouns can be divided into five subclasses, depending on the class-marking vowel they have, as illustrated in Table 5.11.

Table 5.11: Subclasses of Class I nouns and their class marking suffixes

subclass	noun class suffix
Ia	-a
Ib	-á
Ic	-o
Id	-å
Ie	-e,i,á

The first four subclasses behave very similarly, while subclass Ie is unique due to the presence of *j*-suffix vowel harmony, as discussed in detail in §5.4.1.1. For subclasses Ia, Ib, Ic and Id, the class marking suffix is invariable throughout the paradigm, while the class marking suffix for subclass Ie varies due to *j*-suffix vowel harmony.

For nouns with consonant gradation and/or umlaut in Class I, NOM.SG, ILL.SG and ESS are in the strong grade and have *ä* or *ua/uä* in V1 position, while other case/number slots in a paradigm have the weak grade and *ie* or *uo* in V1 position. The gradation pattern and class marking suffixes for Class I are summarized in Table 5.12 on the facing page. Here, V stands for the vowel which comprises the suffix for each class (i.e., *a* for Class Ia, *á* for Class Ib, *o* for Class Ic, *å* for Class Id and *e/i/á* for Class Ie).

Inflectional paradigms can be found on pages 101 and 102 to illustrate subclasses Ia, Ib, Ic and Id. The paradigms for the words *luakkta* 'bay' and *mánná*

5.4 Inflectional classes for nouns

Table 5.12: The consonant gradation pattern and inflectional noun class suffixes for Class I

	SINGULAR		PLURAL	
NOM	str	-V	wk	-V
GEN	wk	-V	wk	-V-
ACC	wk	-V-	wk	-V-
ILL	str	-V-	wk	-V-
INESS	wk	-V-	wk	-V-
ELAT	wk	-V-	wk	-V-
COM	wk	-V-	wk	-V-
ABESS	wk	-V-	wk	-V-
ESS	str		-V-	

'child' are provided in Table 5.13 as an example for Class Ia and Class Ib nouns, respectively. Table 5.14 shows the paradigms for *bäbbmo* 'food', a Class Ic noun, and for *skåvvlå* 'school', a Class Id noun. Because subclass Ie is more complex due to *j*-suffix vowel harmony, it is discussed separately in §5.4.1.1.

Table 5.13: The inflectional paradigms for the Class Ia noun *luakkta* 'bay' and the Class Ib noun *mánná* 'child'

	SINGULAR	PLURAL		SINGULAR	PLURAL
NOM	luakkt-a	luokt-a	NOM	mánn-á	mán-á
GEN	luokt-a	luokt-a-j	GEN	mán-á	mán-á-j
ACC	luokt-a-v	luokt-a-jd	ACC	mán-á-v	mán-á-jd
ILL	luakkt-a-j	luokt-a-jda	ILL	mánn-á-j	mán-á-jda
INESS	luokt-a-n	luokt-a-jn	INESS	mán-á-n	mán-á-jn
ELAT	luokt-a-st	luokt-a-jst	ELAT	mán-á-st	mán-á-jst
COM	luokt-a-jn	luokt-a-j	COM	mán-á-jn	mán-á-j
ABESS	luokt-a-dak	luokt-a-daga	ABESS	n/a	n/a
ESS	luakkt-a-n		ESS	n/a	

5 Nominals I: Nouns

Table 5.14: The inflectional paradigms for the Class Ic noun *bäbbmo* 'food' and the Class Id noun *skåvvlå* 'school'

	SINGULAR	PLURAL		SINGULAR	PLURAL
NOM	bäbbm-o	biebm-o	NOM	skåvvl-å	skåvl-å
GEN	biebm-o	biebm-o-j	GEN	skåvl-å	skåvl-å-j
ACC	biebm-o-v	biebm-o-jd	ACC	skåvl-å-v	skåvl-å-jd
ILL	bäbbm-o-j	biebm-o-jda	ILL	skåvvl-å-j	skåvl-å-jda
INESS	biebm-o-n	biebm-o-jn	INESS	skåvl-å-n	skåvl-å-jn
ELAT	biebm-o-st	biebm-o-jst	ELAT	skåvl-å-st	skåvl-å-jst
COM	biebm-o-jn	biebm-o-j	COM	skåvl-å-jn	skåvl-å-j
ABESS	biebm-o-dak	biebm-o-daga	ABESS	skåvl-å-dak	skåvl-å-daga
ESS	bäbbm-o-n		ESS	skåvvl-å-n	

5.4.1.1 Class Ie

Class Ie nouns are a special subset of class I nouns due to two features:

- *j*-suffix vowel harmony
- allomorphy in the class markers (*e, i, á*)

The inflectional paradigm for the words *guolle* 'fish' and *vágge* 'valley' are provided as examples for Ie nouns in Table 5.15 on the next page; note that *vágge* is not subject to consonant gradation. For nouns with consonant gradation and/or umlaut in Class Ie, NOM.SG, ILL.SG and ESS are in the strong grade and have *ä* or *ua/uä* in V1 position, while other case/number slots have the weak grade and *ie* or *uo* in V1 position, just as with all Class I nouns.

As mentioned above, nouns in Class Ie are subject to *j*-suffix vowel harmony. This refers to non-adjacent regressive vowel harmony triggered by the presence of /j/ in certain case/number suffixes. In this, certain V1 vowels and the V2 vowel are raised in accommodating the palatal position of the /j/ in the suffix. The vowel in V2, which is *e* in Class Ie nouns, is raised to *i*, while the vowel in V1 is raised depending on its initial value: ä→i, uo/uä→u, a→ä, á→ä and å→u. Other V1 vowels in Class Ie are not affected, but the V2 vowel is always raised from /e/ to /i/ in the relevant paradigm slots.

The class marking suffixes and consonant gradation pattern for Class Ie are summarized in Table 5.16 on the facing page.

5.4 Inflectional classes for nouns

Table 5.15: The inflectional paradigms for the Class Ie nouns *guolle* 'fish' and *vágge* 'valley'

	SINGULAR	PLURAL
NOM	guoll-e	guol-e
GEN	guol-e	gul-i-j
ACC	guol-e-v	gul-i-jd
ILL	guoll-á-j	gul-i-jda
INESS	guol-e-n	gul-i-jn
ELAT	guol-e-st	gul-i-jst
COM	gul-i-jn	gul-i-j
ABESS	guol-e-dak	guol-e-daga
ESS	guoll-e-n	

	SINGULAR	PLURAL
NOM	vágg-e	vágg-e
GEN	vágg-e	vägg-i-j
ACC	vágg-e-v	vägg-i-jd
ILL	vágg-á-j	vägg-i-jda
INESS	vágg-e-n	vägg-i-jn
ELAT	vágg-e-st	vägg-i-jst
COM	vägg-i-jn	vägg-i-j
ABESS	vágg-e-dak	vágg-e-daga
ESS	vágg-e-n	

Table 5.16: The consonant gradation pattern and inflectional noun class suffixes for Class Ie

	SINGULAR		PLURAL	
NOM	str	-e	wk	-e
GEN	wk	-e	wk	-i-
ACC	wk	-e-	wk	-i-
ILL	str	-á-	wk	-i-
INESS	wk	-e-	wk	-i-
ELAT	wk	-e-	wk	-i-
COM	wk	-i-	wk	-i-
ABESS	wk	-e-	wk	-e-
ESS	str		-e-	

5 Nominals I: Nouns

5.4.2 Class II

Two features mark nouns in Class II:

- the class marking suffix for NOM.SG is *-Vj*, while for the other case/number slots, the class marker is *-V*

- *wk-str* grade alignment (when relevant)

The inflectional paradigm for the words *båtsoj* 'reindeer' and *ålmaj* 'man' are provided as examples in Table 5.17.

Table 5.17: The class-marker suffix and case/number paradigms for the Class II nouns *båtsoj* 'reindeer' and *ålmaj* 'man'

	SINGULAR	PLURAL		SINGULAR	PLURAL
NOM	båts-oj	buhts-u	NOM	ålm-aj	ålm-a
GEN	buhts-u	buhts-u-j	GEN	ålm-a	ålm-a-j
ACC	buhts-u-v	buhts-u-jd	ACC	ålm-a-v	ålm-a-jd
ILL	buhts-u-j	buhts-u-jda	ILL	ålm-a-j	ålm-a-jda
INESS	buhts-u-n	buhts-u-jn	INESS	ålm-a-n	ålm-a-jn
ELAT	buhts-u-st	buhts-u-jst	ELAT	ålm-a-st	ålm-a-jst
COM	buhts-u-jn	buhts-u-j	COM	ålm-a-jn	ålm-a-j
ABESS	buhts-u-dak	buhts-u-daga	ABESS	n/a	n/a
ESS	båts-o-n		ESS	ålm-a-n	

Note that the grade alignment in the *båtsoj* paradigm is for the most part *wk-str*, i.e., the weak grade is found in NOM.SG and ESS, and the strong grade elsewhere. The lexical item *ålmaj* does not feature consonant gradation, and attempts to elicit the abessive forms resulted in three inconsistent forms. The gradation pattern and class marking suffixes for Class II are summarized in Table 5.18 on the facing page.

There do not appear to be many words in Class II, and the data in the corpus are ultimately inconclusive. There are some irregularities which cannot be explained, for instance why the vowel in V2 position in *båtsoj* is only *o* in NOM.SG and ESS, but otherwise *u*, while the V2 vowel in *ålmaj* is consistently *a*. Furthermore, it is unclear why consonant gradation in the ILL.SG form in the *båtsoj* paradigm does not align with NOM.SG and ESS.

5.4 Inflectional classes for nouns

Table 5.18: The Class II consonant gradation pattern and inflectional noun class suffixes

	SINGULAR		PLURAL	
NOM	wk	-Vj	str	-V
GEN	str	-V	str	-V-
ACC	str	-V-	str	-V-
ILL	str	-V-	str	-V-
INESS	str	-V-	str	-V-
ELAT	str	-V-	str	-V-
COM	str	-V-	str	-V-
ABESS	str	-V-	str	-V-
ESS	wk		-V-	

5.4.3 Class III

Three features mark nouns in Class III:

- the stem is consonant-final
- the NOM.SG form lacks a class suffix
- *wk-str* grade alignment (when relevant)

This class consists of two subclasses (IIIa and IIIb), as discussed in the following two sections.

5.4.3.1 Class IIIa

Class IIIa is the more common Class III subclass. It exhibits a NOM.SG form which lacks a class marker and ends in a closed syllable; in this case, the stem-final consonant is thus the word-final consonant. The paradigms for the nouns *sabek*[12] 'ski' and *vanás* 'boat' are provided in Table 5.19 on the next page as examples for this subclass. The word *vanás* 'boat' is similar to *sabek* 'ski', but is subject to consonant gradation. Finally, denominal nouns derived by the diminutive suffix -*tj* are all in Class IIIa. Table 5.20 on the following page provides a nearly complete paradigm for *guolátj* 'little fish'.

---

[12] In adhering to Pite Saami orthographic conventions, word-final /k/ is spelled with <k>, while intervocalic /k/ is spelled <g>.

Table 5.19: The inflectional paradigms for the Class IIIa nouns *sabek* 'ski' and *vanás* 'boat'

	SINGULAR	PLURAL		SINGULAR	PLURAL
NOM	sabek	sabeg-a	NOM	vanás	vadnás-a
GEN	sabeg-a	sabeg-i-j	GEN	vadnás-a	vadnás-i-j
ACC	sabeg-a-v	sabeg-i-jd	ACC	vadnás-a-v	vadnás-i-jd
ILL	sabeg-i-j	sabeg-i-jda	ILL	vadnás-i-j	vadnás-i-jda
INESS	sabeg-i-n	sabeg-i-jn	INESS	vadnás-i-n	vadnás-i-jn
ELAT	sabeg-i-st	sabeg-i-jst	ELAT	vadnás-i-st	vadnás-i-jst
COM	sabeg-i-jn	sabeg-i-j	COM	vadnás-i-jn	vadnás-i-j
ABESS	n/a	n/a	ABESS	n/a	n/a
ESS	n/a		ESS	n/a	

Table 5.20: The inflectional paradigm for the Class IIIa denominal noun *guolátj* 'little fish'

	SINGULAR	PLURAL
NOM	guolátj	guolátj-a
GEN	guolátj-a	guolátj-i-j
ACC	guolátj-a-v	guolátj-i-jd
ILL	guolátj-i-j	guolátj-i-jda
INESS	guolátj-i-n	guolátj-i-jn
ELAT	guolátj-i-st	guolátj-i-jst
COM	guolátj-i-jn	guolátj-i-j
ABESS	n/a	n/a
ESS	n/a	

5.4.3.2 Class IIIb

The less common subclass of Class III nouns exhibits a NOM.SG form which also lacks a class marker but ends in an open syllable; thus, the stem-final consonant, which is present in all other slots in the paradigm, is lacking. The word *bena* 'dog' is provided in Table 5.21 as a example for this second subclass.

Table 5.21: The inflectional paradigm for the Class IIIb noun *bena* 'dog'

	SINGULAR	PLURAL
NOM	*bena*	*bednag-a*
GEN	*bednag-a*	*bednag-i-j*
ACC	*bednag-a-v*	*bednag-i-jd*
ILL	*bednag-i-j*	*bednag-i-jda*
INESS	*bednag-i-n*	*bednag-i-jn*
ELAT	*bednag-i-st*	*bednag-i-jst*
COM	*bednag-i-jn*	*bednag-i-j*
ABESS	n/a	n/a
ESS	n/a	

5.4.3.3 Class III summary

The gradation pattern and class marking suffixes for Class III are summarized in Table 5.22 on the following page. As with Class II words, the corpus only provides limited data on Class III words, and attempts to elicit abessive and essive forms led to inconsistent results, partly due to uncertain native speaker intuition for these rare forms. However, elicited abessive forms were consistently in the strong grade, while elicited essive forms were sometimes in the strong grade, sometimes in the weak grade, without any seemingly consistent patterns.[13]

5.4.4 Summary of noun classes

Table 5.23 on page 109 is provided to facilitate cross-class comparison of inflectional paradigms for examples from the various noun classes. While the whole

---

[13] One language consultant fairly consistently produced ABESS.SG forms without the stem final consonant for some nouns in this class, but still felt uncertain about this. Specifically, this individual produced the forms *vadnádaga* 'boat-ABESS.SG', *bednadaga* 'dog-ABESS.SG' and *sabedaga* 'ski-ABESS.SG'.

5 Nominals I: Nouns

Table 5.22: The Class III consonant gradation pattern and inflectional noun class suffixes

	SINGULAR		PLURAL	
NOM	wk	-	str	-a
GEN	str	-a	str	-i-
ACC	str	-a-	str	-i-
ILL	str	-i-	str	-i-
INESS	str	-i-	str	-i-
ELAT	str	-i-	str	-i-
COM	str	-i-	str	-i-
ABESS	str	n/a	str	n/a
ESS	n/a		n/a	

paradigm for each word is not listed due to a lack of space, the forms for NOM.SG, NOM.PL, ACC.SG, GEN.PL, ILL.SG and ELAT.SG are more than sufficient to convey the relevant morphological differences between the classes.

5.5 Possessive suffixes

A special set of possessive suffixes exists in Pite Saami which indicate, in addition to case and number for the host noun, the person and number of the possessor of the referent of the host noun. While the possessive suffixes go back to Proto-Saami (Sammallahti 1998: 73), they seem to have nearly fallen out of use in contemporary Pite Saami, and are only attested in three recordings from the corpus. These examples from the corpus are presented first, and a discussion follows.

While there are technically nine tokens of possessive pronouns in the corpus, these nine tokens can be grouped into two identical sets, so that effectively only two examples are available. Specifically, there are three tokens of *áhttjes* 'my father' in nominative case by one speaker in two different recordings, and three tokens of the parallel construction *mammaset ja pahpaset* 'your mother and your father' by another speaker in one recording. An example from the first speaker is provided in (39), and an example[14] from the second speaker in (40).

---

[14] The example in (40) is essentially identical to the other utterance with four tokens of these same noun stems with possessive suffixes (pit100703a.034).

5.5 Possessive suffixes

Table 5.23: Comparison of noun class examples

class		NOM.SG	NOM.PL	ACC.SG	GEN.PL	ILL.SG	ELAT.SG	
I	a	luakkt-a	luokt-a	luokt-a-v	luokt-a-j	luakkt-a-j	luokt-a-st	'bay'
	b	mánn-á	mán-á	mán-á-v	mán-á-j	mánn-á-j	mán-á-st	'child'
	c	bäbbm-o	biebm-o	biebm-o-v	biebm-o-j	bäbbm-o-j	biebm-o-st	'food'
	d	skåvvl-å	skåvl-å	skåvl-å-v	skåvl-å-j	skåvvl-å-j	skåvl-å-st	'school'
	e	guoll-e	guol-e	guol-e-v	gul-i-j	guoll-á-j	guol-e-st	'fish'
		vágg-e	vágg-e	vágg-e-v	vágg-i-j	vágg-á-j	vágg-e-st	'valley'
		sábm-e	sám-e	sám-e-v	sám-i-j	sábm-á-j	sám-e-st	'Saami'
II		båts-oj	buhts-u	buhts-u-v	buhts-u-j	buhts-u-j	buhts-u-st	'reindeer'
		ålm-aj	ålm-a	ålm-a-v	ålm-a-j	ålm-a-j	ålm-a-st	'man'
III	a	sabek	sabeg-a	sabeg-a-v	sabeg-i-j	sabeg-i-j	sabeg-i-st	'ski'
		vanás	vadnás-a	vadnás-a-v	vadnás-i-j	vadnás-i-j	vadnás-i-st	'boat'
	b	bena	bednag-a	bednag-a-v	bednag-i-j	bednag-i-j	bednag-i-st	'dog'
		gáma	gábmag-a	gábmag-a-v	gábmag-i-j	gábmag-i-j	gábmag-i-st	'shoe'

5 Nominals I: Nouns

(39) áhttjes   dá lä   gähtjamin jus gävdnij
     áhttje-s   dá lä   gähtja-min jus gävdni-j
     father-1SG.POSS\NOM.SG then be\3SG.PRS look-PROG if exist-3SG.PST
     aktak, nag   getjokmiesse
     aktak nagin getjok-miesse
     any   some unmarked-calf\NOM.SG
     'My father is checking if there are any unmarked calves.'   [pit080909.004]

(40) *nå   dä hulij,   nå   hälset   del mammaset   ja*
     nå   dä huli-j   nå   hälse-t   del mamma-set   ja
     well then say-3SG.PST well greet-PL.IMP then mother-2PL.POSS\ILL.SG and
     pahpaset
     pahpa-set
     father-2PL.POSS\ILL.SG
     'Well then she said "well, say hello to your mother and your father".'
                                                                 [pit100703a.038]

Just as with the other case/number suffixes, the possessive case/number suffixes follow the inflectional class marker, as illustrated in (41).

(41)   Σ + class-marker + possession/case/number

The three examples from the corpus can thus be parsed morphologically as in (42) through (44):

(42) *áhttj-e-s*
     father-Ie-1SG.POSS\NOM.SG
     'my father'

(43) *mamm-a-set*
     mother-Ia-2PL.POSS\ILL.SG
     'to your (PL) mother'

(44) *pahp-a-set*
     father-Ia-2PL.POSS\ILL.SG
     'to your (PL) father'

While these three examples do not provide enough evidence for case and number marking in addition to possession, the thorough paradigm for *åbba* 'sister' and a very partial paradigm for *áhttje* 'father' in Lehtiranta (1992: 158–159)[15] indicate that the possessive suffixes are best described as portmanteau suffixes which

---

[15] Note that Lehtiranta (1992) uses a different orthography: *ååp'paa* for 'sister' and *aah'tjie* for 'father'.

indicate the number and case of the host noun as well as the person and number of the external possessor.[16] As substitutes for the external possessor NP, they fill a pronominal function, as well.

It should be pointed out that the possessive suffixes above do not correspond to the equivalent examples in the Lehtiranta paradigms: Lehtiranta has *aah'tjaam* for 'father-1SG.POSS\NOM.SG', while *aah'tjies* is listed as 'father-3SG.POSS\NOM.SG', a form which is much closer to the form in (42), but means 'his/her father'.[17] Furthermore, Lehtiranta indicates that *ååp'paasetieh* is 'sister-2PL.POSS\ILL.SG, which has an additional -*ieh* word-finally not found in (43) or (44).

In all other cases in the corpus, NP-internal possession is expressed using a noun or pronoun in the genitive case, as in (45), which is from the same speaker and recording as in (40) above.

(45) ja dä lij mijan sessa Kärin
 ja dä li-j mijan sessa Kärin
 and then be-3SG.PST 1PL.GEN paternal.aunt\NOM.SG Karin
 'And then it was our paternal aunt Karin.' [pit100703a.014]

It is likely the case that alienability plays (or played) a role in determining which nouns can be marked with possessive suffixes. It is also possible that certain nouns with possessive suffixes have been lexicalized in current usage. While the lack of possessive suffixes in the corpus seems to indicate that they are no longer used regularly, the fact that the two obvious loan words in (43) and (44)[18] have possessive suffixes, indicates that they may still be productive somehow, or at least retrievable via analogy. At any rate, the corpus does not provide nearly enough data on the possessive suffixes and any conclusions on their current state this topic must be left to future research.

---

[16] Lagercrantz (1926: 110) only lists six possessive suffixes (1/2/3SG.POSS, 3DU.POSS and 3PL.POSS), but he does not provide any further information concerning possessive suffixes.
[17] Lagercrantz (1926: 110) also indicates that the 3SG.POSS suffix is -*s*.
[18] From Swedish *mamma* 'mother' and *pappa* 'father'.

6 Nominals II: Pronouns

Pite Saami has a closed class of pronouns consisting of personal, demonstrative, reflexive, interrogative and relative pronouns. Pronouns are nominals and are defined syntactically by their ability to substitute a nominal phrase. As nominals, all pronouns inflect for case (cf. §5.2 on the case system); concerning number, personal and reflexive pronouns inflect for singular, dual and plural, while demonstrative, interrogative and relative pronouns only inflect for singular and plural. The Pite Saami pronouns are described below, in the order listed above; paradigms for each pronoun type are also included. The pronouns are written using the working Pite Saami orthography. The corpus does not provide sufficient data about the status of any pronouns in the abessive and essive cases,[1] so this must be left for future study. Note that there are also a number of non-nominal interrogative pro-forms which do not inflect for case or number; although not nominals, these pro-forms are covered in §6.4.4, after the interrogative pronouns.

6.1 Personal pronouns

Personal pronouns inflect for person and number (singular, dual or plural) as well as for case. They are listed in Table 6.1 on the following page. Personal pronouns do not inflect for the biological sex of their referents, but are restricted in referring only to humans (demonstrative pronouns are used when the referent is not human). The nominative forms all have two possible forms, e.g. *mån~månnå* '1SG.NOM'. In general, the monosyllabic form is the default, while the bisyllabic form is typically used as a citation form and when the pronoun is emphasized.

The person marking morphemes in personal pronouns are completely systematic and are listed in Table 6.2 on the next page. Case and number marking is not quite as systematic, but certain segmental patterns are present which closely resemble the singular case/number suffixes for nouns, particularly those in inflectional class I (cf. §5.4.1). Specifically, note the lack of a final consonant for all full forms of nominative pronouns (cf. the lack of a NOM.SG or NOM.PL nominal case suffix), genitive pronouns in dual and plural (cf. the lack of a GEN.SG

---

[1] Neither Lagercrantz (1926) nor Lehtiranta (1992) provide sufficient data, either.

6 Nominals II: Pronouns

Table 6.1: Personal pronouns

	1ˢᵀ	2ᴺᴰ	3ᴿᴰ	
NOM	mån~månnå	dån~dånnå	sån~sånnå	SINGULAR
GEN	muv	duv	suv	
ACC	muv	duv	suv	
ILL	munje	dunje	sunje	
INESS	muvne	duvne	suvne	
ELAT	muvvste	duvvste	suvvste	
COM	mujna	dujna	sujna	
NOM	måj~måjå	dåj~dåjå	såj~såjå	DUAL
GEN	munuo	dunuo	sunuo	
ACC	månov	dånov	sånov	
ILL	munnuj	dunnuj	sunnuj	
INESS	munuon	dunuon	sunuon	
ELAT	munuost	dunuost	sunuost	
COM	munujn	dunujn	sunujn	
NOM	mij~mija	dij~dija	sij~sija	PLURAL
GEN	mijá	dijá	sijá	
ACC	mijáv	dijáv	sijáv	
ILL	mijjaj	dijjaj	sijjaj	
INESS	maján	diján	siján	
ELAT	mijást	dijást	sijást	
COM	mijájn	dijájn	sijájn	

Table 6.2: Person morphemes in personal pronouns

1ˢᵀ	m-
2ᴺᴰ	d-
3ᴿᴰ	s-

nominal case suffix), the final -v in the accusative personal pronouns (cf. -v for nouns in ACC.SG), a final or nearly final j-element for illative pronouns (cf. -j for nouns in ILL.SG), a final or nearly final n-element for inessive pronouns (cf. -n for nouns in INESS.SG), a final or nearly final st-element for elative pronouns (cf. -st for nouns in ELAT.SG and ELAT.PL) and a final or nearly final jn-element for comitative pronouns (cf. -jn(a) for nouns in COM.SG).

6.2 Demonstrative pronouns

Demonstrative pronouns are based on the stem d-. They inflect for case and number (singular and plural, but not dual), as well as the proximity of the entity they refer to. The data from the corpus indicate that there is a three-way distinction between referents close to the speaker (proximal), those away from the speaker (distal), and those particularly far away (remote). The demonstrative pronouns are listed in Table 6.3. Note that due to a lack of sufficient data on the remote forms in the corpus (either no forms exist or speakers were too uncertain to warrant inclusion here), this part of the paradigm is not complete; forms based on tentative data are marked by a question mark.

Table 6.3: Demonstrative pronouns

	SINGULAR			PLURAL		
	PROX	DIST	RMT	PROX	DIST	RMT
NOM	dát	dat	dut	dá(h)	da(h)	du(h)
GEN	dán	dan	dun	dáj	daj	duj
ACC	dáv	dav	duv	dájt	dajt	dujt
ILL	dása	dasa	?dun	dájda	dajda	n/a
INESS	dán	dan	dun	dájtne	dajtne	?duj
ELAT	dásste	dasste	?duj	dájste	dajste	?duj
COM	dájna	dajna	dujn	dáj	daj	duj

Morphologically, demonstrative pronouns consist of the stem d-, followed by -á-, -a- or -u- for proximal, distal and remote, respectively. This is then followed by a case/number suffix, as summarized in Table 6.4 on the next page.

Both distal and remote demonstrative pronouns have a referent which is away from the speaker, but remote demonstrative pronouns indicate a greater distance than distal demonstrative pronouns so that the referent of a remote demonstrative pronoun is clearly not located near the addressee. On the other hand, the

6 Nominals II: Pronouns

Table 6.4: Case/number suffixes for demonstrative pronouns

	SG	PL
NOM	-t	(-h)
GEN	-n	-j
ACC	-v	-jt
ILL	-sa	-jda
INESS	-n	-jtne
ELAT	-sste	-jste
COM	-jna	-j

referent of a proximal demonstrative pronoun is very close to the speaker. Distal demonstrative pronouns are not as specific in indicating the location of the referent, and do not necessarily rule out a referent which is near the addressee. Indeed, distal demonstrative pronouns are the most common in the corpus and are a sort of unmarked default demonstrative pronoun. Note that demonstratives are identical in form to demonstrative pronouns, but differ syntactically because they modify the head of an NP; they are discussed in §7.8.

Demonstrative pronouns typically have non-human referents, as in (1).

(1) *muhtin   sa del   vuoptin   dajt*
    muhtin   sa del   vuopti-n   d-a-jt
    sometimes so then sell-1DU.PST DEM-DIST-ACC.PL
    'So sometimes we sold those.'   [pit080924.300]

However, they can also be used to refer to third-person human referents, as in the example in (2).

(2) *da   lä   jabmam,   ber   muv*
    d-a   lä   jabma-m   ber   mu-v
    DEM-DIST\NOM.PL be\3PL.PRS   die-PRF   only   1SG.GEN
    äddne'l   viessomin   dále
    äddne=l   viesso-min   dále
    mother\NOM.SG=be\3SG.PRS   live-PROG   now
    'They have died, only my mother is living today.'   [pit100310b.145]

Distal demonstrative pronouns can also be used for anaphoric text deixis. For instance, *dat* in example (3) refers to the fact that the speaker has just dropped her ski pole.

(3) oj! ij   dat   aktagav   dága
    oj ij   d-a-t   aktaga-v   dága
    oh NEG\3SG.PRS DEM-DIST-NOM.SG none-ACC.SG make\CONNEG
    'Oh! That's no problem.' (lit.: that makes nothing)   [pit100404.156]

6.3 Reflexive pronouns

The reflexive pronouns in Pite Saami are based on the stem *etj-* and inflect for the number (singular, dual and plural) and person of the noun they are coreferential with. Reflexive pronouns also inflect for case. These are listed in Table 6.5 on the following page. The stem *etj-* can be translated as 'self', which could imply that it is a noun, but it is different from nouns for several reasons: 1) it is monosyllabic, 2) it has its own case and number marking suffixes, and 3) it inflects for dual number. Note that reflexive pronouns are not common in the spontaneous language recordings in the corpus, but are mostly found in elicitation sessions. Even in elicitation sessions, my main consultant was not completely sure about some of the forms for less common cases (i.e., everything except nominative, accusative[2] and genitive). Furthermore, a number of the elicited forms deviate from the forms provided in the complete paradigm in Lehtiranta (1992: 162).[3]

For these reasons, the forms in Table 6.5 on the next page should be considered preliminary at this point, and potentially subject to modification as a result of more thorough study. My consultants were particularly uncertain about the forms marked by a question mark, while forms listed in parenthesis are not attested in the corpus, but taken from the paradigms in Lehtiranta (1992: 162) and adapted to the current Pite Saami orthography.

---

[2] However, note the form *etjav* 'REFL-1SG.ACC' was provided by a different speaker (A) than the speaker (B) who provided the forms in the rest of the paradigm, and speaker A was very uncertain of this form. Lehtiranta (1992: 162) lists *etjam* and *etjamav*, and I suspect that the form *etjav* indicates that a simplification of the system has taken place (at least for speaker A) in which the root *etj-* is simply treated as a noun (such as 'self') which inflects using standard nominal case/number suffixes (here the ACC.SG suffix *-v*), but ultimately more data are needed to verify this.

[3] But note also that the paradigm in Lehtiranta (1992: 162) indicates a lack of consensus in the reflexive pronouns across speakers, as well. Whether the forms found in the Pite Saami Documentation Project corpus indicate a simplification of the system or simply another speaker's ideolect is impossible to determine at this point.

6 Nominals II: Pronouns

Table 6.5: Reflexive pronouns

	1ST	2ND	3RD	
NOM	etj	etj	etj	SINGULAR
GEN	etjan	etjad	etjas	
ACC	?etjav	etjavt	etjavs	
ILL	etjanij	etjasad	etjasis	
INESS	ehtjanen	etjanat	etjanis	
ELAT	ehtjanist	etjastit	etjastis	
COM	etjajnen	(etjajnat)	(etjajnis)	
NOM	etja	etja	etja	DUAL
GEN	etjanij	etjade	etjajsga	
ACC	(etjamenen)	etjajd	etjajdisa	
ILL	ehtjasimen	ehtjasiden	ehtjasijga	
INESS	(etjanenen)	?etjajdin	(etjaneská)	
ELAT	etjanis	etjastit	etjastis	
COM	(etjajnenen)	(etjajneten)	(etjajneská)	
NOM	etja	etja	etja	PLURAL
GEN	etjajme	etjajde	etjajse	
ACC	(ehtjameh)	etjajd	etjajdisa	
ILL	etjasijme	etjasida	etjasise	
INESS	?ehtjanen	?etjajdin	?etjajnisan	
ELAT	?etjanist	?etjastist	?etjajsist	
COM	(etjajneneh)	(etjajneteh)	(etjajneseh)	

One example of a reflexive pronoun is shown in (4).

(4) mån ságastav etjan birra
    mån ságasta-v etja-n birra
    1SG.NOM speak-1SG.PRS REFL-1SG.GEN about
    'I talk about myself.' [pit110521b2.010]e

Reflexive pronouns are frequently used to add emphasis to the noun phrase they are coreferential with (as an intensifier), as in (5).

(5) mån lev etj sábme
    mån le-v etj sábme
    1SG.NOM be-1SG.PRS REFL\1SG.NOM Saami\NOM.SG
    'I myself am Saami.' [pit080703.023]

6.4 Interrogative pronouns

The noun phrase that a reflexive pronoun is coreferential with does not have to be realized overtly, as illustrated by the utterance in (6) (here as an intensifier as well).

(6)   etj   lä   lerram
      etj   lä   lerra-m
      REFL\2SG.NOM be\2SG.PRS learn-PRF
      '(You) yourself have learned.'   [pit080924.407]

6.4 Interrogative pronouns

Pite Saami has several classes of interrogative pronouns as well as a set of interrogative pro-forms which do not refer to NPs. While the latter set of non-nominal pro-forms refer to other word classes, they are covered in this section nonetheless due to their syntactic status as pro-forms. The pronouns can be divided into those with human referents (cf. §6.4.1), which use the stem *ge-*, and those with non-human referents (cf. §6.4.2), which use the stem *m-*. Furthermore, there are two classes of interrogatives which enquire about the selection of a particular item (semantically equivalent to English 'which'; described in §6.4.3): the first refers to a choice from a selection in general and uses the stem *mikkir-*, while the other refers to a choice of one or two items and uses the stem *gåb-*. Interrogative pro-forms not referring to NPs mostly feature the stem *g-* (cf. §6.4.4). This classification is summarized in Figure 6.1, which also indicates the stem for each type.

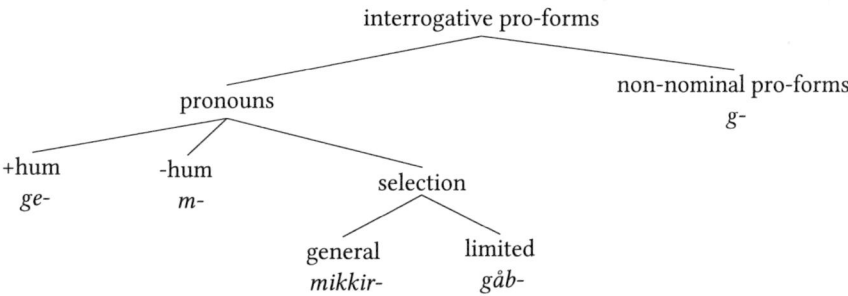

Figure 6.1: A taxonomy of interrogative pro-form types and their stems

6.4.1 Interrogative pronouns with human referents

Interrogative pronouns with human referents use the stem *ge-* and inflect for the number (singular or plural) of the intended referent and for case. These pronouns are listed in Table 6.6; examples are provided in (7) and (8).

(7) nå, gejna dä tjuovo?
nå ge-jna dä tjuovo
well who-COM.SG then accompany\2SG.PST
'Well, who did you go with?' [pit080924.071]

(8) gen gabmaga lä dá?
ge-n gabmag-a lä d-á
who-GEN.SG shoe-NOM.PL be\3PL.PRS DEM-PROX\NOM.PL
'Whose shoes are these?' [pit100404.326]

Table 6.6: Interrogative pronouns with human referents

	SG	PL
NOM	ge	ge
GEN	gen	gej
ACC	gev	gejd
ILL	gesa	gejda
INESS	genne	gejdne
ELAT	gesste	gejsste
COM	gejna	gej

6.4.2 Interrogative pronouns with non-human referents

Interrogative pronouns with non-human referents use the stem *m-* and inflect for the number (singular or plural) of the intended referent and for case. These pronouns are listed in Table 6.7 on the facing page; an example is provided in (9).

(9) mav dån sida?
ma-v dån sida
what-ACC.SG 2SG.NOM want\2SG.PRS
'What do you want?' [pit090519.194]

6.4.3 Interrogative pronouns concerning a selection

The two selective interrogative pronouns are used to enquire about the selection or choice of an item. The stem *mikkir-* refers to a selection in general, while the

Table 6.7: Interrogative pronouns with non-human referents

	SG	PL
NOM	mij	ma(h)
GEN	man	mej
ACC	mav	mejd~majd
ILL	masa	mejda
INESS	manne	majdne
ELAT	masste	majsste
COM	majna	mej

stem *gåb-* limits the selection to one or two choices. These are described in the following two sections.

6.4.3.1 General selection using *mikkir-*

Interrogative pronouns based on the stem *mikkir-* are used to enquire about a choice or selection in general. They inflect for the number (singular and plural) of their referent and for case. These forms are listed in Table 6.8 on the next page. Note that the inessive forms are not attested in the corpus. Two examples are provided in (10) and (11).

(10)   *mikkirist*   *lä*   *dat*   *dágaduvvum?*
      mikkir-ist   lä   d-a-t   dága-duvv-um
      which-ELAT.SG be\3SG.PRS DEM-DIST-NOM.SG make-PASS-PRF
      'What is that made of?'   [pit110521b1.203]e

(11)   *nå, mikkira*   *lidjin*   *dan*   *Ákabakten?*
      nå   mikkir-a   lidji-n   d-a-n   Ákabakte-n
      well which-NOM.PL be-3PL.PST DEM-DIST-INESS.SG Åkkabakkte-INESS.SG
      'Well which (people) were in Ákkabakkte?'   [pit080924.032]

They can also modify the head of an NP, and are then a 'pro-adjective'[4] enquiring after a further characterization of the referent. In this case, they do not inflect for number or case (as is true of all attributive adjectives), and so the form is always *mikkir*, as illustrated by the examples in (12) and (13).

---

[4] Cf. Schachter & Shopen (2007: 31–34) for more on non-pronoun 'pro-forms'.

Table 6.8: Interrogative pronouns with a demonstrative referent using the *mikkir-* stem

	SG	PL
NOM	*mikkir*	*mikkira*
GEN	*mikkira*	*mikkirij*
ACC	*mikkirav*	*mikkirijd*
ILL	*mikkirij*	*mikkirijda*
INESS	n/a	n/a
ELAT	*mikkirist*	*mikkirijst*
COM	*mikkirijna*	*mikkirij*

(12)   *mikkir málle   lij?*
       mikkir málle   li-j
       which blood\NOM.SG be-3SG.PST
       'Which (kind of) blood was it?'   [pit080924.256]

(13)   *mikkir gulijd   åtjojde?*
       mikkir guli-jd   åtjo-jde
       which fish-ACC.PL buy-2PL.PST
       'Which (kinds of) fish did you buy?'   [pit080924.025]

Another possible form of the stem seems to be *makkar-*, but this is only attested twice in the corpus and by one speaker, while *mikkir-* was consistently preferred in elicitation sessions. An example with *makkar* is provided in (14); here, *makkar* is a pro-adjective modifying a noun in a subordinate interrogative clause.

(14)   *ja dä lä   aj väha gähtjamin makkar sarvajd*
       ja dä lä   aj väha gähtja-min makkar sarva-jd
       and then be\3SG.PRS also a.little look-PROG which reindeer.bull-ACC.PL
       gilgin   njuovat   aj
       gilgi-n   njuova-t   aj
       will-3PL.PST slaughter-INF also
       'And then he is also checking a bit which reindeer bulls they should also slaughter.'   [pit080909.006]

6.4.3.2 Limited selection using *gåb-*

A further interrogative pronoun used to limit a selection to only one or two is based on the stem *gåb-*. It inflects for case and for number (singular and plural), as described below. Table 6.9 lists the various forms.

Table 6.9: Interrogative pronouns with a demonstrative referent using the *gåb-* stem

	SG	PL
NOM	gåbba	n/a
GEN	gåban	gåbaj
ACC	gåbav	gåbajd
ILL	gåbbaj	gåbajda
INESS	gåban	gåbajn
ELAT	gåbast	gåbajst
COM	gåbajn(a)	gåbaj

When marked for singular, it indicates a selection of one out of two possible choices, as in (15).

(15) gåban sajen lä dån årrom?
gåba-n saje-n lä dån årro-m
which-INESS.SG place-INESS.SG be\2SG.PRS 2SG.NOM be-PRF
'At which of the two places have you been?' [pit110521b1.161]e

When marked for plural, it indicates a selection of two out of three or more choices, as in (16).

(16) gåbaj birra ságasta?
gåba-j birra ságasta
which-GEN.PL about speak\2SG.PRS
'Which two are you talking about?' [pit110521b1.037]e

This interrogative pronoun is only attested in elicitation sessions in the corpus. A more thorough description must be left to future research.

6.4.4 Non-nominal interrogative pro-forms

There are a number of non-nominal interrogative pro-forms. These enquire about information typically expressed by a clause-level adverbial, an adjunct or a complement clause. They are listed and glossed in Table 6.10, and three examples are provided in (17) through (19).

Table 6.10: Non-nominal interrogative pro-forms

gåsse	'when'
gusa~guse	'to where'
gånne	'where'
guste	'from where'
manen	'why'
man (+adj.)	'how (big)'
maktes~gukte	'how'
galla	'how many'

(17) gånne dajt   tjogijdä?
gånne d-a-jt   tjogi-jdä
where DEM-DIST-ACC.PL pick-2PL.PST
'Where did you pick them?' [pit080924.168]

(18) gukte almatj   hålla   'reta'?
gukte almatj   hålla   reta
how person\NOM.SG say\3SG.PRS 'reta'
'How does one say 'reta'?' [pit080924.377]

(19) man mälgat lij   gu lij   hiejman,   iv
man mälgat li-j   gu li-j   hiejm-an,   i-v
how far   be-3SG.PST when be-3SG.PST home-INESS.SG neg-1SG.PRS
mån   diede
mån   diede
1SG.NOM know\CONNEG
'How far it was, when one was home, I don't know' [pit100404.317]

The list in Table 6.10 is likely not complete, as there are several other non-nominal interrogative pro-forms listed in the Pite Saami wordlist (cf. §1.2.3.4) which are not attested in the corpus. Furthermore, the data do not indicate what the difference is between the various alternate forms for 'to where' and 'how'.

6.5 Relative pronouns

Relative pronouns in Pite Saami are identical in form to the interrogative pronouns with non-human referents (cf. §6.4.2). However, unlike interrogative pronouns, relative pronouns do not reflect the human-ness of their referents. They agree in number with their referent, and inflect for the case required by their syntactic function within the relative clause. The relative pronouns are listed in Table 6.11. See §14.2.4 for a number of examples with relative pronouns as well as a description of relative clauses.

Table 6.11: Relative pronouns

	SG	PL
NOM	mij	ma(h)
GEN	man	mej
ACC	mav	mejd~majd
ILL	masa	mejda
INESS	manne	majdne
ELAT	masste	majsste
COM	majna	mej

7 Adjectivals

Adjectivals in Pite Saami are defined syntactically by their ability to head an adjectival phrase (AP). They can be divided into four sub-categories based on both syntactic and morphological behavior, as summarized in Table 7.1.

Table 7.1: Summary of syntactic and morphological features for the four types of adjectivals

	syntactic	morphological
attributive adjectives	attributive position within an NP	no inflection (except in elliptic constructions)
predicative adjectives	predicative position (complement of *årrot* 'be')	inflect for number
demonstratives	initial attributive position within an NP	inflect for number & case
numerals	attributive or predicative position	never inflect

While attributive adjectives generally do not inflect, in elliptical phrases in which the head of an NP is not realized overtly, they do inflect for case and number. Predicative adjectives are marked for number, and are morphologically similar to nominals. Demonstratives agree in number and case with the noun they modify. Numerals, on the other hand, are consistently uninflected. Finally, the two types of adjectives form an open sub-class, while numerals are a closed sub-class.

The rest of this chapter covers adjectives, demonstratives and numerals as follows: §7.1 provides a description of attributive adjectives, while §7.2 deals with predicative adjectives, before §7.3 takes up the formal relationship between these two types. §7.4 then goes on to describe comparative and superlative forms, before §7.5 illustrates the implementation of such forms in making comparisons. Syntactic restrictions on the adjectives corresponding to 'small, little' are described in §7.6. Quantifiers (a semantic sub-class of adjectives) are discussed in §7.7, while demonstratives are presented in §7.8. Finally, §7.9 covers numerals.

7 Adjectivals

7.1 Attributive adjectives

Attributive adjectives form the head of an AP modifying the head of the matrix nominal phrase, and are normally not subject to inflectional morphology. As part of an attributive AP, an attributive adjective occurs before the head noun it modifies, but after a demonstrative, if present (cf. §11.2 on the structure of NPs). Examples are provided in (1) through (3).

(1) dat   lä   tjähppis båtsoj   ja villges
d-a-t   lä   tjähppis båtsoj   ja villges
DEM-DIST-NOM.SG be\3SG.PRS black   reindeer\NOM.SG and white
ájjve
ájjve
head\NOM.SG
'It is a black reindeer and a white head.' [pit100405b.043]

(2) guolle'l   nåv njalga bäbbmo
guolle=l   nåv njalga bäbbmo
fish\NOM.SG=be\3SG.PRS so tasty food\NOM.SG
'Fish is such tasty food.' [pit100310b.025]

(3) dat   villges båtsoj
d-a-t   villges båtsoj
DEM-DIST-NOM.SG white reindeer\NOM.SG
'that white reindeer' [pit090930a.014]e

As the head of an AP, attributive adjectives can be modified by adverbs of grade, as illustrated by the AP *hoj buorak* 'really good' in (4), or *nåv njalga* 'so tasty' in (2) above.

(4) ja dat   lä   årrom hoj buorak giesse
ja d-a-t   lä   årro-m hoj buorak giesse
and DEM-DIST-NOM.SG be\3SG.PRS be-PRF really good summer\NOM.SG
'And it has been a really good summer.' [pit080909.009]

A number of adjectives end in -s (cf. the two adjectives *tjähppes* 'black' and *villges* 'white' in (1)), which is often considered an 'attribution' marking suffix in the literature.[1] However, as *njalga* 'tasty' in (2) illustrates, not all adjectives

---

[1] Rießler (2011: 215–228) deals in detail with this final -s, which is common to all Saami languages. Rießler claims that it was grammaticalized from a 3SG possessive suffix, and originally only marked the attributive form of adjectives. However, note that Rießler also points out that

are marked this way. Furthermore, corresponding predicative adjective forms (cf. §7.2 below) often also have a final -s, sometimes even to the exclusion of the attributive adjective form. Because no consistent relationship between forms with and forms without a final -s exists, it is no longer a productive way to mark or derive either attributive or predicative adjectives. For this reason, it is not considered to be morphologically meaningful in the present discussion. Nonetheless, it is worth noting that adjectival forms (both attributive and predicative) ending in -s are common.

Note also that some attributive adjectives appear to have two possible forms. For instance, *guhka* and *guhkes* 'long' were both encountered in elicitation sessions with a single speaker who insisted that both forms were equally valid (cf. recording pit080819a starting at 33m14s).

7.1.1 Attributive adjectives in elliptic constructions

If the context of the wider discourse is sufficiently unambiguous, it is possible that the nominal head of an NP is not realized, but implied. When such elliptic constructions (sometimes called 'headless NPs') feature an AP, the head adjective is then inflected for case and number.

For instance, in the elliptic construction in (5), the adjective *ruopsis* 'red' is marked for singular number and as the object of the verb form *bårov* 'I eat' for accusative case. In (6), the subject NP also lacks an overt nominal head, but features the adjective *tjähppis* 'black' (cf. the example in (1) above), which receives NOM.PL marking.

(5) båråv   ruopsisav
    bårå-v   ruopsisa-v
    eat-1SG.PRS   red-ACC.SG
    'I eat the red one.'   [pit090930a.119]e

(6) tjähppisa   lä   njallge
    tjähppis-a   lä   njallge
    black-NOM.PL   be\3PL.PRS tasty\NOM.SG
    'The black ones are tasty.'   [pit090930a.112]e

Adjectives in elliptic NPs can be preceded by a demonstrative, as in (7).

"the system of attributive and predicative marking is highly irregular in the Saamic languages" (Rießler 2011: 215).

7 Adjectivals

(7) dat   tjábba   máhtta   sáme
    d-a-t   tjábba   máhtta   sáme
    DEM-DIST-NOM.SG beautiful\NOM.SG can\3SG.PRS Saami\GEN.SG
    gielav
    giela-v
    language-ACC.SG
    'That beautiful one can (speak) the Saami language.' (referring to a girl)
    [pit090930a.148]e

As the host of case/number inflection, such adjectives look morphologically like nouns. However, syntactically, these adjectives remain adjectives for two reasons. First, they can be modified by adverbs of grade, while nouns cannot be. Second, they generally have a referential antecedent that is the bearer of the property they denote.[2] Semantically, they do not denote an entity (as nouns do), but a property, as with all adjectives. A further example is provided in (8). Here, the choice of the attributive adjective form *tjábba* 'beautiful' (as opposed to the corresponding predicate adjective form *tjábbe*) indicates that this is indeed an elliptical NP construction, and not predication.

(8) lä   huj tjábba,   dat,   dat
    lä   huj tjábba   d-a-t   d-a-t
    be\3SG.PRS quite beautiful\NOM.SG DEM-DIST-NOM.SG DEM-DIST-NOM.SG
    lä   jävvja
    lä   jävvja
    be\3SG.PRS white.reindeer\NOM.SG
    'It is a quite beautiful one, it, it is a white reindeer.' (referring to a reindeer)
    [pit100405b.036-037]

7.2 Predicative adjectives

While attributive adjectives form the head of an attributive AP embedded in an NP, predicative adjectives form the head of an AP which is the complement of the copular verb *årrot* 'be' and ascribe a property to the subject referent. In (9) and (10), for instance, the predicative adjective corresponding to the attributive adjective *tjáhppis* 'black' (cf. the example in (1) above) is *tjáhpat*.

---

[2] The quantifier *aktak* 'none, any' can be used in an elliptic NP without a referential antecedent; cf. §7.7, specifically example (37).

7.2 Predicative adjectives

(9) *fáhttsa   lä   tjáhpat*
    fáhttsa   lä   tjáhpat
    mitten\NOM.SG be\3SG.PRS black\SG
    'The mitten is black.'   [pit090930a.062]e

(10) *fáhtsa   lä   tjáhpada*
     fáhtsa   lä   tjáhpad-a
     mitten\NOM.PL be\3PL.PRS black-PL
     'The mittens are black.'   [pit090930a.063]e

Morphologically, predicative adjectives are much like nouns because they inflect for number. In fact, many predicative adjectives inflect for number in ways that clearly align with the NOM.SG~NOM.PL inflectional marking of certain noun classes. The case could be made that they also inflect for case, although they are always in nominative case (cf. §13.1.4 on copular clauses). However, because no paradigmatic opposition to other case forms exists for predicative adjectives (they are only attested in the corpus as a nominative complement to a copular clause), I conclude that they only inflect for number.

Nonetheless, these are syntactically adjectives, as they head adjectival phrases and can be modified by adverbs of grade, such as *nav* 'so' as in (11).

(11) *buhtsu   lä   nav buojde ja   tjábbe*
     buhtsu   lä   nav buojde ja   tjábbe
     reindeer\NOM.PL be\3PL.PRS so fat\PL   and beautiful\PL
     'The reindeer are so fat and beautiful.'   [pit080703.014]

Table 7.2 on the next page lists a number of attributive adjectives and the corresponding predicative adjectives; the latter clearly align with noun classes in their number marking. The table is divided into subgroups of word forms (indicated by small Roman numerals) that feature the same morphological relationship between attributive and predicative adjectives.

As is evident from the examples in Table 7.2, the attributive forms and the predicative forms correspond in a variety of ways. These correspondence patterns (numbered i-vii) are described here:

i   The attributive form differs from the predicative form in the choice of stem allomorph concerning V1, consonant center, V2 and the final consonant. Number marking like class IIIa nouns.
ii The attributive form and the plural predicative form have the same V1 and consonant center, as opposed to the singular predicative adjective; the attributive form has a stem final -s, while the predicative forms have an open final syllable. Number marking like class I nouns.

7 Adjectivals

Table 7.2: Some attributive and predicative adjective sets, including the noun class corresponding to the number marking pattern exhibited by the predicate adjectives

no.	attributive adjective	predicative adjectives SINGULAR	PLURAL	corresp. N-class	
i	tjáhpis	tjáhpat	tjáhpada	IIIa	'black'
	rusjgis	russjgat	russjgada		'red'
ii	nievres	návvre	nievre	Ie	'bad'
	vastes	vasste	vaste		'ugly'
	buosjes	buossje	buosje		'fearless'
	fávros	fávvro	fávro	Ic	'attractive'
iii	dájges	dájges	dájgesa	IIIa	'cowardly'
	åvros	åvros	åvrosa		'nervous'
	vuoras	vuoras	vuorasa		'old'
	gujos	gujos	gudjosa		'frozen solid'
	luvas	luvas	luvvasa		'wet'
	nanos	nanos	nannosa		'sturdy'
iv	sádnes	sádnes	sádna	II	'true'
v	bivvalis	bivval	bivvala	IIIa	'warm' (weather)
	buoragis	buorak	buoraga		'good'
vi	ånegis	ådne	åne	Ie	'short'
vii	jallga	jallgat	jallgada	IIIa	'flat'
	njuallga	njuallgat	njuallgada		'straight'
	lägga	lieggas	läggasa		'warm'
	galbma	galmas	galbmasa		'cold'

iii The attributive form and the singular predicative form are syncretic and have a stem-final -s, while the plural predicative form's stem is also identical, but marked for plural by a final -a. Number marking like class IIIa nouns.

iv The attributive form and the singular predicative form are syncretic and have a stem-final -s, while the plural predicative form is marked by a final -a instead of the final es in the other forms. Only one example in the corpus; number marking like a class II noun.

v   The bare stem in the singular predicative form, an additional final -*is* for the attributive form and -*a* for the plural predicative form. Number marking like class IIIa nouns.

vi The singular and plural predicative forms differ only in the choice of stem allomorph (in the consonant center), while the attributive form is in the 'weak' grade (like predicative plural) but with a stem-final *gis*. Only one example in the corpus; number marking like a class Ie noun.

vii The predicative forms have a stem-final -*t* or -*s*, which is lacking in the attributive form. The plural predicative form is marked with a final -*a*. In the case of *galbma*, the attributive form and plural predicative form have the 'strong' stem form, as opposed to the singular predicative form, which is 'weak'. Number marking like class IIIa nouns.

Despite the similarities with nouns described above, it is important to point out that there are a number of predicative adjectives which do *not* inflect for number. Moreover, this lack of number marking cannot be assigned to any specific noun class, particularly since noun classes with similar segmental structures exhibit clear number marking strategies. Examples of such predicative adjectives are presented in Table 7.5 on the following page.

The paradigms in Table 7.5 are divided into two sub-groupings, again based on the relationship between the attributive form and the predicative forms. They are summarized here:

viii The attributive form ends in -*a*, while the predicative form ends in -*e*.[3]
ix   All forms are syncretic. The first two examples have a closed final syllable, while the last three examples have an open final syllable.

The variety evident in morphological correlations between the attributive and the predicative forms indicates that there is no regular form-to-function relationship between the attributive and predicative forms. Therefore, on formal grounds, the attributive and predicative forms of these property words are assigned to different, though formally and semantically related, adjectival lexemes, as argued for in the following section (§7.3).

---

[3] Cf. §7.6 for more details on *unna/unna* and *smáve/smáve*, the words for 'small'.

Table 7.5: Some attributive and predicative adjective sets for which the predicative adjective does not inflect for number

no.	attributive adjective	predicative adjective	
viii	tjábba	tjábbe	'beautiful'
	guhka	guhke	'long'
	unna	unne	'small' (only SG)
	smáva	smáve	'small' (only PL)
ix	tjåskes	tjåskes	'cold' (weather)
	låjes	låjes	'tame'
	gårå	gårå	'bad'
	räkta	räkta	'correct'
	buorre	buorre	'good'

7.3 A note on attributive and predicative adjectives

In the literature on Saami languages, a convention prevails by which predicative adjectives are treated as having more or less derivable attributive forms.[4] From a historical point of view, this may be reasonable, particularly if there was a point in the history of the Saami languages at which attributive forms were derived by adding -s and selecting the phonologically relevant stem allomorph, and thus the attributive forms were derivable from the predicative forms. For Pite Saami, however, there is no clear or consistent morphological relationship synchronically between attributive adjectives and the corresponding predicative adjectives, as shown above. This is particularly exemplified by the existence of more than one acceptable attributive form, (as pointed out in §7.1 for the attributive adjective forms guhkes~guhka 'long'), as well as by the existence of a number of predicative forms ending in -s, but attributive forms lacking -s (cf. pattern vii above). Due to cases like those illustrated by subgrouping ix in Table 7.5, it is not clear that it is sensible to claim that *all* adjectives have corresponding predicative adjectives that differ at all. Because of the wide variety of and the inconsistencies in morphological patterns between corresponding attributive and predicative adjectives, it is ultimately more elegant to analyze these two sets of adjectives simply as semantically and etymologically related – but not morphologically derivable – adjectives.

---

[4] Cf. Sammallahti (1998: 71), Svonni (2009: 74–76;98) and Feist (2010: 179).

7.4 Comparatives and superlatives

The comparative and superlative forms of attributive and predicative adjectives are derived using suffixes. It seems that, morphosyntactically speaking, comparative and superlative forms can be derived from all adjectives, even when a semantic restriction could lexically prevent such forms from occurring; cf., e.g., *guäktegierdakap* 'more pregnant' (pit090927.07m01s).

The singular comparative or superlative predicative form is identical to the respective comparative or superlative attributive form. However, the plural comparative or superlative predicative form is always marked by a suffix consisting of a single vowel (mostly *-a*). In many cases, the stem to which comparative and superlative suffixes are attached is identical to the stem of the positive plural predicative form, but a number of exceptions exist.

Table 7.6 on the next page provides some example paradigms. To help illustrate the morphophonemic relationship to positive forms, the singular predicative adjective form is also indicated. Furthermore, the paradigms are divided into subgroupings (each marked with a Roman numeral) based on suffix allomorph patterns. The third and fifth columns in Table 7.6 provide the singular comparative and superlative adjectives (the attributive and predicative singular forms are syncretic), respectively, while the fourth and sixth columns only indicate the suffix used to mark the plural predicative comparative and superlative adjectives, respectively. Note that there are allomorphic alternations in the superlative suffix for subgroupings *iii* and *iv*.

Comparative adjectives are derived in a relatively straightforward way: the suffix *-p*[5] is added to an adjective root. If the root has a closed final syllable, then an epenthetic vowel *-u-* is inserted between the root and the suffix. In predicative position, plural is always marked by a suffix consisting of a vowel; in most cases (groups *i*, *ii* and *iv*), the vowel is *-a*, but sometimes it is *-o* (group *iii*). It is not clear what determines the choice of plural suffix for comparative forms. While all forms marked by *-o* in the corpus have a stem final *-s*, not all forms with a stem final *-s* are marked by *-o* (cf. *nanos* 'strong').

The superlative suffix has four allomorphs. For the attributive and the singular predicative forms, the allomorph *-mos* is chosen when the root has a closed final syllable, as in groups *iii* and *iv*. Roots with an open final syllable have either the superlative suffix allomorph *-mus* or *-jmus*; however, it is not clear what drives the selection of these latter two allomorphs.

---

[5] Note that, in the current working orthography, the comparative suffix *-p* is written *-b-* when intervocalic, such as in plural predicative forms.

7 Adjectivals

Table 7.6: Some comparative and superlative adjective paradigms

no.	positive PRED.SG	comparative ATTR/PRED.SG	PRED.PL	superlative ATTR/PRED.SG	PRED.PL	
i	nävvre	nievre-p	-a	nievre-mus	-a	'bad'
	ådne	åne-p	-a	åne-mus	-a	'short'
	guhke	guhke-p	-a	guhke-mus	-a	'long'
ii	tjábbe	tjábba-p	-a	tjábba-jmus	-a	'beautiful'
	vasste	vasste-p	-a	vasste-jmus	-a	'ugly'
	gårå	gårå-p	-a	gårå-jmus	-a	'bad'
	fávvro	fávro-p	-a	fávro-jmus	-a	'attractive'
iii	luvas	luvasu-p	-o	luvasu-mos	-bmus-a	'wet'
	garras	garrasu-p	-o	garrasu-mos	-bmus-a	'hard'
iv	nanos	nanosu-p	-a	nanosu-mos	-bmus-a	'strong'
	bivval	bivvalu-p	-a	bivvalu-mos	-bmus-a	'warm'
	tjáhpat	tjáhpadu-p	-a	tjáhpadu-mos	-bmus-a	'black'
	galmas	galbmasu-p	-a	galbmasu-mos	-bmus-a	'cold'
	vuoras	vuorasu-p	-a	vuorasu-mos	-bmus-a	'old'
	njuallgat	njuallgadu-p	-a	njuallgadu-mos	-bmus-a	'correct'

The allomorph -bmus- occurs whenever the resulting form has an odd number of syllables, as is the case for roots with a final odd syllable in the plural predicative form. Essentially, the superlative suffix always forms the final foot of a word, and thus is the location for consonant gradation alternations. If a final, odd syllable is present (e.g., for the plural predicative form), then the -bmus- allomorph is chosen.[6]

Examples for comparative and superlative adjectives in attributive position can be found in (12) and (13), respectively. Instances for predicative usage can be found in (18) and (19) in §7.5.

(12) bivvalup   dállke
      bivvalu-p   dállke
      warm-COMP weather\NOM.SG
      'warmer weather'   [pit090926.23m22s]e

(13) så dä   lä   vuorasumos   saddje
      så dä   lä   vuorasu-mos   saddje
      so then be\3SG.PRS old-SUPERL   place\NOM.SG
      'So then it's the oldest place.'   [pit0906_Ahkajavvre_a.123]

---

[6] Cf. §2.2.2 on prosodic domains and §4.1.2.1 on consonant gradation.

7.5 Comparing NP referents

As with positive adjectives, comparative and superlative adjectives can occur in elliptic NPs, in which case they inflect for case and number (cf. §7.1.1). Examples are provided in (14) and (15). Note that in the second example, the superlative suffix allomorph is *-bmus* because the adjective has an odd number of syllables.

(14) *mån uvadav tjábbabuv*
mån uvada-v tjábba-b-uv
1SG.NOM kiss-1SG.PRS beautiful-COMP-ACC.SG
'I kiss the more beautiful one.' (referring to 'beautiful girl')

[pit090930a.166]*e*

(15) *buhtsu lin mälgadubmusin*
buhtsu li-n mälgadu-bmus-in
reindeer\3PL.NOM be-3PL.PST far-SUPERL-INESS.SG
'The reindeer were farthest away.' (lit.: in the farthest one (place))

[pit090927.88m34s]*e*

7.5 Comparing NP referents

Predicative adjectives can be used to compare the referents of nominal phrases. If both referents are considered equal concerning the characteristic of comparison, then the NP of comparison is the subject of a copular predicate which is complemented by a construction using the numeral *akta* 'one' and the relevant predicative adjective, while the NP of reference is in the comitative case. An example is provided in (16). In such constructions, *akta* can be shortened to *akt*.

(16) *Svenna lä akta vuoras Ingerijn*
Svenna lä akta vuoras Ingeri-jn
Sven\NOM.SG be\3SG.PRS one old\SG Inger-COM.SG
'Sven is as old as Inger.' (lit.: Sven is one old with Inger) [pit110331b.135]*e*

Alternatively, both referents can be included in the subject NP, as in (17).

(17) *måj lin akta vuorasa*
måj li-n akta vuoras-a
1DU.NOM be-1DU.PRS one old-PL
'We two are the same age.' (lit.: we are one old) [pit080621.65m00s]

When comparing two referents that are not considered equal, the NP of comparison is the subject of a copular predicate which is complemented by a comparative predicative adjective and the NP of reference in the elative case, as in the example in (18).

(18) *Inger   lä   stuorap   várest*
     Inger   lä   stuora-p   váre-st
     Inger\NOM.SG be\3SG.PRS big-COMP\SG mountain-ELAT.SG
     'Inger is bigger than a mountain.'   [pit110331b.144]*e*

To indicate that a referent is the most extreme concerning the characteristic of comparison (at least within the group being compared), the relevant NP is the subject of a copular predicate which is complemented by the superlative predicative adjective. The quantifier *gajk* 'all' can be added for emphasis,[7] as in (19).

(19) *dát   lä   vanj   dä   gajk vuorasumos*
     d-á-t   lä   vanj   dä   gajk vuorasu-mos
     DEM-PROX-NOM.SG be\3SG.PRS probably then all old-SUPERL\SG
     dágaduvvum
     dága-duvvu-m
     make-PASS-PRF
     'This was probably the absolute oldest made.'
                                              [pit0906_Ahkajavvre_a.120]

7.6 Restrictions on *smáva* and *unna* 'small'

The paradigms for the two Pite Saami words for 'small' provided in Table 7.5 on page 134 do not sufficiently indicate the restrictions placed on these specific adjectives. The root *smáv-*, a North Germanic loan word, only modifies plural nouns, while *unn-*, the native word (Sammallahti 1998: 265), usually only modifies singular nouns. No other Pite Saami adjectives underlie such a restriction; however, the Swedish adjective *små* (cognate with the source of *smáv-*) is also restricted to modifying plural nouns.[8] Therefore, it seems that this syntactic restriction was probably also borrowed. While a few examples exist in the corpus of *unn-* modifying a plural noun, *smáv-* is the preferred item and much more frequent in the corpus.[9] Examples are provided in (20) through (23).

---

[7] The construction *gajk vuorasumos* 'absolute oldest' in (19) is possibly a calque based on North Germanic; cf. Swedish *allra äldst* 'absolute oldest'. In both cases, the adverbial modifier is based on the word for 'all' and precedes the superlative adjective.

[8] The Swedish adjective stem *lite-* is used for singular nouns.

[9] A corpus search (including elicitation sessions) resulted in 1 token of *unn-* and 10 tokens of *smáv-* modifying a plural noun (carried out on 12th November 2012).

7.6 Restrictions on smáva and unna 'small'

(20) já, månnå aj mujhtav gu liv unna
 já månnå aj mujhta-v gu li-v unna
 yes 1SG.NOM also remember-1SG.PRS when be-1SG.PST small
 mánátj
 máná-tj
 child-DIM\NOM.SG
 'Yes, I also remember when I was a small child.' [pit080924.632]

(21) bena lä unne
 bena lä unn-e
 dog\NOM.SG be\3SG.PRS small\SG
 'The dog is small.' [pit080819a.126]e

(22) ber akta bällge, ja smáva gisstá, dá
 ber akta bällge ja smáva gisstá d-á
 only one thumb\NOM.SG and small glove\NOM.PL DEM-PROX\NOM.PL
 'only one thumb, and small gloves, these here' [pit080708_Session08.031]

(23) bednaga lä smáve
 bednag-a lä smáve
 dog-NOM.PL be\3PL.PRS small\PL
 'Dogs are small.' [pit080819a.129]e

In non-elicited tokens from the corpus, nouns modified by the adjective *unna* are always diminutive nouns, as in (20) above and in (24) and (25) below.

(24) dát lä dåpe sin, unna dåpátja
 d-á-t lä dåpe sin unna dåpá-tj-a
 DEM-PROX-NOM.SG be\3SG.PRS house\GEN.SG in small house-DIM-GEN.SG
 sin
 sin
 in
 'This is in the house, in the little house.' [pit100310b.070]

(25) ja danne vuojdniv unna jåŋåtjav
 ja danne vuojdni-v unna jåŋå-tj-av
 and there see-1SG.PST small lingonberry-DIM-ACC.SG
 'And I saw a little lingonberry there.' [pit100404.353]

139

7.7 Quantifiers

While quantifiers are semantically similar to numerals, formally they are adjectives. Quantifiers include *edna* 'many, much', *gajk* 'all', *omasse* 'all kinds of', *färt* 'every', *nagin* 'some', *såmes* 'some', *suhta* 'some, several' and *binna* 'a bit, a little'. Some examples of quantifiers in attributive APs are provided in (26) through (30).

(26) *vuojdna   edna guhkajuolgagijd?*
      vuojdna   edna guhka-juolga-gi-jd
      see\2SG.PST many long-leg-NMLZ-ACC.PL
      'Did you see many long-leggers?' (referring to moose) [pit080924.007]

(27) *färt   bäjjve   mij   bårojmä   gulijd*
      färt   bäjjve   mij   båro-jmä   guli-jd
      every day\NOM.SG 1PL.NOM eat-1PL.PST fish-ACC.PL
      'Every day we ate fish.' [pit100310b.024]

(28) *ja dä vållda   nijbev   ja tjuolast   nagin rägijt*
      ja dä vållda   nijbe-v   ja tjuolast   nagin rägi-jt
      and then take\3SG.PRS knife-ACC.SG and cut\3SG.PRS some hole-ACC.PL
      'And then one takes a knife and cuts some holes.' [pit100404.098]

(29) *gajk almatja   lä   Árjepluoven*
      gajk almatj-a   lä   Árjepluove-n
      all person-NOM.PL be\3PL.PRS Arjeplog-INESS.SG
      'All people are in Arjeplog.' [pit100310b.132]

(30) *muvne   lä   binna   vuopta*
      muvne   lä   binna   vuopta
      1SG.INESS be\3SG.PRS little.bit hair\NOM.PL
      'I have a little hair.' [pit080926.02m05s]e

As with any attributive adjectives, quantifiers do not inflect for case or number, as evidenced by the examples above. Note, however, that *gajk* 'all' can optionally be marked for plural in attributive position by adding the suffix *-a*, as shown in (31).

(31) *mån   vaddav   gajka buhtsujda   biebmov*
      mån   vadda-v   gajk-a buhtsu-jda   biebmo-v
      1SG.NOM give-1SG.PRS all-PL reindeer-ILL.PL food-ACC.SG
      'I give all the reindeer food.' [pit110413b.173]e

However, when a quantifier is in an elliptic NP, it inflects for case and number (just as with other attributive adjectives). This is illustrated by *enabu* 'more' in (32), by *gajk* 'all' in (33), and by *nagin* 'some' in (34)

(32) galgav   enabuv   biejat?
     galga-v   ena-b-uv   bieja-t
     shall-1SG.PRS much-COMP-ACC.SG   put-INF
     'Shall I put in more?'   [pit090519.156]

(33) mana   tjasskit   dajd   åjvijd   ja   gajkajd
     mana   tjasski-t   d-a-jd   åjvi-jd   ja   gajk-ajd
     go\2SG.IMP throw-INF DEM-DIST-ACC.PL head-ACC.PL and all-ACC.PL
     duhku
     duhku
     over.there
     'Go throw those heads and all that over there.'   [pit080909.146]

(34) hålå   naginav   mav   galgav   hållåt
     hålå   nagina-v   ma-v   galga-v   hållå-t
     say\2SG.IMP some-ACC.SG REL-ACC.SG shall-1SG.PRS say-INF
     'Say something that I should say.'   [pit100304.001]

The quantifier *aktak* 'none, any' is used to emphasize a negated clause. It seems to be composed of the numeral *akta* 'one' and the suffix -*k*, which is a nominalizer in other cases; however, as illustrated by the examples in (35) and (36), it heads an attributive AP and does not inflect for case and number, unless it is in an elliptic NP, as in (37). It is thus considered an adjective.

(35) muvne   ij   lä   aktak vuopta
     muvne   ij   lä   aktak vuopta
     1SG.INESS NEG\3SG.PRS be\CONNEG none hair\NOM.PL
     'I don't have any hair.' (lit.: on me isn't a single hair) [pit080926.02m02s]e

(36) gu   itjij   almatj   dåbdå   aktak almatjid
     gu   itji-j   almatj   dåbdå   aktak almatji-jd
     when NEG-3SG.PST person\NOM.SG know\CONNEG none person-ACC.PL
     'if one didn't know any people'   [pit080924.342]

(37) itjij   almatj   åbbå hålå   aktagav
     itji-j   almatj   åbbå hålå   aktag-av
     NEG-3SG.PST person\NOM.SG at.all say\CONNEG none-ACC.SG
     'One didn't say anything at all.'   [pit080924.354]

7 Adjectivals

Concerning the status of corresponding predicative quantifiers, there is not enough data in the corpus to come to a certain conclusion. However, at least the attribute adjective *edna* 'many, much' corresponds to the predicative adjective form *ednak*; this is illustrated by (38) and (39). This indicates that attributive and predicative forms of quantifiers also differ in form, just as with other attributive and predicative adjective sets.

(38) bärrgo   lä   ednak.
     bärrgo   lä   ednak
     meat\NOM.SG be\3SG.PRS much\SG
     'There is much meat.' (lit.: meat is much)   [pit090926.113]*e*

(39) biergo   bijta   lä   ednaga
     biergo   bijta   lä   ednag-a
     meat\GEN.SG piece\NOM.PL be\3PL.PRS much-PL
     'There are many pieces of meat.' (lit.: meat pieces are many)
                                                               [pit090926.114]*e*

7.8 Demonstratives

Demonstratives modify a noun phrase by further specifying the head noun concerning the distance of the referent relative to the speaker. Just as with demonstrative pronouns, the corpus data indicate that there is a three-way distinction between referents close to the speaker (proximal), those away from the speaker (distal), and those particularly far away (remote). Indeed, they are identical in form with the demonstrative pronouns listed in Table 6.3 on page 115 in the section on demonstrative pronouns (§6.2), and are therefore not listed separately here. Unlike adjectives, demonstratives always agree with the noun they modify in number (singular and plural, but not dual) and in case. Examples of demonstratives are provided in (40) through (42).

(40) gu   lijmä   vuodjam dajna   traktorijna
     gu   li-jmä   vuodja-m d-a-jna   traktor-ijna
     when be-1PL.PST   drive-PRF DEM-DIST-COM.SG tractor-COM.SG
     'Grållåjn'
     Grållå-jn
     Grålle-COM.SG
     'when we had driven that 'Grålle' tractor'   [pit090702.287]

142

(41) dajd   gulijd   giesijmä   tjielkajn   dik
     d-a-jd   guli-jd   giesi-jmä   tjielka-jn   dik
     DEM-DIST-ACC.PL fish-ACC.PL pull-1PL.PST sled-COM.SG to.here
     'We pulled those fish here with a sled.'   [pit0906_Ahkajavvre_a.043]

(42) men dut   biehtse,   men ånekatj   ja   gassak
     men d-u-t   biehtse   men åneka-tj   ja   gassa-k
     but DEM-RMT-NOM.SG   pine\NOM.SG   but short-DIM   and thick-NMLZ
     'But that pine tree over there, how short and thick!'   [pit090519.284]

7.9 Numerals

Numerals in Pite Saami form a closed class and a distinct closed sub-class of adjectives. Syntactically, they are adjectives because they head an adjectival phrase; however, morphologically, they differ from other adjectives by never inflecting (neither for number in predicative APs, nor for case and number in ellipsis constructions). Furthermore, numerals do not consist of attributive/predicative sets differing in form. Instead, numerals are consistent in form, regardless of being in attributive or predicative position.

Pite Saami numerals form a decimal system consisting of the basic numerals for the numbers one through ten, hundred and thousand. All other numerals are compounds based on these basic terms, with the exception of *nolla* 'zero'. Basic and complex numerals are dealt with in §7.9.1 and §7.9.2, respectively; the derivation of ordinal numerals is described in §7.9.1.1.

7.9.1 Basic numerals

The basic numerals for the numbers one through ten in Pite Saami are reconstructable native Saamic numerals, and *tjuohte* 'hundred' is at least from Proto-Saami.[10] The numerals *nolla* 'zero' and *tuvsan* 'thousand' are likely more recent borrowings, although it is not entirely clear whether they are from North Germanic or Finnic.[11] These basic cardinal numerals are listed on the left side of Table 7.7 on the following page.

---

[10] Sammallahti (1998: 234–235) indicates that *tjuohte* 'hundred' was originally a borrowing from Proto-Indo-European into Proto-Finno-Ugric or Proto-Finno-Saamic.

[11] The entries for the numerals 'zero' and 'thousand' in Álgu (2006) only provide etymologies for North Saami and Inari Saami; however, while Finnic is clearly a contact language for these two languages, North Germanic is a contact language for Pite Saami, and therefore also a potential source for these two numerals; cf. Swedish *nolla* 'zero' and *tusen* 'thousand'.

7 Adjectivals

Table 7.7: Cardinal and ordinal numerals

	cardinal	ordinal	
0	nolla	-	
1	akkta	vuostas	1st
		aktát	$n1^{st}$
2	guäkte	mubbe	2nd
		guoktát	$n2^{nd}$
3	gålbmå	gålmát	$(n)3^{rd}$
4	nällje	nielját	$(n)4^{th}$
5	vihta	vidát	$(n)5^{th}$
6	guhta	gudát	$(n)6^{th}$
7	gietjav	giehtjet	$(n)7^{th}$
8	gakktse	gáktsát	$(n)8^{th}$
9	åktse	åktsát	$(n)9^{th}$
10	lågev	lågát	$(n)10^{th}$
100	tjuohte	n/a	100th
1000	tuvsan	n/a	1000th

7.9.1.1 Derivation and suppletion in ordinal numerals

In general, ordinal numerals, which are listed on the right side of Table 7.7, can be derived from the corresponding cardinal numeral by replacing the vowel in V2 position and any final consonant with the suffix *-át* (and its allomorph *-et* in *giehtjet* 'seventh'). In addition, the weak stem allomorph is selected and umlaut of V1 occurs, if applicable (cf. §4.1.2 on stem allomorphy). The ordinal numerals corresponding to *tjuohte* 'hundred' and *tuvsan* 'thousand' are not attested in the corpus.

However, there are exceptions. First, the ordinals *vuostas* 'first' and *mubbe* 'second' are suppletive forms compared to the corresponding cardinal numerals *akkta* 'one' and *guäkte* 'two'.[12] These two ordinals are used exclusively for the single-digit numbers 'first' and 'second'; any ordinal numeral referring to a number of two or more digits uses a form derived from the cardinal numeral, as described above. This is illustrated in Table 7.8 on the facing page.

Second, the cardinal numeral *giehtjav* 'seven' differs in the final two segments from the ordinal numeral *gietjet* 'seventh' (i.e., *-av* and *-et*).

---

[12] Note that *vuostas* 'first' and *mubbe* 'second' are also reconstructable to at least Proto-Saami (Sammallahti 1998: 257;268).

Table 7.8: Suppletive and derived ordinal numerals

	cardinal			ordinal
1	akkta	$\rightarrow$	1st	vuostas
11	akta-låk-akkta	$\rightarrow$	11th	akta-låk-aktát
21	guäkte-låk-akkta	$\rightarrow$	21st	guäkte-låk-aktát
2	guäkte	$\rightarrow$	2nd	mubbe
12	akta-låk-guäkte	$\rightarrow$	12th	akta-låk-guoktát
22	guäkte-låk-guäkte	$\rightarrow$	22nd	guäkte-låk-guoktát

7.9.2 Complex numerals

Any numerals other than those listed in Table 7.7 on the preceding page are complex numerals formed by combining the basic numerals. Multiples of ten are composed of the relevant cardinal numeral followed by *lågev* 'ten'; examples are provided in Figure 7.1.

guäkte-lågev	*gålbmå-lågev*	*nällje-lågev*	etc.
two-ten	three-ten	four-ten	
20	30	40	

Figure 7.1: Multiples of ten

Note that *lågev* is often shortened to *låk* in fast speech, as in (43).

(43) ... *gokt lij   dánne giehtjavlåk   jage   maŋŋus*
      gokt li-j   dánne giehtjav-låk jage   maŋŋus
      how be-3SG.PST here seven-ten   year\NOM.PL ago
      '... how it was here seventy years ago.'   [pit0906_Ahkajavvre_a.001]

There are two ways to compose two-digit numerals that are not multiples of ten. One method appends the relevant numeral representing the 'ones-digit' to the multiple of ten, while *lågev* 'ten' is shortened to *låk*. This is illustrated in Figure 7.2 on the next page, with examples of two-digit numerals from the corpus presented in (45) and (44).

(44) *sån   lä   gakktselåkgiehtjav   jage*
      sån   lä   gakktse-låk-giehtjav jage
      3SG.NOM be\3SG.PRS eight-ten-seven   year\NOM.PL
      'She is eighty-seven years old.'   [pit100310b.146]

7 Adjectivals

akta-låk-guäkte	gålbmå-låk-guhta	åktse-låk-gakktse	
one-ten-two	three-ten-six	nine-ten-eight	etc.
12	36	98	

Figure 7.2: Two-digit numerals, method A

(45) dä   lij   del   tjuojgadam ja   gåddam nälljalåkgakktse
      dä   li-j   del   tjuojgada-m ja   gådda-m nällja-låk-gakktse
      then be-3SG.PST then ski-PRF   and slay-PRF four-ten-eight
      stalpe   sájtejna
      stalpe   sájte-jna
      wolf\GEN.PL   spear-COM.SG
      'Then he skied and slew forty-eight wolves with a spear.'
      [pit0906_Ahkajavvre_a.088-089]

Alternatively, complex numerals may be formed phrasally. According to this strategy, the 'ones-digit' precedes a postpositional phrase headed by the postposition *nanne*[13] 'on' with the multiple of ten as the dependent *låge* (in GEN.SG case), as illustrated in Figure 7.3. However, this latter method was only attested in elicitation sessions with one consultant, and is not found in non-elicited data from the corpus.

guäkte låge nan	guhta gålbmå-låge nan	gakktse åktse-låge nan	etc.
two ten\GEN.SG on	six three-ten\GEN.SG on	eight nine-ten\GEN.SG on	
12	36	98	

Figure 7.3: Two-digit numerals, method B

Native ordinal numerals referring to numbers between ten and one hundred are only attested in the corpus in elicitation sessions, and speakers are quite inconsistent and unsure about them. The same is true for cardinal numerals larger than one hundred. The only example in the corpus for a numeral larger than one thousand is not native, but a Swedish borrowing (in an NP with Pite Saami case and number marking); this is provided in (46).[14]

---

[13] Note that *nanne* is often shortened to *nan* in rapid speech.

[14] With the exception of the case/number suffix -*n*, the entire phrase *nittonhundratalan* 'in the nineteen-hundreds' in (46) is borrowed from Swedish *nittonhundratalet* 'the nineteen-hundreds'.

(46) nittonhundratálan   álgon   ja dä
nitton-hundra-tála-n   álgo-n   ja dä
nineteen-hundred-century-INESS.SG beginning-INESS.SG and then
viesoj
vieso-j
live-3SG.PST
'He lived in the nineteen-hundreds, at the beginning.'
[pit0906_Ahkajavvre_a.070-072]

7.9.3 Numerals and morphosyntax

Numerals are generally not subject to inflectional morphology. This is illustrated by the examples (43) through (44) above as well as in (47) below.

(47) *mån   vaddav   gålbmå buhtsujda   biebmov*
mån   vadda-v   gålbmå buhtsu-jda   biebmo-v
1SG.NOM give-1SG.PRS three   reindeer-ILL.PL food-ACC.SG
'I give food to three reindeer.'   [pit110413b.156]*e*

Note that this is true even in predicative position and in elliptic constructions, as shown by the examples in (48)[15] through (50).

(48) *så dä   lä   guäkte*
så dä   lä   guäkte
so then be\3SG.PRS two
'So then it's two.'   [pit080924.011]

(49) *ja dä   lä   njeljåt   aprilla uddne*
ja dä   lä   njelj-åt   aprilla uddne
and then be\3SG.PRS four-ORD April   today
'And it is the fourth of April today.'   [pit100404.018]

(50) *ja gålmåt   sjadda   dä Stutjaj*
ja gålm-åt   sjadda   dä Stutja-j
and three-ORD become\3SG.PRS then Stutja-ILL.SG
'And the third one then goes to Stutja.' (referring to a fishing net)
[pit090702.026-027]

---

[15] Note that it is not clear in the example in (48) why the verb does not inflect for dual (*lähpa* 'be-3DU.PRS' would be expected).

7 Adjectivals

However, there are at least two exceptions. First, the numeral *akta* 'one' inflects for ACC.SG case when modifying a noun, as illustrated by (51), as well as when it is in a headless elliptical construction, as in (52).[16]

(51) åtjåjmen aktav guolev
 åtjå-jmen akta-v guole-v
 get-1DU.PST one-ACC.SG fish-ACC.SG
 'We got one fish.' [pit0906_Ahkajavvre_a.182]

(52) men vuotjiv mån aktav
 men vuotji-v mån akta-v
 but shoot-1SG.PST 1SG.NOM one-ACC.SG
 'But I shot one.' [pit080924.008]

Second, the example in (53) indicates that at least the ordinal numeral *vuostas* 'first' can be inflected as a superlative as *vuostamos*, meaning 'the very first'.

(53) dieda, mån vuotjev vuostamos guhkajuolgagav
 dieda mån vuotje-v vuosta-mos guhka-juolga-ga-v
 know\2SG.PRS 1SG.NOM shoot-1SG.PST first-SUPERL long-leg-NMLZ-ACC.SG
 'You know, I shot my very first long-legger.' (referring to a moose)
 [pit080924.079]

---

[16] With this in mind, the word *akta* forms a word-class of its own, strictly speaking.

8 Verbs

Verbs in Pite Saami form an open class of words which are defined syntactically by their ability to head a verb complex, as well as morphologically by inflecting for person, number, tense and mood. Verbs consist of a stem which is followed by a class marker and an inflectional suffix or suffixes, as illustrated in (1).

(1) Σ + class-marker + mood/tense/person/number

Verb stems can have up to five allomorphic forms throughout the verbal paradigm due to a complex combination of morphophonological alternations. Verbs form at least five inflectional classes. The inflectional suffixes are exponents for person, number, tense and/or mood. Pite Saami distinguishes three number categories (singular, dual and plural), two tense categories (present and past) and the three modal categories (indicative, imperative and potential).

The first sections of this chapter (§8.1 on the inflectional categories number, tense and mood; §8.2 on non-finite forms and periphrastically marked categories of future, aspect and negation; §8.3 on passive voice) provide a description of relevant morphological categories as a background for the discussion of morphological marking strategies for verbs in §8.4. Finally, §8.5 draws on the initial sections to posit inflectional classes for verbs.

8.1 Finite verbs and inflectional categories

8.1.1 Person and number

All finite verbs agree in number with the subject of the clause and inflect for singular, dual or plural. Finite verbs in the indicative and the potential mood also agree in person. Inflectional morphology is present even if the subject of the clause is not overt. For instance, in (2), the finite verbs *minne* and *gillge* both agree with *da*, the 3PL subject; in (3), the finite verb *lijmen* agrees with the 1DU subject *månnå ja Jåssjå*.

8 Verbs

(2) ja dä da   tjåhken minne   gu   gillge
    ja dä d-a   tjåhken minne   gu   gillge
    and then DEM-DIST\NOM.PL together go\3PL.PRS when will\3PL.PRS
    gåddålit   nagan juhtusav
    gåddåli-t   nagan juhtusa-v
    kill-INF   some animal-ACC.SG
    'And then they go together when they are going to kill some animal.'
    [pit080703.047-048]

(3) månnå ja Jåssjå   lijmen   ulgon   sirijd
    månnå ja Jåssjå   li-jmen   ulgon   siri-jd
    1SG.NOM and Josh\NOM.SG be-1DU.PST outside blueberry-ACC.PL
    tjåggemin
    tjågge-min
    pick-PROG
    'Josh and I were picking blueberries outside.'   [pit100310b.032]

Note that there are a few examples in the corpus in which speakers do not consistently inflect for dual, but instead use the corresponding plural form.

The imperative is not marked for person, but distinguishes the three number categories singular, dual and plural. For example, in (4) the finite verb *tjaske* is inflected for the implied (2nd person) singular subject.

(4) tjaske   munje sobev
    tjaske   munje sobe-v
    throw\SG.IMP 1SG.ILL pole-ACC.SG
    'Throw a ski-pole to me!'   [pit100404.206]

8.1.2 Tense

For indicative clauses, verbs can inflect for present tense, as in (2), or past, as in (3) above. Verbs marked for present tense generally signify that a situation is true in the present, as in (5) below, or they express general truths, as in example (2) above (which indicates a general truth about wolves' behavior). However, present tense can also be used to indicate historical present, as in (6), or planned future situations, as in (7). It is therefore not strictly a *present* tense and could be considered *non-past*. Nonetheless, the glossing standard 'PRS' is chosen to mark this, as it covers the most common function.

(5) dale lä   bar bievadak   mij   sudda
    dale lä   bar bievadak   mij   sudda
    now be\3SG.PRS only sunshine\NOM.SG which\NOM.SG melt\3SG.PRS
    muahtagav
    muahtaga-v
    snow-ACC.SG
    'Now it's only the sun which melts the snow.'   [pit100405a.036]

(6) *tjävlav   valdav   ja dä   tjanáv   virbmev*
    tjävla-v   valda-v   ja dä   tjaná-v   virbme-v
    bobber-ACC.SG take-1SG.PRS and then tie-1SG.PRS net-ACC.SG
    dan[1]   tjävvlaj   ja   hålåv   raddnaj...
    d-a-n   tjävvla-j   ja   hålå-v   raddna-j
    DEM-DIST-?ILL.SG bobber-ILL.SG and say-1SG.PRS friend-ILL.SG
    'I take the bobber and then I tie the net to that bobber and I say to my friend...'   [pit090702.029]

(7) *ja dä   maŋŋel dä   vuolga   Västeråsaj*
    ja dä   maŋŋel dä   vuolga   Västeråsa-j
    and then after.that then drive\2SG.PRS Västerås-ILL.SG
    'And then after that you'll drive to Västerås.'   [pit080924.677]

8.1.3 Mood

Pite Saami has three moods: indicative, imperative and potential. Indicative mood is by far the most common mood and is considered the default, unmarked mood, as it is not overtly expressed morphologically, as in the examples in §8.1.2 above. The following two sections deal with imperative and potential mood.

8.1.3.1 Imperative mood

Verbs inflectedisinflection!verbal for imperative mood indicate that the speaker is instructing or commanding the addressee to carry out the action referred to by the verb; the implied subject is always 2nd person. Verbs in the imperative are not marked for person, but do inflect for number (singular, dual and plural), as

---

[1] In the example in (6), it is not clear why the demonstrative *dan* is used, as this resembles either the genitive or the inessive demonstratives, but not the expected illative demonstrative *dasa*. Perhaps it is simply an error in natural speech.

8 Verbs

in (4) above as well as in (8) and (9) below; see Table 8.3 on page 160 in §8.4.1 for the imperative number suffixes.

(8) nå, giehto   naginav   dan   Luoddauvre
    nå giehto   nagina-v   d-a-n   Luoddauvre
    well tell\SG.IMP something-ACC.SG DEM-DIST-GEN.SG Luoddauvre\GEN.SG
    birra
    birra
    about
    'Well, say something about this 'Luoddauvre'!'   [pit080924.314]

(9) dáhken   dal dav
    dáhke-n   dal d-a-v
    do-DU.IMP now DEM-DIST-ACC.SG
    'Do that now!'   [pit101208.188]*e*

The example in (10) below indicates that imperative can also be used as a kind performative speech-act.

(10) gijtov   ednet
     gijtov   edne-t
     thank-ACC.SG   have-PL.IMP
     'Thank you all!' (lit.: have thank)   [pit101208.290]*e*

Note that Lehtiranta (1992: 150–155) includes a second imperative category in his verb paradigms that inflects for all three person categories and is marked by a stem-final -*u*-; Lehtiranta terms this 'imperative II'. Lagercrantz (1926: 22) mentions 'imperative II' in passing as well, explaining that it is "less severe and more like a wish" (my translation), but Lagercrantz only includes examples for 2SG. The Pite Saami Documentation Project corpus does not have any tokens of such verbs, so more study is needed to determine their current status.

8.1.3.2 Potential mood

Verbs can also be inflected for potential mood, indicating that the action referred to by the verb is likely to happen. Verbs in the potential mood are marked by a linearly segmentable morpheme -*tj*- followed by a person/number suffix.[2] Examples are provided in (11) through (13).

---

[2] Cf. §13.4 for syntactic aspects of clauses in the potential mood.

8.2 Non-finite verb forms and periphrastically marked verbal categories

(11) nå hålåv, vuolgetjip del
nå hålå-v vuolge-tji-p del
well say-1SG.PRS go-POT-1PL obviously
'Well then I say we should obviously go.' [pit090702.013]

(12) nä, virtitjav nuollat
nä virti-tja-v nuolla-t
no must-POT-1SG undress-INF
'Oh no, I'll probably have to take off some clothes.' [pit090519.029]

(13) ikeb dat vuosjatja káfav
ikeb d-a-t vuosja-tj-a káfa-v
maybe DEM-DIST-NOM.SG prepare.coffee-POT-3SG coffee-ACC.SG
'Perhaps he'll make some coffee.' [pit110404.270]e

As the examples in (14) and (15) illustrate, the potential mood can be used as a friendly request.

(14) vuosjatja káfav
vuosja-tj-a káfa-v
prepare.coffee-POT-2SG coffee-ACC.SG
'Perhaps you could make some coffee.' [pit110404.267]e

(15) gulatja dav mav mån hålåv
gula-tj-a d-a-v ma-v mån hålå-v
hear-POT-2SG DEM-DIST-ACC.SG REL-ACC.SG 1SG.NOM say-1SG.PRS
'Please hear what I am saying!' [pit110404.056]e

The person/number suffixesisinflection!verbal for potential mood are homophonous with those used in present tense for Class V verbs (cf. §8.5.5); cf. §8.4.3 for a discussion of the status of verbs in the potential mood as inflectional and derivational forms.

8.2 Non-finite verb forms and periphrastically marked verbal categories

A number of non-finite verb forms exist in Pite Saami. The most common of these are the infinitive, connegative, perfect and progressive forms. Each of these non-finite verb forms can co-occur with an auxiliary verb to periphrastically express the verbal categories of future tense, perfect or progressive aspect, and negation;

8 Verbs

these categories are described in §8.2.1, §8.2.2 and §8.2.3, respectively. Syntactic aspects of clauses involving these non-finite forms are described in §13.1.5 on declarative clauses with more than one verb form, as well as in §14.2 on clausal subordination. Table 8.1 summarizes the morphological and syntactic features of these four non-finite forms, while examples of verbs in these forms are provided in Table 8.2.

Table 8.1: Common non-finite verb forms and their features

	morphological features	*syntactic features*
infinitive	suffix -*t*, strong grade	co-occurs with auxiliary *galgat* for future; complement to lexical verbs like *sihtat* 'want', *állget* 'begin', etc.
connegative	no suffix, weak grade	co-occurs with negation verb
perfect	suffix -*m*, strong grade	co-occurs with auxiliary *årrot* 'be'
progressive	suffix -*min*, strong grade	co-occurs with auxiliary *årrot* 'be'

Table 8.2: Some non-finite verb forms

infinitive	connegative	perfect	progressive	
tjájbmat	*tjájma*	*tjájbmam*	*tjájbmamin*	'laugh'
viessot	*vieso*	*viessom*	*viessomin*	'live'
båhtet	*både*	*båhtem*	*båhtemin*	'come'
ságastit	*ságaste*	*ságastam*	*ságastamin*	'speak'
bargatjit	*bargatje*	*bargatjam*	*bargatjemin*	'work a little'

The literature on Saami languages often treats non-finite verb forms in addition to those mentioned above. These include the verb genitive, verb abessive or gerunds, for instance.[3] For Pite Saami, Lehtiranta (1992: 95–106) describes the morphological form a number of such non-finite forms,[4] while Lagercrantz (1926) does not describe such verb forms.

With this in mind, it is certainly plausible that Pite Saami has other non-finite

---

[3] Cf. Sammallahti 1998: 103–104 and Svonni 2009: 67–73 for North Saami, or Spiik 1989: 104–111 for Lule Saami.

[4] These non-finite forms are also included in the verb paradigms in Lehtiranta (1992: 150–155).

8.2 Non-finite verb forms and periphrastically marked verbal categories

verb forms other than those mentioned here. However, there is no evidence of such forms in the present corpus. Ultimately, the morphological and syntactic behavior of other non-finite verb forms must be left for future study.

8.2.1 Future

The verb *gallgat* 'will' plus the infinitive form of the lexical verb can together express a future activity. The examples in (16) through (18) illustrate this.

(16) nå gukte galga dåhkå ållit dajna
 nå gukte galga dåhkå ålli-t d-a-jna
 well how will\2SG.PRS to.there reach-INF DEM-DIST-COM.SG
 'Well how are you going to reach it with that?' [pit080909.052]

(17) dä galgav mån gähttot
 dä galga-v mån gähtto-t
 then will-1SG.PRS 1SG.NOM tell-INF
 'Then I will tell a story.' [pit0906_Ahkajavvre_a.115]

(18) man ednag biejve galga danne årrot?
 man ednag biejve galga danne årro-t
 how many day\NOM.PL will\2SG.PRS there be-INF
 'How many days are you going to be there?' [pit080924.658]

Note that, as mentioned in §8.1.2 above, the present tense is also used to express planned future events.

8.2.2 Aspect

Pite Saami features two aspects, perfect and progressive, as described in §8.2.2.1 and §8.2.2.2 below. Both aspects are formed periphrastically using a combination of the auxiliary verb *årrot* 'be' and the relevant non-finite verb form. See also §13.1.5.2 on the syntactic structure of clauses with perfective and progressive verbs.

8.2.2.1 Perfect

The perfect verb form is marked by the suffix *-m* (glossed as PRF); the verb stem is in the strong grade when consonant gradation is relevant. Verbs in the perfect generally indicate that an action in the past still has relevancy in the present situation. For instance, in (19) the speaker is slaughtering a reindeer, and is now able

8 Verbs

to cut out the stomach because the esophagus has been tied in a knot, preventing the stomach's contents from running out.

(19)   men mån   lev   tjåjvev   ruhtastemin ullgus,
        men mån   le-v   tjåjve-v   ruhtaste-min ullgus
        but 1SG.NOM be-1SG.PRS stomach-ACC.SG cut-PROG   out
        tjådågov   lev   tjadnam   tjieboten
        tjådågo-v   le-v   tjadna-m tjiebote-n
        esophagus-ACC.SG be-1SG.PRS knot-PRF neck-INESS.SG
        'But I am cutting out the stomach, I have knotted the esophagus in the neck.'   [pit080909.054-055]

In (20), the speaker indicates that one can dip potatoes in fish fat only after one has fried the fat, thus melting it.

(20)   gu   lä   dav   bassam, dä   máhta
        gu   lä   d-a-v   bassa-m dä   máhta
        when be\2SG.PRS DEM-DIST\ACC.SG fry-PRF then can\2SG.PRS
        pironijd   budnjut
        pironi-jd   budnju-t
        potato-ACC.PL dip-INF
        'Once you have fried it, you can dip potatoes (in it).'   [pit090702.088]

Finally, in (21), the perfect form of the verb *jábmet* 'die' is used to mark the state of being dead resulting from the event of dying as opposed to the present state of being alive.

(21)   da   lä   jábmam, ber   muv
        d-a   lä   jábma-m ber   muv
        DEM-DIST\NOM.PL be\3PL.PRS die-PRF only 1SG.GEN
        äddne'l   viessomin   dále
        äddne=l   viesso-min dále
        mother\NOM.SG=be\3SG.PRS live-PROG   now
        'They have died, only my mother is still living now.'   [pit100310b.145]

8.2.2.2 Progressive

Verbs in the progressive indicate that an activity is ongoing. The progressive verb form is marked by the suffix *-min* (glossed as PROG) appended to the verb stem, which is in the strong grade when consonant gradation is relevant. In (19) above, the speaker uses the progressive form *rhtastemin* because he is in the middle of cutting out the stomach as he utters the sentence. In (21), the speaker's mother is still living, as opposed to the deceased. The action expressed by a progressive verb does not have to be simultaneous with the moment of the utterance, but can be past tense, as shown by the example in (22). Here, the speaker is describing a picture which was taken while picking blueberries.

(22) månnå ja Jåssjå, lijmen ulgon sirijd
månnå ja Jåssjå li-jmen ulgon siri-jd
1SG.NOM and Josh\NOM.SG be-1DU.PST outside blueberry-ACC.PL
tjåggemin
tjågge-min
pick-PROG
'Josh and I were picking blueberries outside.' [pit100310b.032]

8.2.2.3 Progressive verb forms used adverbially

The progressive form of a verb can also be used in an adverbial function. For instance, *tjájbmamin* 'laughing' in (23) and *gullamin* 'listening' in (24) are each used as a modal adverbial to indicate a simultaneous activity.

(23) tjájbmamin vádtsa
tjájbma-min vádtsa
laugh-PROG go\3SG.PRS
'She walks while laughing.' [pit110522.29m10s]e

(24) gullamin mån tjálav
gulla-min mån tjála-v
listen-PROG 1SG.NOM write-1SG.PRS
'I write while listening.' [pit110404.089]e

8.2.3 Negation

Negation in Pite Saami is expressed periphrastically by a finite negation verb and a non-finite verb form. The inflectionalisinflection!verbal behavior of the negation verb is presented in §8.5.8, while syntactic aspects of negation in Pite Saami are covered in more detail in §13.1.5.3; however, a brief description of negation is provided here.

As with any finite verb, the negation verb agrees in person and number with the subject of the sentence and inflects for tense or mood. The complement verb occurs in a special non-finite verb form called the connegative (glossed as

8 Verbs

CONNEG), which is in the weak grade (when gradation is relevant) and otherwise lacks any additional morphological marking. Examples for present and past indicative as well as imperative forms are provided in (25) through (27).

(25) mån   iv   vasja   lipsusijd   ja   daggarijd
     mån   i-v   vasja   lipsusi-jd   ja   daggari-jd
     1SG.NOM NEG-1SG.PRS feel.like\CONNEG rumen.fat-ACC.PL and such-ACC.PL
     válldet   dán   muddon
     vállde-t d-á-n   muddo-n
     take-INF DEM-PROX-INESS.SG   time-INESS.SG
     'I don't feel like taking the rumen fat and stuff at this time.' [pit080909.091]

(26) nå   ittjij   Henning   dä   skihpá,   gu
     nå   ittji-j   Henning   dä   skihpá   gu
     well NEG-3SG.PST Henning\NOM.SG then become.sick\CONNEG when
     lij   nåv gållum
     li-j   nåv gållu-m
     be-3SG.PST so freeze-PRF
     'Well Henning didn't get sick after he had been freezing like that.'
     [pit090702.373]

(27) ele   tsábme!
     ele   tsábme
     NEG\SG.IMP hit\CONNEG
     'Don't hit!' (said to a child)   [sje20121009.11m27s]e

8.3 Passive voice

Verbs in the passive voice can be derived from other verbs by the derivational suffix -duvv. Note that the vowel immediately following this suffix is the class marking morpheme for Class IV verbs; cf. §8.5.4. Examples are provided in (28) through (30).

(28) dat   huvvsa   bidtjiduvvuj   Nisest
     d-a-t   huvvsa   bidtji-duvvu-j   Nise-st
     DEM-DIST-NOM.SG   house\NOM.SG   build-PASS-3SG.PST   Nils-ELAT.SG
     'That house was built by Nils.'   [pit110522.33m03s]e

(29) ja   dat   lä   etjaláhkaj dä   dat
     ja   d-a-t   lä   etjaláhkaj dä   d-a-t
     and   DEM-DIST-NOM.SG be\3SG.PRS different then DEM-DIST-NOM.SG
     lij   dal   navte   gårroduvvum
     lij   dal   navte   gårro-duvvu-m
     be\3SG.PST now   like.that sew-PASS-PRF
     'And that is different as it has been sewn like that.'
     [pit080708_Session08.011]

(30) men dá   buhtsu   ij   lä
     men d-á   buhtsu   ij   lä
     but DEM-PROX\NOM.PL reindeer\NOM.PL NEG\3PL.PRS be\CONNEG
     mierkeduvvum
     mierke-duvvu-m
     mark-PASS-PRF
     'But these reindeer have not been marked.'   [pit080703.030]

The data from the corpus concerning passive verbs are quite limited, but indicates that passive verbs can be finite verbs inflecting for tense, person and number, as in (28), or non-finite forms, such as the perfect, as in (29) and (30). However, due to a lack of data, it is not clear whether passives can be used for progressive aspect, or inflect for either imperative or potential mood.

That being said, these examples do make clear that the passive marker is restricted to lexical verbs. Passives are therefore not considered to be part of inflectional paradigms, but instead valency-decreasing verbal derivations. See also §10.2.5 in the chapter on derivational morphology and §13.1.1.1 on syntactic aspects of clauses in the passive voice.

Note that Ruong (1945) includes other derivational suffixes which create passive verbs that are not attested in the corpus.

8.4 Morphological marking strategies on verbs

As shown in §8.1 above, finite verbs can be marked for four inflectional categories:

- agreement in person with the subject
- agreement in number with the subject
- tense
- mood

8 Verbs

Just as with nouns, inflectional categories for verbs can be expressed by suffixes and by non-linear morphology, and frequently a combination of both. In the following, §8.4.1 focusses on inflectional suffixes, while §8.4.2 goes on to describe the behavior of non-linear morphology found in stem-consonant alternations (consonant gradation), stem-vowel alternations (umlaut), and vowel harmony. The final section (8.5) then uses the various morphophonological inflectional patterns found across verb paradigms to posit five preliminary inflectional classes for verbs.

8.4.1 Inflectional suffixes for verbs

The portmanteau suffixes expressing agreement in person and number as well as tense or mood in finite verbs are listed in Table 8.3. In this table, if only one suffix is given in a slot, then it is found in all inflectional classes. When more than one suffix is included in a slot, then the first allomorph is for inflectional classes I, II and III, the second allomorph for class IV, and the third allomorph for class V verbs. The suffixes for the non-finite infinitive, connegative and perfect verb forms are included here and in the following sections because they are common verb forms in the corpus and particularly useful in recognizing patterns in verb paradigms.

Table 8.3: Inflectional verb suffixes

		SG	DU	PL
PRS	1st	-v	-n/-jin/-n	-p
	2nd	-	-bähten/-bähten/-hpen	-ähtet/-bähtet/-hpit
	3rd	-/-ja/-	-ba	-/-je/-
PST	1st	-v/-jiv/-jiv	-jmen	-jmä/-jme/-jme
	2nd	-/-je/-je	-jden	-jdä/-jde/-jde
	3rd	-j	-jga	-n/-jin/-n
IMP	2nd	-	-n/n/a/-hten	-t/n/a/-htet
INF	-t		CONNEG	-
PRF	-m			

8.4.1.1 Verbal suffixes and syncretism

Several of the verbal inflectional suffixes, considered by themselves, are homophonous:

8.4 Morphological marking strategies on verbs

- *-v* for 1SG.PRS and 1SG.PST in classes I, II and III
- *-n* for 1DU.PRS, 3PL.PST in all classes, and also DU.IMP in classes I, II and III
- *-t* for INF and PL.IMP in classes I, II and III
- *no suffix* for 2SG.PRS, SG.IMP and CONNEG in all classes; 3SG.PRS, 3PL.PRS in classes I, II, III and V; and 2SG.PST in classes I, II and III

Despite these similarities, only the morphology of 1DU.PRS and 3PL.PST verb forms is syncretic in all verb classes because in most cases homophonous suffixes combine with different non-linear morphology and/or with different class marking suffixes.

8.4.2 Non-linear morphology in verbs

In addition to using the inflectional suffixes described above, inflectional categories for verbs can be marked by one or more of the following stem allomorphy strategies:

- stem consonant alternations (consonant gradation)
- V1 vowel alternations (umlaut)
- V1 vowel raising when followed by a close/close-mid V2 vowel (vowel harmony)

Because 2SG.PRS, 3SG.PRS, 3PL.PRS, 2SG.PST, 3SG.PST, SG.IMP and CONNEG forms often lack suffixes (cf. §8.4.1.1 above), verbs in these inflectional categories are typically marked exclusively by these essentially non-linear morphological marking strategies. To illustrate this, the inflectional paradigm for the verb *buälldet* 'ignite, burn' is provided in Table 8.4 on the next page and described here.

Note that the vowel in V2 position (*a*, *e* and *i*) in all forms is the inflectional class marker for Class III verbs (cf. §8.5.3); thus the stem has five allomorphs: *buälld-*, *buald-*, *buold-*, *bulld-* and *buld-*.[5] This reflects a consonant gradation pattern that alternates between strong *lld* and weak *ld*, and an umlaut pattern that alternates between *ua/uä* and *uo* in the vowel in V1 position.[6] Furthermore, the forms for 1DU.PRS, 3PL.PRS and all past forms are subject to vowel harmony;

---

[5] The examples used in this description of non-linear verb morphology is based on the current Pite Saami orthography, which is still a work in progress. Because the orthography is to a great extent phonemic, orthographic representations are sufficient for the current discussion.

[6] Note that *ua* and *uä* are allophones of /ua/; cf. §3.2.1.9.

Table 8.4: The inflectional paradigm for the verb *buälldet* 'ignite, burn'

		SG	DU	PL
PRS	1ˢᵗ	*buold-a-v*	*bulld-e-n*	*buälld-e-p*
	2ⁿᵈ	*buold-a*	*buälld-e-bähten*	*buälld-e-bähtet*
	3ʳᵈ	*bualld-a*	*buälld-e-ba*	*bulld-e*
PST	1ˢᵗ	*bulld-i-v*	*buld-i-jmen*	*buld-i-jmä*
	2ⁿᵈ	*bulld-e*	*buld-i-jden*	*buld-i-jdä*
	3ʳᵈ	*buld-i-j*	*buld-i-jga*	*bulld-e-n*
IMP	2ⁿᵈ	*buold-e*	*buälld-e-n*	n/a
INF	*buälld-e-t*	CONNEG	*buold-e*	
PRF	*bualld-a-m*			

here, the vowel in V1 position is raised to *u* in the presence of a close-mid front (*e*) or a close front (*i*) vowel in V2 position. Note, however, that this vowel harmony is morphologically selected by these slots in the paradigms; the *e* in V2 in other inflected forms does not trigger vowel harmony (cf. 2DU.PRS or DU.IMP forms).

In summary, the inflectional paradigm for *buälldet* 'ignite, burn' is characterized by consonant gradation, umlaut and vowel harmony in the stem, and the morphological environment determines which of these allomorphs is selected. For instance, as a result, the 1SG.PRS form *buoldav* is marked for person, number and tense/mood by the weak *buold-* stem (with the *-uo-* umlaut form) and the *-v* suffix simultaneously, and the 1PL.PST form *buldijmä* is marked by the weak *buld-* stem subjected to vowel harmony, and the *-jmä* suffix.

The pattern of non-linear inflectional marking throughout the paradigm for *buälldet* is illustrated in Table 8.5 on the facing page. The patterns for both consonant gradation and for umlaut in verb classes subject to these morphophonological strategies align seamlessly. However, each of the two verbal inflection classes subject to vowel harmony has its own unique vowel harmony pattern.

8.4 Morphological marking strategies on verbs

Table 8.5: Non-linear morphological marking in the paradigm for the verb *buälldet* 'ignite, burn'

		SG	DU	PL
PRS	1st	*uo*+wk	*VH*+str	*uä*+str
	2nd	*uo*+wk	*uä*+str	*uä*+str
	3rd	*ua*+str	*uä*+str	*VH*+str
PST	1st	*VH*+str	*VH*+wk	*VH*+wk
	2nd	*VH*+str	*VH*+wk	*VH*+wk
	3rd	*VH*+wk	*VH*+wk	*VH*+str
IMP	2nd	*uo*+wk	*uä*+str	n/a
INF		*uä*+str	CONNEG	*uo*+wk
PRF		*ua*+str		

Not every verb undergoes consonant gradation and/or umlaut; instead, their presence are determined by the phonological form of a verb.[7] Some examples of verbs with umlaut alternations and consonant gradation are shown in Table 8.6 below and Table 8.7 on the next page, respectively. Note that *ua* and *uä* are allophones of /ua/; cf. §3.2.1.9.

Table 8.6: Umlaut alternation patterns for verbs, with 3SG.PRS and 2SG.PRS example pairs

x	-	y	3SG.PRS		2SG.PRS	
ɛ	-	e	/kɛʰtʃa/	-	/ketʃa/	'look'
			gähtja		gietja	
u͡a	-	o	/pu͡aːta/	-	/polta/	'ignite, burn'
			buallda		buolda	

---

[7] Consonant gradation is described in detail in §4.1.2.1 and umlaut in §4.1.2.2.

8 Verbs

Table 8.7: Consonant gradation patterns for verbs, with 3SG.PRS and 2SG.PRS example pairs

strong	-	weak	3SG.PRS		2SG.PRS	
ʰx	-	x	/pɔʰta/ båhta	-	/pɔta/ båda	'come'
x:	-	x	/paːla/ bálla	-	/paːla/ bála	'dig'
			/maːʰta/ máhtta	-	/maːʰta/ máhta	'be able to'
x:y	-	xy	/parːka/ barrga	-	/parka/ barga	'work'
xy	-	y	/atnaː/ adná	-	/anaː/ aná	'have'
xyz	-	xz	/tʃaːjpma/ tjájbma	-	/tʃaːjma/ tjájma	'laugh'

8.4.2.1 Vowel harmony patterns for verbs

Vowel harmony in verb forms refers to a regressive assimilation of place of articulation between the two vowels of the final foot in a word. Specifically the raising of the vowel in V1 position triggered by the presence in specific, class-dependent paradigmatic slots of a close-mid /e/ (orthographic *e*) or a close front /i/ (orthographic *i*) vowel in V2 position. There are six attested vowel harmony patterns in the V1 vowel of a verb stem from Class II or Class III, as illustrated by Table 8.8 on the facing page.

The data from the corpus indicate that Class I and Class IV verbs do not exhibit vowel harmony, but there are no tokens of Class I or Class IV verbs with one of the vowels listed in Table 8.8 on the next page in V1 position. Consequently, the data must be considered inconclusive in this respect. On the other hand, it is quite evident that Class V verbs are not affected by vowel harmony because the V2 vowel in Class V verbs is never subject to the allomorphic alternations which trigger vowel harmony in the V1 vowel.

It is not clear why *á* and *a* have different vowel harmony alternations (*i/ä* and *i/e*, respectively, as illustrated by the first four examples in Table 8.8); these alternation patterns do not align with verb classes. Further research is needed to come to a better understanding of this vowel harmony.

Table 8.8: Vowel harmony alternation patterns for verbs (Class II and III), with INF and 2SG.PRS example pairs

A	→	B	INF	2SG.PST	
á	→	i	tjájbmat	tjijbme	'laugh'
á	→	ä	sávvat	sävve	'wish'
a	→	i	barrgat	birrge	'work'
a	→	e	adnet	edne	'have'
å	→	u	bårråt	burre	'eat'
uä	→	u	buälldet	bullde	'ignite'

8.4.3 The potential mood: inflection or derivation?

The potential mood[8] is not attested very often in the corpus, particularly outside elicitation settings, and was not considered in most elicitation sessions focussing on verb paradigms. As a result, the amount of data from the corpus available to inform a description of the inflectional behavior of the potential forms are quite limited. Nonetheless, the paradigm for the potential forms of the verb *gullat* 'hear' is provided in Table 8.9.

Table 8.9: Potential forms for the verb *gullat* 'hear'

	SG	DU	PL
1st	gulatjav	gulatjen	gulatjep
2nd	gulatja	gulatjähpen	gulatjehpit
3rd	gulatja	gulatjäba	gulatje

Taking the potential forms presented in the verb paradigms in Lehtiranta (1992: 150–155) and in the examples in Lagercrantz (1926: 22–24) into consideration, the paradigm of class marking suffixes and person/number suffixes used for potential verb forms is presented in Table 8.10 on the next page. The stem allomorph of the verb is in the weak stage, when applicable.

In the literature on Saami languages, potential mood is normally treated as an inflectional category,[9] and, for this reason as well as due to its seeming opposition

---

[8] Cf. §8.1.3.2 for a general description, including examples, of the potential mood.
[9] Cf., e.g., Sammallahti (1998: 76–84), Lehtiranta (1992: 88–89,150–153), Lagercrantz (1926: 118–122) and Feist (2010: 115).

8 Verbs

Table 8.10: Class marking suffixes and person/number suffixes for potential verb forms

	SG	DU	PL
1st	-a-v	-e-n	-e-p
2nd	-a	-ä-hpen	-e-hpit
3rd	-a	-ä-ba	-e

to imperative or tense-marked forms, is treated as such in the present study.

However, three morphosyntactic aspects of potential mood verb forms make its classification as an inflectional category potentially questionable. First, verbs in the potential mood feature a segmentally separable marker (*-tj-*), rather than being part of a portmanteau morpheme simultaneously indicating mood/tense, number and normally person as is the case for other tenses and moods. Second, the stem allomorph chosen in all potential forms is consistently the weak form, which is quite consistent with the morphosyntactic behavior of other derived verbs which consistently have a specific consonant gradation type, while the mood and tense paradigms for non-derived verbs contain both strong and weak stem allomorphs. Finally, it is striking that the potential mood class marking suffixes and person/number suffixes (listed in Table 8.10) are homophonous with the class marking and present tense person/number suffixes for Class V verbs (cf. Table 8.23 on page 177).[10] In all of these three aspects, the potential forms of verbs are identical in behavior to a number of derivational verb forms (cf. §10.2.1, §10.2.2 and §10.2.3), and unlike other inflectional tense/mood forms. At this point, the only morphological motivation to classify the potential mood as an inflectional category is its complementary distribution with other tense and mood forms. These characteristics are summarized in Table 8.11 on the facing page.

---

[10] Note that 3SG potential forms in Lehtiranta (1992: 150–154) do not have a class marker or person/number suffix. This deviates from the 3SG.PRS forms of Class V verbs (even though Lehtiranta (1992: 88) mentions that the potential forms are inflected in the same way as indicative present forms). On the other hand, all instances of 3SG potential forms in the Pite Saami Documentation Project corpus are marked with *-a*, just like the 3SG.PRS forms of Class V verbs. Perhaps this 3SG potential marker is a recent change to the Pite Saami potential verb forms based on analogy to these present tense forms.

8.4 Morphological marking strategies on verbs

Table 8.11: Features of potential verb forms characterized as typical for inflectional or derivational forms

	consistent with	
features of potential forms	inflection	derivation
consistently linearly segmentable marker		✓
consistently occurs with specific Σ-allomorph		✓
person/number marking like Class-V verbs		✓
complementary distribution with tense/mood forms	✓	

With these facts in mind, potential forms could be analyzed as derived verb forms consisting of a lexical verbal root plus a verbalizer (the potential mood morpheme) followed by Class V inflectional suffixes. This possible analysis is illustrated in (31), in which the morphological components of the form *gulatjav* 'I will likely hear' are parsed and labeled.

(31) *gula-tj-a-v*
hear-POT-V-1SG
Σ-mood-class-person/number

In such an analysis, potential verbs no longer stand in opposition to tense and imperative mood forms, but instead are subject to a semantic restriction to a non-past time, and are thus only marked for present (i.e., non-past) tense, and are marked according to the present tense slots of the inflectional paradigm for Class V verbs.

It should be pointed out that the corpus contains insufficient data concerning the potential forms of any verbs in Class V. This is relevant because Class V verbs have bisyllabic stems that, together with the potential marker, may trigger allomorphy in other person/number suffixes, in which case not all potential forms would follow the standard Class V paradigm. Such information would be essential in fully evaluating the analysis proposed here. Due mainly to this lack of truly conclusive data, I continue to follow the standard classification of the potential mood as an inflectional category for the means of the present study, but point out this potentially problematic analysis for Pite Saami as described above as a topic worthy of future study.

8.5 Inflectional classes for verbs

Verbs in Pite Saami can be grouped into inflectional classes based on recurring patterns across inflectional paradigms.[11] Each verb is marked by a class suffix which is attached directly after the verb stem and precedes inflectional suffixes (cf. Figure 1 on page 149). Unlike nouns, the potential to have umlaut alternations and/or consonant gradation present for a given verb is dependent on the verb's membership in a specific class. However not every verb in the umlaut/gradation classes is subject to these alternations, as that is determined by whether the phonemes occupying the V1 position and the consonant center of the final foot, respectively, are susceptible to umlaut and/or consonant gradation. Furthermore, some derivational suffixes (such as the diminutive suffix -*tj*) can block consonant gradation and umlaut from occurring in the derived form. Membership in a specific verb class does not seem to be semantically motivated.

As described in the previous section, Pite Saami verb paradigms present complex combinations of linear morphology (inflectional suffixes) and non-linear morphology (consonant gradation, umlaut, vowel harmony), and consist of a minimum of 21 finite forms and several non-finite forms. This minimum includes 1st, 2nd and 3rd person forms for singular, dual and plural in both present and past, as well as singular, dual and plural forms for imperative.[12] These are by far the most common forms in non-elicited data from the corpus. Furthermore, the three non-finite forms infinitive, connegative and perfect were also considered in determining inflectional classes. The non-elicited portions of the Pite Saami Documentation Project corpus are simply too limited to even come close to providing complete paradigms for even a single verb, and so a majority of the verb forms composing the paradigms for the current study are from elicitation sessions. Approximately 30 more or less complete verb paradigms were recorded, which provides sufficient data to posit five inflectional classes. However, the true extent and finer details of the morphophonological patterns found across verb paradigms in Pite Saami must be left to future study; it is possible that, with more research, more verb classes may result, or that the present classes may need revision. As a result, what follows must be considered of a preliminary nature.

There are five main criteria for positing five different verb classes:

---

[11] I am indebted to phonologist and Lule Saami scholar Bruce Morén-Duolljá for inspiring me to consider an approach to the data involving post-stem class marking morphology.

[12] Because of insufficient data concerning the potential forms of verbs, but also due to their regular predictability across classes (cf. §8.4.3), these were not considered in determining inflectional classes for verbs.

8.5 Inflectional classes for verbs

- the regularity of the pattern of vowels occurring between the stem and inflectional suffixes (i.e., the class marking suffix)
- the number of syllables in the infinitive form
- the presence of deviant person/number suffixes relative to the other verb classes
- V1 and consonant center stem allomorphy patterning throughout the inflectional paradigm (i.e., umlaut and consonant gradation)
- whether some verb forms are subject to vowel harmony, and which slots trigger such vowel harmony

To summarize these differences, it is sufficient to look at the class suffix and the syllable count in the infinitive form, the regularity of person/number suffixes across classes, the presence of consonant gradation ('C-grad') and umlaut, and the presence/absence of vowel harmony,[13] as illustrated in Table 8.12.

Table 8.12: Verb classes and their defining features

class	infinitive class suffix	σ-count	deviant agr. sx.	C-grad / umlaut	VH (pattern)
I	-o	2		✓	
II	-a/å	2		✓	✓(A)
III	-e	2		✓	✓(B)
IV	-V	2	✓		
V	-i	3			

Class I is the least complex class, and is therefore dealt with first in §8.5.1, while classes II, III, IV and V are described in §8.5.2 through §8.5.5. §8.5.6 briefly discusses the possibility of the existence of other verb classes. The verb *årrot* 'be' and the negation verb are dealt with in §8.5.7 and §8.5.8. The final section (§8.5.9) provides a brief summary of the verb classes, including a table listing examples from each of the verb classes.

---

[13] Note that, particularly historically, the verbs in inflectional classes I, II and II are similar to nouns in inflectional class I, while verbs in class IV are similar to nouns in class II, and verbs in class V correspond to nouns in class III. Cf. §5.4 for inflectional classes for nouns.

8 Verbs

8.5.1 Class I

Verbs in Class I are relatively simple, and characterized as follows:

- a bisyllabic infinitive form
- the class marking suffix is consistently -o
- potentially subject to consonant gradation and umlaut, but not vowel harmony

The verb *viessot* 'live, feel' is provided in Table 8.13 as an example. Other examples of Class I verbs include: *årrot* 'reside', *gårrot* 'sew', *gähttjot* 'tell', *lávvlot* 'sing' and *såggot* 'drown'.

Table 8.13: The inflectional paradigm for the Class I verb *viessot* 'live, feel'

		SG	DU	PL
PRS	1st	vies-o-v	viess-o-n	viess-o-p
	2nd	vies-o	viess-o-bähten	viess-o-bähtet
	3rd	viess-o	viess-o-ba	viess-o
PST	1st	viess-o-v	vies-o-jmen	vies-o-jme
	2nd	viess-o	vies-o-jden	vies-o-jde
	3rd	vies-o-j	vies-o-jga	viess-o-n
IMP	2nd	vies-o	viess-o-n	viess-o-t
INF		viess-o-t	CONNEG	vies-o
PRF		viess-o-m		

Table 8.14 on the facing page summarizes the gradation pattern and class suffixes for Class I verbs. Note that umlaut alternations align with consonant gradation alternations.

There are a number of verbs which seem to be marked by -u as a class marker in infinitive, such as *gävdnut* 'exist' and *pruvkut* 'use; usually do'. While the data in the corpus are incomplete, such verbs likely pattern in essentially the same way as the verbs mentioned above marked by -o, only they are consistently marked with -u as the class marking suffix.

8.5 Inflectional classes for verbs

Table 8.14: The consonant gradation pattern and inflectional verb class suffixes for Class I

		SINGULAR		DUAL		PLURAL	
PRS	1st	wk	-o-	str	-o-	str	-o-
	2nd	wk	-o	str	-o-	str	-o-
	3rd	str	-o	str	-o-	str	-o
PST	1st	str	-o-	wk	-o-	wk	-o-
	2nd	str	-o	wk	-o-	wk	-o-
	3rd	wk	-o-	wk	-o-	str	-o-
IMP	2nd	wk	-o	str	-o-	str	-o-
INF		str	-o-	CONNEG		wk	-o
PRF		str	-o-				

8.5.2 Class II

The characteristics of verbs in Class II are:

- a bisyllabic infinitive form with a class suffix *-a* or *-å*
- potentially subject to consonant gradation, umlaut and vowel harmony

For most inflected forms, the class marking suffix is consistent with the class marking suffix in the infinitive form; however, eight forms are assigned a specific class-marking vowel, as listed in Table 8.15.

Table 8.15: Specific class marking suffixes for all Class II verbs

form		form	
3SG.PRS	-a	1DU.PRS	-e
1SG.PST	-i	2SG.PST	-e
3PL.PRS	-e	3PL.PST	-e
2DU.IMP	-e	2PL.IMP	-i

8 Verbs

Class II verbs can further be divided into two sub-classes, based on the class marking suffix in the infinitive form: Class IIa is marked by *a*, while Class IIb is marked by *å*. The verb *bassat* 'wash' is provided in Table 8.16 as an example for a Class IIa verb, and *bårråt* 'eat' for a Class IIb verb in Table 8.17.

Table 8.16: The inflectional paradigm for the Class IIa verb *bassat* 'wash'

		SG	DU	PL
PRS	1st	bas-a-v	biss-i-n	bass-a-p
	2nd	bas-a	bass-a-bähten	bass-a-bähtet
	3rd	bass-a	bass-a-ba	biss-e
PST	1st	biss-i-v	bas-a-jmen	bas-a-jmä
	2nd	biss-e	bas-a-jden	bas-a-jdä
	3rd	bas-a-j	bas-a-jga	biss-i-n
IMP	2nd	bas-a	bass-e-n	bess-i-t
INF	bass-a-t		CONNEG	bas-a
PRF	bass-a-m			

Table 8.17: The inflectional paradigm for the Class IIb verb *bårråt* 'eat'

		SG	DU	PL
PRS	1st	bår-å-v	burr-e-n	bårr-å-p
	2nd	bår-å	bårr-å-bähtin	bårr-å-bähtet
	3rd	bårr-a	bårr-å-ba	burr-e
PST	1st	burr-e-v	bår-å-jmen	bår-å-jme
	2nd	burr-e	bår-å-jden	bår-å-jde
	3rd	bår-å-j	bår-å-jga	burr-e-n
IMP	2nd	bår-å	bårr-e-n	burr-i-t
INF	bårr-å-t		CONNEG	bår-å
PRF	bårr-å-m			

Other examples of Class IIa verbs include: *juhkat* 'drink', *tjájbmat* 'write', *barrgat* 'work', *gullat* 'hear', *gähtjat* 'look' and *sávvat* 'wish'. The corpus only provides sufficient data for the Class IIb verb *bårråt*; the verbs *dåbbdåt* 'recognize', *gåpptjåt* 'close', *hållåt* 'say' and *låhkåt* 'read' are also likely candidates for Class IIb. Verbs in Class IIb all have *å* as the initial stem vowel while the class marking post-stem vowel is also *å*, just as the nouns in noun Class Id (also marked by *å*).

Table 8.18 summarizes the gradation pattern, class suffixes and locations for vowel harmony for Class II verbs; here, **V** stands for the vowel which marks the infinitive form (*a* for Class IIa and *å* for Class IIb). Note that umlaut alternations align with consonant gradation alternations.

Table 8.18: The consonant gradation pattern, inflectional verb class suffixes and vowel-harmony features for Class II

		SINGULAR			DUAL			PLURAL		
PRS	1st	wk	-V-		str	-i-	+VH	str	-V-	
	2nd	wk	-V		str	-V-		str	-V-	
	3rd	str	-a		str	-V-		str	-e	+VH
PST	1st	str	-i-	+VH	wk	-V-		wk	-V-	
	2nd	str	-e	+VH	wk	-V-		wk	-i-	
	3rd	wk	-V-		wk	-V-		str	-i-	+VH
IMP	2nd	wk	-V		str	-e-		str	-i-	+VH
INF		str	-V-			CONNEG		wk	-V	
PRF		str	-V-							

8.5.3 Class III

Verbs in Class III are characterized as follows:

- a bisyllabic infinitive form with a class suffix *-e*
- potentially subject to consonant gradation, umlaut and vowel harmony

Twelve forms are subject to vowel harmony (the same six as for Class II verbs, plus six more). The verb *basset* 'fry' is provided in Table 8.19 on the next page as an example for a Class III verb. Other examples of Class III verbs include: *vádtset* 'go', *adnet* 'have, possess', *diehtet* 'know', *båhtet* 'come', *buälldet* 'ignite, burn' and *máhttet* 'can'. When the consonant center of a Class III stem consists of a single segment in the 1SG.PRS and 2SG.PRS forms and the V1 vowel is neither *á* nor *ua/uä/uo*, the class marking vowel is *á* instead of *a*, as illustrated in Table 8.19.

Table 8.20 on the following page summarizes the gradation pattern, class suffixes and locations for vowel harmony for Class III verbs. Note that umlaut alternations align with consonant gradation alternations.

Table 8.19: The inflectional paradigm for the Class III verb *basset* 'fry'

		SG	DU	PL
PRS	1st	bas-á-v	biss-i-n	bass-e-p
	2nd	bas-á	bass-e-bähten	bass-e-bähtet
	3rd	bass-a	bass-e-ba	biss-e
PST	1st	biss-i-v	bis-i-jmen	bis-i-jmä
	2nd	biss-e	bis-i-jden	bis-i-jdä
	3rd	bis-i-j	bis-i-jga	biss-i-n
IMP	2nd	bas-e	bass-e-n	biss-i-t
INF		bass-e-t	CONNEG	bas-e
PRF		bass-a-m		

Table 8.20: The consonant gradation pattern, inflectional verb class suffixes and vowel-harmony features for Class III

		SINGULAR			DUAL			PLURAL		
PRS	1st	wk	-a/á-		str	-i-	+VH	str	-e-	
	2nd	wk	-a/á		str	-e-		str	-e-	
	3rd	str	-a		str	-e-		str	-e	+VH
PST	1st	str	-i-	+VH	wk	-i-	+VH	wk	-i-	+VH
	2nd	str	-e	+VH	wk	-i-	+VH	wk	-i-	+VH
	3rd	wk	-i-	+VH	wk	-i-	+VH	str	-i-	+VH
IMP	2nd	wk	-e		str	-e-		str	-i-	+VH
INF		str	-e-			CONNEG		wk	-e	
PRF		str	-a-							

8.5.4 Class IV

Class IV verbs are characterized by:

- a bisyllabic infinitive form
- no allomorphic variation in the stem and in the class marker
- deviant person/number suffixes with a -j- element

The stem and the class marking suffix are consistent in all forms throughout a paradigm, i.e., there is no allomorphy in the stem or class marker. The person/number suffixes for 3SG.PRS, 1DU.PRS, 3PL.PRS, 1SG.PST, 2SG.PST and 3PL.PST deviate from the corresponding person/number suffixes in other verb classes in featuring an initial -j- element. A nearly complete paradigm for the verb *välldut* 'marry' is provided in Table 8.21.

Table 8.21: The inflectional paradigm for the Class IV verb *välldut* 'marry'

		SG	DU	PL
PRS	1st	välld-u-v	välld-u-jin	välld-u-p
	2nd	välld-u	välld-u-bähten	välld-u-bähtet
	3rd	välld-u-ja	välld-u-ba	välld-u-je
PST	1st	välld-u-jiv	välld-u-jmen	välld-u-jme
	2nd	välld-u-je	välld-u-jden	välld-u-jde
	3rd	välld-u-j	välld-u-jga	välld-u-jin
IMP	2nd	n/a	n/a	n/a
INF	välld-u-t		CONNEG	välld-u
PRF	välld-u-m			

However, the data in the corpus are not nearly sufficient to provide much more than the paradigm in Table 8.21. Class IV is likely a relatively small class of verbs; other potential candidates are *årrat*[14] 'fall asleep', *ádnot* 'request' and *tjerrot* 'cry'. Lehtiranta (1992: 154) includes a paradigm for *tjerrot*, which appears to pattern like *välldut*.[15] The class marking vowel in the infinitive form is thus not restricted to the -u- indicated in Table 8.21.

---

[14] The verb *årrat* 'fall asleep' should not be confused with the Class III verb *årret* 'sleep'.
[15] But even the paradigm in Lehtiranta (1992: 154) for *tjerrot* is marked by inconsistent forms across dialects. Furthermore, one of my main consultants from the northern side of the Pite Saami territory stated that her dialect does not use the lexeme *tjerrot*, but instead *vállut* 'cry'.

8 Verbs

Table 8.22 summarizes the preliminary class suffix pattern for Class IV verbs, as well as the presence of a person/number suffix which deviates from the corresponding person/number suffixes in other verb classes. This is based on the paradigm for *välldut* in Table 8.21 on the previous page and the paradigm for *tjerrot* provided in Lehtiranta (1992: 154).[16]

Table 8.22: The preliminary inflectional verb class suffix and deviant person/number suffix features (marked by ✓) for Class IV

		SINGULAR		DUAL		PLURAL	
PRS	1st	-V-		-V-	✓	-V-	
	2nd	-V		-V-		-V-	
	3rd	-V-	✓	-V-		-V-	✓
PST	1st	-V-	✓	-V-		-V-	
	2nd	-V-	✓	-V-		-V-	
	3rd	-V-		-V-		-V-	✓
IMP	2nd	n/a	n/a	n/a	n/a	n/a	n/a
INF		-V-		CONNEG		-V	
PRF		-V-					

8.5.5 Class V

Verbs in Class V are characterized by:

- a trisyllabic infinitive form with the class marking suffix *-i*
- absence of consonant gradation, umlaut and vowel harmony

Many Class V verbs are derived verbs based on a bisyllabic verb (cf. *gullat* 'hear' and *gulladit* 'be in touch' (lit.: let someone hear from you)).[17] The paradigm in Table 8.23 on the facing page provides an example for the verb *ságastit* 'speak'; other Class V verbs include *bargatjit* 'work a little', *gatjadit* 'ask', *gullalit* 'listen', *málestit* 'cook, boil', *gávnadit* 'meet' and *leradit* 'teach'. Table 8.24 then summarizes the gradation pattern and class suffixes for Class V verbs.

---

[16] Note the difference in orthographic forms between those used here, with *tjerrot* for the infinitive form, and the forms used in Lehtiranta (1992), with *tjier'rut* for the infinitive form.

[17] Because many derived verbs are in Class V, the semantic aspects accompanying the relevant derivational suffixes align in Class V, but their membership in Class V is due to their (morpho-)phonemic structure, not their semantics. Cf. §10.2 on verbal derivation.

8.5 Inflectional classes for verbs

Table 8.23: The inflectional paradigm for the Class V verb *ságastit* 'speak'

		SINGULAR	DUAL	PLURAL
PRS	1st	ságast-a-v	ságast-e-n	ságast-e-p
	2nd	ságast-a	ságast-ä-hpen	ságast-e-hpit
	3rd	ságast-a	ságast-ä-ba	ságast-e
PST	1st	ságast-i-jiv	ságast-i-jmen	ságast-i-jme
	2nd	ságast-i-je	ságast-i-jden	ságast-i-jde
	3rd	ságast-i-j	ságast-i-jga	ságast-e-n
IMP	2nd	ságast-e	ságast-ä-hten	ságast-ä-htet
INF		ságast-i-t	CONNEG	ságast-e
PRF		ságast-a-m		

Table 8.24: The inflectional verb class suffixes for Class V

		SINGULAR	DUAL	PLURAL
PRS	1st	-a-	-e-	-e-
	2nd	-a	-ä-	-e-
	3rd	-a	-ä-	-e
PST	1st	-i-	-i-	-i-
	2nd	-i-	-i-	-i-
	3rd	-i-	-i-	-e-
IMP	2nd	-e	-ä-	-ä-
INF		-i-	CONNEG	-e
PRF		-a-		

8 Verbs

8.5.6 Other possible verb classes

The data in the corpus are unfortunately not sufficient to be entirely confident concerning the five inflectional classes for verbs proposed here. With this in mind, the data concerning several verbs seem unusual, but also contradictory and inconsistent. Specifically, limited data on the verbs *årret* 'sleep', *årrat* 'fall asleep' and *ádnot* 'request' exist in the corpus indicating that these may belong to Class IV or some subset of Class IV verbs. Furthermore, a number of verbs with bisyllabic infinitive forms marked by *-i-* as a post-stem class-marking suffix exist in the data in the wordlist compiled by the Wordlist Project (cf. §1.2.3.4); however, in many cases, it seems that these verbs in fact belong to Class III, and the *-i-* class marker is simply an inconsistent spelling of *e*, as the realizations of /i/ and /e/ in unstressed syllables are more centralized, and thus easily confusable, particularly when applying what are otherwise Swedish graphemes representing more distinctly front Swedish vowels. For instance, the verb *virrtit* 'must' should perhaps be spelled *virrtet* and likely belongs to Class III. More data on this and other bisyllabic verbs with the *-i-* spelling need to be gathered to determine whether another inflectional class exists, or if these are only subclasses for Class IV and perhaps Class I, II or III.

8.5.7 The verb *årrot* 'be'

The verb *årrot* 'be' can be used both as a copula (cf. §13.1.4) and as an auxiliary (cf. §13.1.5.2); its paradigm is presented in Table 8.25. It is an unusual verb in a number of ways; these are listed on the following page.

Table 8.25: The inflectional paradigm for the verb *årrot* 'be'

		SG	DU	PL
PRS	1st	lev	lin	lep
	2nd	lä/'l	lähpen	lehpet
	3rd	lä/'l	lähpa	lea/'l
PST	1st	lidjiv	lijmen	lijme
	2nd	lidje	lijden	lijde
	3rd	lij	lijga	lidjen
IMP	2nd	n/a	n/a	n/a
INF		årrot	CONNEG	lä
PRF		urrum/lam		

- *årrot* 'be' is suppletive, featuring the two stems *årr-* and *l-*.
- Many of the *l-* stem forms are monosyllabic.
- The 2SG.PRS, 3SG.PRS and 3PL.PRS forms can be shortened to *'l* and encliticized onto the preceding word of an utterance if the preceding word has an open final syllable, as in (32).

(32)   *duvne'l*   *aj*   *'svála'*   *båkså*
       duvne=l   aj   svála   båkså
       2SG.INESS=be\3PL.PRS also arctic.fox\GEN.SG pant\NOM.PL
       'You also have *Fjällräven*[18] pants on.'   [pit090519.073]

- The 1SG.PST form *lidjiv* is often shortened to *lijiv*, and the 3PL.PST form *lidjin* is often shortened to *lin*.
- The infinitive and perfect forms are the only forms in this basic paradigm which use the *årr-* stem, which is homophonous (and cognate) with the verb *årrot* 'reside, live'.
- Finally, the verb *årrot* 'be' is unique in having a contracted connegative and perfect form: *lam* 'be-PRF\CONNEG' is a shortened form of *lä* 'be\CONNEG' and *urrum* 'be-PRF', and is thus only used in conjunction with the verb of negation, as illustrated by the example in (33).

(33)   *men*   *iv*   *lam*   *dä*   *månnå*   *del*
       men   i-v   l-am   dä   månnå   del
       but NEG-1SG.PRS be-PRF\CONNEG then 1SG.NOM then
       skålån   *giesen*
       skålå-n   giese-n
       school-INESS.SG summer-INESS.SG
       'But I haven't been in school during the summer.'   [pit080924.622]

8.5.8 The negation verb

The negation verb is unique because it only exists as a finite verb; thus there are no non-finite forms. Table 8.26 on the following page presents the paradigm for the negation verb. Concerning the imperative forms, both forms indicated for each number slot are attested in the corpus.

---

[18] *Fjällräven* refers to a Swedish clothing company named after 'the arctic fox' (lat.: *Vulpes lagopus*); in (32), the speaker literally translates the company's name into Pite Saami.

Table 8.26: The inflectional paradigm for the negation verb

		SINGULAR	DUAL	PLURAL
PRS	1st	iv	en	ep
	2nd	i	ehpen	ehpet
	3rd	ij	eba	eh
PST	1st	ittjiv	ettjijmen	ittjijme
	2nd	ittje	ettjijden	ittjijde
	3rd	ittjij	ettjijga	ittjin
IMP	2nd	ele/ilu	ellen/illun	ellet/illut

8.5.9 Summary of verb classes

Table 8.27 on the next page is provided to facilitate a cross-class comparison of inflectional paradigms with examples from the various inflectional classes for verbs, as well as the verb *årrot* 'be' and the negation verb. While the whole paradigm for each word is not listed due to a lack of space, the forms for INF, 2SG.PRS, 3SG.PRS, 2SG.PST, 3SG.PST and CONNEG are sufficient to convey the relevant morphological differences between the classes.

8.5 Inflectional classes for verbs

Table 8.27: Comparison of verb class examples

class		INF	2SG.PRS	3SG.PRS	2SG.PST	3SG.PST	CONNEG	
I		viess-o-t	vies-o	viess-o	viess-o	vies-o-j	vies-o	'live, feel'
		årr-o-t	år-o	årr-o	årr-o	år-o-j	år-o	'live, reside'
		gårr-o-t	går-o	gårr-o	gårr-o	går-o-j	går-o	'sew'
II	a	tjåjbm-a-t	tjåjm-a	tjåjbm-a	tijibm-e	tjåjm-a-j	tjåjm-a	'laugh'
		gähtj-a-t	gietj-a	gähtj-a	gihtj-e	gietj-a-j	gietj-a	'look'
		bass-a-t	bas-a	bass-a	biss-e	bas-a-j	bas-a	'wash'
	b	bårr-å-t	bår-å	bårr-a	burr-e	bår-å-j	bår-å	'eat'
III		bass-e-t	bas-á	bass-a	biss-e	bis-i-j	bas-e	'fry'
		buälld-e-t	buold-a	buälld-a	bulld-e	buld-i-j	buold-e	'ignite, burn'
		adn-e-t	an-á	adn-a	edn-e	en-i-j	an-e	'have'
IV		vådts-e-t	våts-e	vådts-a	vådts-e	våts-i-j	våts-e	'go'
V		välld-u-t	välld-u	välld-u-ja	välld-u-je	välld-u-j	välld-u	'marry'
		ságast-i-t	ságast-a	ságast-a	ságast-e	ságast-i-j	ságast-e	'say'
		málest-i-t	málest-a	málest-a	málest-e	málest-i-j	málest-e	'cook, boil'
		bargatj-i-t	bargatj-a	bargatj-a	bargatj-e	bargatj-i-j	bargatj-e	'work a little'
copula		årrot	lä	lä	lidje	lij	lä	'be'
negation		-	i	ij	ittje	ittjij	-	'NEG'

9 Other word classes

This chapter describes the word classes:

- adverbs in §9.1,
- adpositions in §9.2,
- conjunctions in §9.3,
- and interjections in §9.4

The information provided here is of a preliminary nature due to limited data in the corpus, and stands to gain much from future research.

9.1 Adverbs

Adverbs compose an open word class and are defined by their ability to head an adverbial phrase; they can be further divided into two main groups:

- derived adverbs
- lexical adverbs

Here, §9.1.1 deals with the former, while §9.1.2 presents with the latter.

9.1.1 Derived adverbs

At least one derivational affix seems to exist which derives an adverb from an adjective: the suffix *-t*, as illustrated by Table 9.1 on the following page.
 The adverbializing suffix *-t* triggers the weak consonant grade, when applicable. Two examples from the corpus are provided in (1) and (2) below.

(1) dån   virte   várogit   válldet
     dån   virte   várogi-t   vállde-t
     2SG.NOM must\2SG.PRS careful-ADVZ take-INF
     'You have to take it carefully.'   [pit080909.062]

9 Other word classes

Table 9.1: Derived adverbs and their adjectival stems

ATTR-adjective		adverb	
várogis	→	várogit	'careful(ly)'
buoragis	→	buoragit	'good/well'

(2) viesojmä   vanj   ganska buoragit   dajna
    vieso-jmä   vanj   ganska[1] buoragi-t d-a-jna
    live-1PL.PST definitely quite   good-ADVZ DEM-DIST-COM.SG
    guollemijn   aj
    guollemi-jn   aj
    fishing-COM.SG also
    'We definitely lived pretty well with the fishing, too.'

[pit0906_Ahkajavvre_a.164]

9.1.2 Lexical adverbs

A group of lexical items exclusively used as adverbs in Pite Saami forms a subset of adverbs. A list of some lexical adverbs is provided in Table 9.2 on the next page.[2] Examples containing the sentence adverbs *ber* 'only', *kan* 'maybe', *aj* 'too' and *vanj* 'definitely' are provided in (3) through (6).

(3) buhtsu   mielkest   ijtjen   ber vuostajd
    buhtsu   mielke-st   ittj-in   ber vuosta-jd
    reindeer\GEN.SG milk-ELAT.SG NEG-3PL.PST only cheese-ACC.PL
    dága
    dága
    make\CONNEG
    'They didn't only make cheese from reindeer milk.'

[pit080708_Session03.001]

(4) kan   Edde   diehta
    kan   Edde   diehta
    maybe Edgar\NOM.SG know\3SG.PRS
    'Maybe Edgar knows.'

[pit090519.355]

---

[1] Note that *ganska* is a nonce borrowing from Swedish; cf. Swedish *ganska* 'quite'.
[2] The adverbs *ber~bar*, *kan* and *så* are Swedish loans; cf. Swedish *bara* 'only', *kanske* 'maybe' and *så* 'so'.

Table 9.2: A selection of lexical adverbs

aj	'also, too'
ber~bar	'only'
del	'obviously'
dä	'then'
gal	'actually'
ihkep	'maybe'
ilá	'too' (excessive)
kan	'maybe'
mudiŋ	'sometimes'
så	'so'
vanj	'really'
åbbå	'quite'

(5) ja dä bedja dun nubbe bielen aj
 ja dä bedja d-u-n nubbe biele-n aj
 and then put\3SG.PRS DEM-RMT-INESS.SG other side-INESS.SG also
 risijd
 risi-jd
 twig-ACC.PL
 'And then one puts twigs on the other side, too.' [pit100404.228]

(6) *gajk vuorasumos saddje'l vanj dát*
 gajk vuoras-umos saddje=l vanj d-á-t
 all old-SUPERL place\NOM.SG=be\3SG.PRS definitely DEM-PROX-NOM.SG
 urrum dulutjist
 urru-m dulutji-st
 be-PRF old.days-ELAT.SG
 'This was definitely the absolute oldest place from the old days.'
 [pit0906_Ahkajavvre_a.059]

A further lexical adverb is *gal* 'actually', which can be used to emphasize a contradiction or surprise, as in (7). The interjection *nä* 'no', a borrowing from Swedish,[3] is also used in this example, in addition to the native Saamic negation verb.

---

[3] < Swedish *nej* 'no'; cf. local dialect pronunciation [nɛː].

9 Other word classes

(7) A: *udtju   sáme   gielav   danne sagastit?*
       udtju   sáme   giela-v   danne sagasti-t
       be.allowed\2SG.PST Saami\GEN.SG   language-ACC.SG   there   speak-INF
       'Were you allowed to speak the Saami language there?'
    B: *nä, ij   gal,   ittjiv   åtjo*
       nä   ij   gal   i-ttjiv   åtjo
       no   NEG\3SG.PRS actually NEG-1SG.PST be.allowed\CONNEG
       'No, actually no, I wasn't allowed to.'   [pit080924.351-352]

In (8), the adverb *ilá* 'too' modifies the adjective *nuora* 'young'.

(8) *ilá   nuora   lijme*
    ilá   nuora   li-jme
    too   young\PL be-1PL.PST
    'We were too young.'   [pit080924.437]

9.1.2.1 The question marker *gu~gus*

In several Saami languages, including closely related Lule Saami, a grammatical unit often referred to in the literature as a 'question particle' is used to mark polar interrogative clauses.[4] For Pite Saami, Lagercrantz (1926: 20–21) indicates that Pite Saami also has a question marker *gu* identifying polar interrogatives, although he shows that it is not obligatory.[5] In the entire Pite Saami Documentation Project corpus, there are only three clear tokens of a polar interrogative with the question marker, and even then, the marker has two forms: *gu* and *gus*. These tokens are provided in examples (9)[6] through (11).

(9) *lä   gu nällgomin?*
    lä   gu nällgo-min
    be\2SG.PRS   Q hunger-PROG
    'Are you hungry?' (lit.: are you hungering)   [pit110518a.18m36s]*e*

---

[4] Cf. North Saami *-go* (cf. Svonni 2009: 90) and Lule Saami *-ga/-k/-ge* (cf. Spiik 1989: 94–94), which are cognate with Pite Saami *gu~gus*. According to Sammallahti (1998: 245), the question marker was originally borrowed from Finnish. Skolt Saami also has a question marker *-a* (cf. Feist 2010: 319–320), which is not cognate.

[5] Lagercrantz (1926: 21) notes that polar questions often are only marked by being verb-initial, so even in 1921 (when he conducted fieldwork for his book) the question marker was not obligatory in Pite Saami.

[6] Note that the question marker in example (9) was recorded serendipitously in an elicitation session concerning a different topic.

(10) aná   gus dån   naginav,   mujtojd?
     aná   gus dån   nagina-v   mujt-o-jd
     have\2SG.PRS Q 2SG.NOM something-ACC.SG remember-NMLZ1-ACC.PL
     'Do you have something, memories?'   [pit090702.483]

(11) nå, juga   gu guäsmagav?
     nå juga   gu guäsmaga-v
     well drink\2SG.PRS Q coffee-ACC.SG
     'Well, do you drink coffee?'   [sje20130530b.015]

Based on this lack of data, and on the description provided in Lagercrantz (1926), one can only conclude that the question marker is no longer required to identify polar interrogative clauses, and has all but disappeared from current Pite Saami usage.

In determining which word class the question marker belongs to, several facts should be considered. Most importantly, like the adverbs in examples (3) through (6) above, the scope of the question marker is the entire sentence; gu~gus indicates an epistemic lack on behalf of the speaker concerning the proposition expressed by the interrogative clause it marks. While its monosyllabicity is remarkable, and implies a strong degree of grammaticalization (since lexical items in general are minimally bisyllabic), a number of other monosyllabic lexical adverbs also exist (cf. Table 9.2 on page 185). On this basis, the question marker can be classified as a lexical adverb.

However, although the data are much too limited to be certain, the question marker in all three examples occurs directly after the finite verb. If it indeed can only occur here, then this may be sufficient reason to consider the question marker to be the sole member of a unique word class (perhaps best named 'particle') defined by its clause-level scope and syntactic position restriction.[7]

9.2 Adpositions

Adpositions in Pite Saami constitute a closed class of words that are defined syntactically by their ability to head an adpositional phrase (abbreviated 'PP' as these are either postpositional or prepositional phrases). Postpositions, which are clearly preferred over prepositions, are covered in §9.2.1. The limited data on

---

[7] Note that the brief description of the cognate Lule Saami 'question particle' in Spiik (1989: 95) indicates that the Lule Saami equivalent may in fact be a focus particle used exclusively in polar interrogatives, as it "is placed near the word on which the most emphasis rests", while always occurring "after the helping verb" (my translations).

9 Other word classes

prepositions, which, with one exception, can all be used as postpositions as well, are described in §9.2.2.

9.2.1 Postpositions

Table 9.3 provides a selection of postpositions found in the corpus and includes English translation equivalents. It is possible that other postpositions also exist but were not attested in the corpus.

Table 9.3: A selection of postpositions and their English translation equivalents

badjel, bajel	'above; over'
birra	'about; around'
duogen	'behind'
gaskan	'between'
guoran	'next to; near'
lahka	'near'
nala	'upon, up, towards'
nanne~nan	'on'
sidån	'next to; beside'
sinne~sin	'inside'
sissa~sis	'into'
siste	'out of'
tjadá	'throughout'
vuolen	'under'
vusste	'against'
åvdon	'in front of'
åvdost	'for'

Postpositions are complemented by NPs in the genitive case. Two examples are provided in (12) and (13); for more on the syntactic behavior of postpositions in postpositional phrases as well as more examples, see §11.5.

(12) *ja tsáhpat biergov   káfa   sis*
      ja tsáhpa-t biergo-v   káfa   sis
      and cut-INF meat-ACC.SG coffee\GEN.SG into
      'and to cut meat into the coffee'   [pit100405a.136]

(13) ja dä skåvlåmáná   minnin   dan   bajel
     ja dä skåvlå-máná   minni-n d-a-n   bajel
     and then school-child\NOM.PL go-3PL.PST DEM-DIST-GEN.SG over
     sparkijin
     sparki-jin
     kick.sled-COM.SG
     'And then the school children went over that by kick-sled.' [pit090915.031]

9.2.2 Prepositions

With the exception of *dugu* 'like', which governs a noun in either the essive or the nominative case (cf. §5.2.9), a few words that are normally used as postpositions may also occur as prepositions. The corpus provides only a very limited amount of data concerning the existence and behavior of prepositions; the two examples are presented here.

In (14), *birra* 'about, around' is used as a preposition, and governs the genitive case on the complement demonstrative.

(14) ja badde,   åsto   badde   birra
     ja badde   åst-o   badde   birra
     and ribbon\NOM.SG buy-NMLZ1\NOM.SG ribbon\NOM.SG around
     danne
     d-a-nne
     DEM-DIST-GEN.SG
     'and ribbon, purchased ribbon around that'   [pit080708_Session08.012]

In (15), *badjel* 'over' is used as a preposition. However, the complement *nällje kronor* 'four crowns' (referring to the Swedish currency) consists of the Pite Saami numeral *nällje* and a Swedish borrowing *kronor* which is inflected according to Swedish grammar (*kron-or* 'crown-PL'), and not Pite Saami grammar, so it is impossible to know with these data which case *badjel* governs as a preposition.

(15) så åtjojmä   badjel nällje kronor tjilos   dalloj
     så åtjo-jmä   badjel nällje kronor tjilos   dalloj
     so receive-1PL.PST over   four   crowns kilogram   at.that.time
     'So we received more than four Swedish crowns per kilogram back then.'
                                                    [pit0906_Ahkajavvre_a.159]

Note that there are numerous examples for both *birra* and *badjel* as postpositions. It is not surprising that prepositions are infrequent and marginal in Pite

9 Other word classes

Saami as other Saami languages also only have a small set of prepositions with significant restrictions in frequency and meaning.[8]

9.3 Conjunctions

Conjunctions in Pite Saami form a closed class of words that connect phrases or clauses. A list of some conjunctions, what they can connect, as well as their English translation equivalents can be found in Table 9.4. Note that the conjunctions *att*, *eller* and *men* are borrowings from Swedish.

Table 9.4: Some Pite Saami conjunctions and their English translation equivalents, as well as whether these connect phrases and/or clauses

		phrases	clauses
att	'(in order) to'		✓
eller	'or'	✓	✓
gu	'when'	✓	✓
ja	'and'	✓	✓
jala	'or'	✓	✓
jus	'if'		✓
maŋŋel	'after'		✓
men	'but'		✓
vaj	'or'		✓
åvdål	'before'		✓

Conjunctions connecting clauses are discussed in §14.1 on coordination and §14.2 on subordination. Conjunctions connecting phrases are briefly described here. NPs, APs and verbs can be connected to another phrase of the same type by a conjunction; however, it is not clear from the data whether PPs or AdvPs can be connected. Some examples can be found in (16) through (21).

In (16) and (17), *ja* 'and' connects NPs and APs, respectively.

---

[8] Cf. Spiik (1989: 91–92) for Lule Saami, Svonni (2009: 84–85) for North Saami and Feist (2010: 314–317) for Skolt Saami. As for Pite Saami, neither Lagercrantz (1926) nor Lehtiranta (1992) mention anything about prepositions or the syntactic behavior (constituent order) of adpositions in general.

(16) dájste   åtjojmä   mielkev,   vuojav,   vuostav
     d-á-jste   åtjo-jmä   mielke-v   vuoja-v   vuosta-v
     DEM-PROX-ELAT.PL get-1PL.PST milk-ACC.SG butter-ACC.SG cheese-ACC.SG
     ja biergov
     ja biergo-v
     and meat-ACC.SG
     'We got milk, butter, cheese and meat from these.'   [pit080825.015]

(17) buhtsu   lä   nav buojde ja tjábbe
     buhtsu   lä   nav buojde ja tjábbe
     reindeer\NOM.PL be\3PL.PRS so fat\PL and beautiful\PL
     'The reindeer are so fat and beautiful.'   [pit080703.014]

In (18), *jala* 'or' connects numeral-APs, while in (19) it connects NPs.

(18) men mån   jahkav   gu   lidjiv   mån   aktalåknelldje
     men mån   jahka-v   gu   li-djiv   mån   akta-låk-nelldje
     but 1SG.NOM believe-1SG.PRS when be-1SG.PST 1SG.NOM one-ten-four
     jala aktalåkvihta   jáge...
     jala akta-låk-vihta jáge
     or   one-ten-five   year\NOM.PL
     'But I believe when I was fourteen or fifteen years (old)...'
     [pit100404.273-274]

(19) válda   káfav   suhkorijn   jala suhkorahta?
     válda   káfa-v   suhkor-ijn   jala suhkor-ahta
     take\2SG.PRS coffee-ACC.SG sugar-COM.SG or sugar-ABESS.SG
     'Do you take coffee with or without sugar?'   [pit110509b.11m42s]e

The conjuction *jala* 'or' can also connect non-finite verbs, as in (20).

(20) ja dálasj   ájgen   ij   almatj,   aktak
     ja dálasj   ájge-n   ij   almatj   aktak
     and nowadays time-INESS.SG NEG\3SG.PRS person\NOM.SG none
     almatj   danne vieso   jala åro
     almatj   danne vieso   jala åro
     person\NOM.SG there live\CONNEG or reside\CONNEG
     'And nowadays no one lives or resides there.'   [pit100310b.131]

Finally, in (21), the loan conjunction *eller* 'or'[9] connects NPs.

---

[9] < Swedish *eller* 'or'.

(21)   *inijmä*   *eller bårojmä*   *sirijd*   *ja*   *láddagijd*
        ini-jmä   eller båro-jmä   siri-jd   ja   láddagi-jd
        have-1PL.PST or   eat-1PL.PST blueberry-ACC.PL and cloudberry-ACC.PL
        'We had or ate blueberries and cloudberries.'   [pit100310b.035]

9.4 Interjections

An interjection is an individual word that is syntactically an utterance of its own at the same level as entire clauses. As such, interjections are not a part of another clause. Interjections often indicate a speaker's feelings or attitude towards an event. The data in the corpus are quite limited, and it is beyond the scope of the current study to describe interjections in detail, so the list of interjections and their English translation equivalents provided in Table 9.5 is preliminary and subject to amendment pending future study. Nonetheless, examples from the

Table 9.5: Some Pite Saami interjections and their English translation equivalents

burist	'hello' (greeting)
jaha	'ok, I see' (understanding)
jå	'yes, definitely'
mmm	'hmmm' (pondering)
nå	'well, yes'
nä	'no'
så	'so'
å~oj	'oh' (surprise)

corpus of *nå* and *jå* are provided below. Note that the interjections *jå, nä, så, å/oj, mmm* and *jaha* are borrowings from Swedish.

The interjection *nå* 'well, yes, ok' is very common in the corpus. It has at least three possible meanings. At the beginning of the conversation presented in (22), *nå* is a kind of declaration that a speaker is beginning to speak. As in the final utterance in this example, *nå* also indicates a switch to a new topic.

(22)   A: *nå*   *buris, Henning*
           nå   buris Henning
           well hello Henning
           'Well hello, Henning!'

B: *nå, buris dä*
   nå   buris dä
   well hello then
   'Well hello there!'
A: *nå, guste   dån   bådá?*
   nå   guste   dån   bådá
   well from.where 2SG.NOM come\2SG.PRS
   'Well where are you coming from?'   [pit080924.001-003]

The interjection *nå* can also be a confirmation of the preceding utterance, as in (23).

(23) A: *ja dä muv   bena   Rahka*
        ja dä muv   bena   Rahka
        and then 1SG.GEN dog\NOM.SG Rahka
        'And then my dog Rahka.'
     B: *nå, duv   bena   aj*
        nå   duv   bena   aj
        well 2SG.GEN dog\NOM.SG also
        'Ok, your dog, too.'   [pit080924.037-038]

Finally, *nå* can be used to indicate that a speaker is finished speaking, usually at the conclusion of a narrative and after a pause. One example can be found in the narrative in the recording 'pit100404' between utterance '.324' and utterance '.361'; due to space constraints, only the last two utterances of this long narrative are presented in (24).

(24) A: *så dä   måj   mähtijmen, måj   Jåsjåjn   mähtijmen*
        så dä   måj   mähti-jmen måj   Jåsjå-jn   mähti-jmen
        so then 1DU.NOM can-1DU.PST 1DU.NOM Josh-COM.SG can-1DU.PST
        dä   tjuäjjgat dán   Stuornjárga   nalá.
        dä   tjuäjjga-t d-á-n   Stuor-njárga   nalá
        then ski-INF   DEM-PROX-GEN.SG big-point\GEN.SG onto
        '...so then we were able to, Josh and I were able to ski up to this here Big Point.'
     B: *nå.*
        nå
        well
        'That's all.'   [pit100404.360-361]

9 Other word classes

The interjection *jå* 'yes', also a Swedish borrowing,[10] is often used to confirm something, or contradict a negative utterance, as in (25), in which two speakers debate about what the correct Pite Saami word for 'esophagus' is.

(25) A: *'tjåddjåk',   nä, ij   lä   'tjåddjåk'*
        tjåddjåk   nä ij   lä   tjåddjåk
        esophagus\NOM.SG no NEG\3SG.PRS be\CONNEG esophagus\NOM.SG
        '"tjåddjåk", no, it's not "tjåddjåk".'
     B: *jå, lä   tjåddjåk*
        jå lä   tjåddjåk
        yes be\3SG.PRS esophagus\NOM.SG
        'Yes, it's "tjåddjåk".'   [pit080909.115-116]

---

[10] < Swedish *jå*, a common pronunciation of *ja* 'yes'.

10 Derivational morphology

Pite Saami is rich in derivational morphology. While it is beyond the scope of the present work to provide a thorough description of all the various derivational processes and of their semantic nuances and productivity,[1] the following should provide a general impression of how derivational morphology works in Pite Saami, as well as an overview of some of the more common derivational morphemes attested in the corpus and extant in the wordlist compiled by the Wordlist Project (cf. §1.2.3.4).

In the following, derivational meanings are assigned to suffixes for simplicity in classification; however, as with inflectional suffixes, derivational suffixes coincide with non-linear morphology when the derivational base is subject to non-linear morphological alternations. There are many nominalizing and verbalizing derivational processes, and derivations can apply to already derived forms. On the other hand, there are only two adjectivizers and one adverbializer.

Nominal derivation and verbal derivation are especially complex because the semantics of a derived word do not consistently equal the sum of the meanings of its components. Furthermore, the borderline between polysemy and homonymy of suffixes cannot always be clearly determined, and the decision whether two formally identical, but semantically different forms should be ascribed to the same morpheme or to distinct morphemes is not always obvious. This is reflected in the glossing standards used here in which most nominalizers and verbalizers are simply allotted numbers, as in NMLZ1 or VBLZ3, as opposed to more meaningful glosses such as DIM.

In the following, nominal derivation is dealt with first, in §10.1, before moving on to verbal derivation in §10.2, while adjectival and adverbial derivation are described briefly in §10.3 and §10.4, respectively. The final section (§10.5) provides a summary of the derivational morphemes discussed here.

Note that examples in the present chapter include references to either the documentation corpus or an entry in the database from the Wordlist Project (cf. §1.2.3.4). Nearly all references to the documentation corpus are for elicita-

---

[1] Israel Ruong (himself a native speaker of Pite Saami) dedicated his entire PhD thesis to verbal derivation in Pite Saami (Ruong 1943).

10 Derivational morphology

tion sessions, and these are marked accordingly. Unlike examples in the other chapters, in which references indicate a particular utterance of a recording, references here may not be not more specific than the recording name alone because the relevant data were obtained during the course of a longer discussion, and not just in a single utterance. References referring to the Wordlist Project's database consist only of the four-digit entry number.

10.1 Nominal derivation

Nouns can be derived from verbs, adjectives, or other nouns. Some of the more common derivational suffixes are -*tj*, -*k*, -*o*, -*däddje*, -*vuohta*, and these are discussed in the following sections. The bases they can be applied to are summarized in Table 10.1.

Table 10.1: The nominal derivation suffixes discussed here and the bases these can suffix to

suffix	nominal	verbal	adjectival
-tj	✓		
-k	✓	✓	✓
-o		✓	
-däddje	✓	✓	
-vuohta	✓		✓

10.1.1 The diminutive suffix -*tj*

The diminutive suffix -*tj* (glossed as DIM) can be affixed to a nominal base to form a denominal noun with a diminutive meaning. Examples can be found in (1) through (6).

(1) vájbmo   →   vájmu-tj   'little heart'
     heart\NOM.SG   heart-DIM\NOM.SG   [pit110413a]*e*

(2) guolla   →   guola-tj   'little testicle'
     testicle\NOM.SG   testicle-DIM\NOM.SG   [pit110413a]*e*

(3) guolle   →   guolá-tj   'little fish'
     fish\NOM.SG   fish-DIM\NOM.SG   [pit110413a]*e*

10.1 Nominal derivation

(4) *båtsoj* → *buhtsu-tj* 'little reindeer'
    reindeer\NOM.SG   reindeer-DIM\NOM.SG   [pit110413b]*e*

(5) *sabek* → *sabega-tj* 'little ski'
    ski\NOM.SG   ski-DIM\NOM.SG   [pit090525b]*e*

(6) *bena* → *bednaga-tj* 'little dog'
    dog\NOM.SG   dog-DIM\NOM.SG   [pit080819a]*e*

The diminutive form features the same stem found in the NOM.PL form of a noun paradigm (differences in the segments occurring between the consonant center and the right edge of the nominal base in these examples are due to regular alternations in inflectional noun class suffixes on the base). The resulting diminutive nouns are class IIIa nouns; a nearly complete paradigm for the derived noun *guolátj* 'little fish' is provided in Table 5.20 in §5.4.3. Note also that there is a diminutive verbalizer suffix *-tj*; cf. §10.2.1.

10.1.2 The general nominalizer suffix *-k*

The nominalizer suffix *-k* (spelled *-g-* intervocalically; glossed as NMLZ[2]) can be affixed to a noun, a verb or an adjective. The resulting derived nouns have a wide variety of meanings, but generally have a referent which is someone or something with a property referred to by the base. A number of examples are provided in (7) through (17) below, but this is hardly an exhaustive sample.

In (7) the derived noun *guhkajuolgagijd* 'long-legger-ACC.PL' is based on a compound noun *guhka-juällge* 'long-leg', and is used several times in the corpus to refer to moose.

(7) *vuojdne   edna   guhkajuolgagijd?*
    vuojdne   edna   guhka-juolga-g-ijd
    see\2SG.PST some long-leg-NMLZ-ACC.PL
    'Did you see some moose?'   [pit080924.007]

The derivation of the base compound's head *guhka-juällge* 'long-leg' into the derived form is illustrated in (8).

(8) *guhka-juällge* → *[guhka-juolga]-k* 'long-legger'
    long-leg\NOM.SG   [long-leg]-NMLZ\NOM.SG   [pit080924.007]

---

[2] Due to its frequency and extensive use as a general nominalizer, the nominalizer *-k* is glossed simply as NMLZ without any additional number to specify it, unlike the other, less frequent nominalizers described in §10.1.3 through §10.1.5.

10 Derivational morphology

Two other examples of denominal nouns derived with *-k* are the word *jagak* 'yearling, one-year-old', which is derived from the nominal base *jahke* 'year', as given in (9), and the word *nástak* 'police', which is derived from the nominal base *násste* 'star':

(9)   jahke   →   jaga-k   'yearling'
        year\NOM.SG   year-NMLZ\NOM.SG   [4911]

(10)   násste   →   násta-k   'police, police officer'
        star\NOM.SG   star-NMLZ\NOM.SG   [1249]

The word *máhtak* 'knowledgable person' is derived from the verb *máhttet* 'can':

(11)   máhtte-t   →   máhta-k   'knowledgable person'
        can-INF   can-NMLZ\NOM.SG   [1110]

The word *villguk* 'white reindeer' is based on a form *vällg-* 'white' (cf. the attributive adjective *villgis* and predicative adjective *vällgat* 'white'):

(12)   vällg-   →   villgu-k   'white reindeer'
        white   white-NMLZ\NOM.SG   [2219]

Similarly, the word *suojmek* 'slow person' is derived from the stem *suajbm-* 'slow' (cf. the attributive adjective *suojmas* and the predicative adjective *suajbma* 'slow'):

(13)   suajbm-   →   suojmek   'slow person'
        slow   slow-NMLZ\NOM.SG   [2650]

The word *vidak* 'five-crown coin' is derived from the numeral base *vihta* 'five', while *vidalågåk* 'fifty-crown bank note' is derived from the numeral base *vidalåhkå* 'fifty':

(14)   vihta   →   vida-k   'five-crown coin'
        five   five-NMLZ\NOM.SG   [4051]

(15)   vidalåhkå   →   vidalågå-k   'fifty-crown banknote'
        fifty   fifty-NMLZ\NOM.SG   [4053]

There are still other cases of nouns derived by *-k* which are based on a verb form at the deepest level, but feature subsequent derivational affixes between the root lexeme and the final nominalizing suffix *-k*, so that it is not clear what base lexeme *-k* is directly attached to. For instance, the noun *gaskaldak* 'bite, bit' is ultimately based on the verb *gassket* 'bite', but it is not clear what the derivational affix or affixes expressed by the segments *-alda-* could indicate:

(16)	*gasske-t*	→	*gask-alda-k*	'bite, bit'
	bite-INF		bite-VBLZ?-NMLZ\NOM.SG	[3278]

Finally, several place names are also likely derived using *-k*. For instance, the name *Tjårvek* 'Lake Hornavan'[3] is derived from the nominal base *tjårrve* 'horn, antler':

(17)	*tjårrve*	→	*tjårve-k*	'Lake Hornavan'
	antler\NOM.SG		antler-NMLZ\NOM.SG	[pit110517b2.083]

It is clear that, morphophonologically, the suffix *-k* triggers the weak consonant grade, when applicable. The vowel immediately preceding the suffix *-k* is not consistent; this could be due to various noun class bases, or perhaps there are in fact more than one nominalizing suffixes of the form *-Vk*. These questions as well as other questions concerning the variety of uses of this very flexible and common derivational morpheme must be left for future study.

10.1.3 The action nominalizer suffix *-o*

The nominalizer suffix *-o* (glossed as NMLZ1) can be affixed to a verbal base to form a deverbal noun. In general, the resulting noun refers to the action or the result of the action denoted by the stem, as in (18) through (23).

(18)	*barrga-t*	→	*barrg-o*	'job, work'
	work-INF		work-NMLZ1\NOM.SG	[pit110404]e
(19)	*bivvde-t*	→	*bivvd-o*	'catch (fishing)'
	catch-INF		catch-NMLZ1\NOM.SG	[6574]
(20)	*gähtto-t*	→	*gähtt-o*	'story, report'
	tell-INF		tell-NMLZ1\NOM.SG	[6686]
(21)	*lávvlo-t*	→	*lávvl-o*	'song, hymn'
	sing-INF		sing-NMLZ1\NOM.SG	[pit080825.030]
(22)	*dårro-t*	→	*dårr-o*	'fight, battle'
	fight-INF		fight-NMLZ1\NOM.SG	[pit080701b]e

---

[3] *Tjårvek* is the large lake on which Arjeplog, the main Pite Saami community, is located. Even the Swedish name *Hornavan* seems to refer to antlers or horns (cf. Swedish *horn* 'horn') and could be the result of a loan translation.

10 Derivational morphology

(23) dårrjo-t → dårrj-o 'support'
support-INF support-NMLZ1\NOM.SG [4732]

However, as (24) and (25) indicate, the deverbalized noun does not have to refer exactly to the action or result of the verb, but only to a related concept.

(24) gåjjkå-t → gåjjk-o 'drought; thirst'
dry-INF dry-NMLZ1\NOM.SG [4225]

(25) jáhkke-t → jáhkk-o 'belief'
believe-INF believe-NMLZ1\NOM.SG [0909]

Such nouns are in nominal inflectional class Ic; these examples present the nominal singular forms, and are thus in the strong stage of consonant gradation. As the example in (26) shows, these are full fledged nouns that inflect for case and number and can fill syntactic slots reserved for NPs (here, the object of the transitive verb *adnet* 'have').

(26) jut almatj adna jáhkov
jut almatj adna jáhk-o-v
if person\NOM.SG have\3SG.PRS believe-NMLZ1-ACC.SG
'if one has faith' [sje20130523.158]

10.1.4 The agent nominalizer suffix *-däddje*

The nominalizing suffix *-däddje* (glossed as NMLZ2) creates an agent noun, indicating that the referent of the noun is involved in the activity denoted by the base. Examples are provided in (27) through (31).

(27) vuäjdne-t → vuojna-däddje 'clairvoyant'
see-INF see-NMLZ2\NOM.SG [6532]

(28) åhpå-t → åhpa-däddje 'teacher'
learn-INF learn-NMLZ2\NOM.SG [2243]

(29) málesti-t → máles-däddje 'cook, chef'
cook-INF cook-NMLZ2\NOM.SG [5377]

(30) gieles → gieles-däddje 'liar'
lie\NOM.SG lie-NMLZ2\NOM.SG [4826]

(31) jåhta-t → báhko+jåde-däddje 'chairperson'
drive-INF word+drive-NMLZ2\NOM.SG [0109]

10.1 Nominal derivation

The base is typically a verb, but can be a noun, as in (30). The stem of the derived agent noun is in the weak grade. As illustrated by (28) and (29), the resulting agent noun (with a root *máles* and *åhpa*) may no longer be directly derivable from the comparable verb (there is no verb **málle-t* 'cook-INF', only *málestit*, nor a verb **åhpa-t*, but instead *åhpådit* 'teach-INF').

Note that the noun *báhkojådedäddje* 'chairperson' in (29) is a compound calque based on the Swedish equivalent *ordförande*, which literally means 'word-driver'. It is not clear whether *?jådedäddje* 'driver' exists on its own.

10.1.5 The state nominalizer suffix *-vuohta*

The nominalizing suffix *-vuohta* (glossed as NMLZ3) typically derives nouns from adjectives, as in (32) through (34).

(32) vassjalis → vassjalis-vuohta 'activity'
     active   active-NMLZ3\NOM.SG   [3082]

(33) sádnes → sádnes-vuohta 'truth'
     true   true-NMLZ3\NOM.SG   [1476]

(34) luossis → luossis-vuohta 'melancholy'
     heavy   heavy-NMLZ3\NOM.SG   [2519]

The suffix *-vuohta* can also be applied to a derived adjectival base. In (35), the stem *máhtelis* 'possible' is itself a derived adjectival based on the verb *máhttet* 'can'. The deepest derivational base in the example in (36) is roughly analogous, but one step farther removed from the final derived form: the highest-level base *bargodis* 'unemployed' is an adjectival form of the noun *bargo* 'work', which itself is a deverbal form based on the verb *barrgat* 'work' (cf. example (18) in §10.1.3 above).

(35) máhtelis → máhtelis-vuohta 'possibility'
     possible   possible-NMLZ3\NOM.SG   [6533]

(36) bargodis → bargodis-vuohta 'unemployment'
     unemployed   unemployed-NMLZ3\NOM.SG   [3131]

Much as with (36) above, the base *tjalmedis* 'blind' in (37) is itself based on the noun *tjalbme* 'eye' derived by the suffix *-dis* indicating a lack of the base referent. Thus, *tjalmedisvuohta* could be literally translated as 'eye-less-ness'.

10 Derivational morphology

(37) tjalmedis → tjalmedis-vuohta 'blindness'
blind blind-NMLZ3\NOM.SG [6201]

However, as (38) indicates, the base from which -vuohta derives a new noun can also be a noun.

(38) mánná → mánná-vuohta 'childhood'
child\NOM.SG child-NMLZ3\NOM.SG [3221]

10.2 Verbal derivation

Verbal derivation in Pite Saami is a particularly complex area, and the interested reader is first and foremost referred to Israel Ruong's PhD thesis *Lappische Verbalableitung dargestellt auf Grundlage des Pitelappischen*[4] (Ruong 1943). This work presents a comprehensive typology of non-derived verbs and verbal derivation suffixes in Pite Saami. It includes an extensive semantic sub-classification of the derivational suffixes into the varied and overlapping meanings each one can have. The forty suffixes Ruong presents, and the myriad functions he assigns them to, further attest to the complicated nature of verbal derivation in Pite Saami.

The present discussion cannot hope to improve on Ruong's work, and instead attempts to use the Pite Saami Documentation Project corpus to achieve the following:

- Using the diminutive verbalizer -tj as a starting point, illustrate the complexity of verbal derivation in Pite Saami due to the persistent irregularities between forms and functions (§10.2.1);

- Present a sample of verbal derivations (§10.2.2 through §10.2.4);

- Provide a basic description of the important valency-decreasing verbal derivation creating passive verb forms (§10.2.5).

10.2.1 The diminutive verbalizer suffix -tj and the complexities of Pite Saami derivational verb morphology

The diminutive verbalizing suffix -tj (glossed as DIM) expresses doing the activity referred to by the verbal base a little bit or to a limited extent, as in (39) through (41).[5]

---

[4] 'Saami verbal derivation as illustrated by the Pite Saami language' (my translation).
[5] Note the similarity in form and semantics to the diminutive nominalizing suffix -tj discussed in §10.1.1.

10.2 Verbal derivation

(39) *barrga-t* → *barga-tji-t* 'work a little bit'
work-INF work-DIM-INF [pit110404]e

(40) *vádtse-t* → *vádtsa-tji-t* 'walk slowly'
walk-INF walk-DIM-INF [2047]

(41) *bällke-t* → *bielka-tji-t* 'have a small quarrel'
quarrel-INF quarrel-DIM-INF [4698]

The weak form of the base verb is selected by *-tj*, and the final vowel in the base becomes *a*. The *i* following the *-tj* suffix is the verb class marker for the resulting Class V verb.

Note, however, that other derivational suffixes can produce diminutive meanings as well, as illustrated by the examples in (42) through (44).

(42) *gähtja-t* → *gietja-sti-t* 'glance'
see-INF see-VBLZ1-INF [2530]

(43) *gåsså-t* → *gåsså-di-t* 'cough a little bit'
cough-INF cough-VBLZ2-INF [4898]

(44) *rassjo-t* → *rässjo-dalla-t* 'rain lightly'
rain-INF rain-VBLZ3-INF [5073]

In these three examples, the derivational suffixes *-st*, *-d* and *-dall*, respectively,[6] also derive deverbal verbs which add similar diminutive meanings to the base.

If these suffixes were restricted to a diminutive meaning, then this would simply be a case of many forms corresponding to a single function. However, these suffixes, which are all quite common, only occasionally carry a diminutive meaning. In other instances, they impart a variety of different meanings to the base form. This is illustrated by just a few examples below, and is even more obvious throughout Ruong (1943). Despite the variety of and inconsistencies in the meanings that verbal derivational suffixes express, their limited number relative to the number of functions they fulfill is reason enough to describe each of these suffixes as a single derivational affix with multiple functions, rather than multiple, homonymous affixes, each aligned to a separate function.

---

[6] The vowel following each of these verbalizers is a class marker.

10.2.2 The verbal derivational suffix -st

In addition to the diminutive meaning in (42) above, the derivational suffix -st (glossed as VBLZ1) is applied to a postposition in (45), and functions as a verbalizer. In (46), the nominal base is not only verbalized, but has a causative or perhaps an inchoative meaning. The derived verb in (47) is a figurative extension of the verbal base's meaning. Furthermore, -st can indicate that an action is carried out briefly or for a short period of time, as in (48).

(45) *birra* → *bira-sti-t* 'cruise around'
 around around-VBLZ1-INF [0185]

(46) *dållå* → *dålå-sti-t* 'start a fire'
 fire\NOM.SG fire-VBLZ1-INF [0422]

(47) *båhtje-t* → *båtje-sti-t* 'wring out'
 milk-INF milk-VBLZ1-INF [0262]

(48) *basse-t* → *base-sti-t* 'fry quickly'
 fry-INF fry-VBLZ1-INF [5501]

Note that the *i* following the -st suffix is the verb class marker for the resulting Class V verb.

10.2.3 The verbal derivational suffix -d

In addition to the diminutive meaning in (43) above, each of the two examples of the verbalizer -d (glossed as VBLZ2) in (49) and (50) has a reflexive meaning; note that the base in (50) is a noun, not a verb. The example in (51) has a transitivizing effect on the verbal base, while there is no clear difference in meaning between the base and the resulting derived form in (52) and (53). The last example, *sykel*[7] 'bicycle' in (54), illustrates that this suffix is quite productive, as it is used as a verbalizer for a loanword serving as a nominal base. Note that the *i* following the -d suffix is the verb class marker for the resulting Class V verb.

(49) *bassa-t* → *basá-di-t* 'wash oneself'
 wash-INF wash-VBLZ2-INF [pit090910]*e*

(50) *gárrvo* → *gärvo-di-t* 'dress oneself'
 clothing\NOM.SG clothing-VBLZ2-INF [0793]

---

[7] < Swedish *cykel* 'bicycle'.

10.2 Verbal derivation

(51) busso-t → buso-di-t 'blow out'
 blow-INF blow-VBLZ2-INF [4704]

(52) bulle-t → bulle-di-t 'ignite'
 ignite-INF ignite-VBLZ2-INF [2664]

(53) tjájbma-t → tjájma-di-t 'laugh, smile'
 laugh-INF laugh-VBLZ2-INF [1865]

(54) sykel → sykel-di-t 'ride a bicycle'
 bicycle\NOM.SG bicycle-VBLZ2-INF [1810]

10.2.4 The verbal derivational suffix -*dall*

In addition to the diminutive meaning in (44) above, the first two examples (55–56) of the verbalizer -*dall* (glossed as VBLZ3) show deadjectival verbs which express being characterized by the base adjective. The adjectival base is even semantically restricted in the derived form in example (56). Similarly, the denominal verb in (57) is based on the 3SG.NOM reflexive pronoun *etjas* 'oneself', and expresses a more forceful state of being the meaning of the base noun. The final two examples also restrict the semantic scope of the verbal base. The *a* following the -*dall* suffix is the verb class marker for the resulting Class IIa verb.

(55) lajjkes → lajkas-dalla-t 'be lazy'
 lazy lazy-VBLZ3-INF [2959]

(56) bahás → bahás-dalla-t 'be against something'
 evil evil-VBLZ3-INF [4705]

(57) etjas → etjas-dalla-t 'be stubborn'
 oneself\NOM.SG oneself-VBLZ3-INF [0460]

(58) gähtja-t → giehtja-dalla-t 'check out, look into'
 see-INF see-VBLZ3-INF [3875]

(59) tjehka-t → tjehka-dalla-t 'play hide and seek'
 hide-INF hide-VBLZ3-INF [1889]

10.2.5 Passivization with the derivational suffix -*duvv*

Transitive verbs can be passivized using the suffix -*duvv* (glossed as PASS). The resulting derived verb belongs to the inflectional verb Class IV, and thus features

10 Derivational morphology

the class marker -*a* following the passivizing suffix in the infinitive form, and -*u* in the perfect form. For instance, compare the verb in (60) (in the active voice) with the equivalent passivized verb in (61), including the oblique agent (in ELATIVE case).

(60) *máná lä tsiggim gådev*
máná lä tsiggi-m gåde-v
child\NOM.PL be\3PL.PRS build-PRF hut-ACC.SG
'Children have built the hut.' [pit110518a.28m14s]*e*

(61) *gåhte lä tsiggijduvvum mánájst*
gåhte lä tsiggij-duvvu-m máná-jst
hut\NOM.SG be\3SG.PRS build-PASS-PRF child-ELAT.PL
'The hut has been built by children.' [pit110518a.28m41s]*e*

Passivization is a valency-decreasing device because the resulting verb is intransitive, as it only features the patient-like argument as its sole core argument in nominative case. Note that Svonni (2009: 92) claims, for North Saami, that "one cannot indicate the agent in any way" (my translation) in passive clauses using the cognate North Saami passivizing suffix. Pite Saami differs significantly from North Saami in this respect, as Ruong – himself a native speaker of Pite Saami – verifies (cf. Ruong 1943: 41). It is very possible that the Pite Saami strategy of placing the agent in an oblique case could be due to extensive language contact with Swedish, a language which clearly allows the agent in a passivized clause to be expressed obliquely using a prepositional phrase headed by the preposition *av* 'of, from'. Indeed, Swedish PPs headed by *av* in other contexts are best translated into Pite Saami as an NP in elative case, the same oblique case in which the agent NP in a passive Pite Saami sentence is found.

Some other examples of transitive verbs and their passivized equivalents using -*duvv* are shown in (62) through (64).

(62) *tjåvvde-t* → *tjåvde-duvva-t* 'be liberated'
untie-INF untie-PASS-INF [3233]

(63) *dahka-t* → *daga-duvva-t* 'be made'
make-INF make-PASS-INF [pit110331b]*e*

(64) *adne-t* → *ane-duvva-t* 'be used'
utilize-INF utilize-PASS-INF [2682]

There are not sufficient data in the corpus to state any more about passive derivation, particularly concerning morphophonological effects of passivization

10.3 Adjectival derivation

on verb stems, and this and other related topics must be left for future study. The reader is referred to Ruong (1943) for a more thorough morphological and semantic account of Pite Saami passives. Inflectional aspects of passivized verbs are treated in §8.3, while syntactic aspects of clauses with passive verbs are presented briefly in §13.1.1.1.

Note that the derivational suffix -*duvv* can have meanings other than passive when attached to a nominal or adjectival base. Typically it then expresses a change of state that is related to the referent of the root involved. A few examples are provided in (65) through (68).

(65) *vuoras* → *vuoras-duvva-t* 'age (verb)'
    old   old-PASS-INF   [2188]

(66) *bevas* → *bevas-duvva-t* 'become sweaty'
    sweat\NOM.SG   sweat-PASS-INF   [6084]

(67) *giella* → *giela-duvva-t* 'become hoarse'
    language\NOM.SG   language-PASS-INF   [3876]

(68) *tjálbme* → *tjálme-duvva-t* 'become blind'
    eye\NOM.SG   eye-PASS-INF   [1876]

10.3 Adjectival derivation

Only two derivational processes exist for adjectivals: the non-productive derivation of adjectives by -*s*, and the productive derivation of ordinal numerals from cardinal ones. These are described below.

10.3.1 Adjective derivation

It seems conceivable that adjectives can be derived by the suffix -*s* (glossed as ADJZ). For instance, *bahá* is a nominal meaning 'evil', as in (69), and *bahás* is the equivalent attributive adjective form, as in (70).

(69) *dat   almatj   lä   bahá*
    d-a-t   almatj   lä   bahá
    DEM-DIST-NOM.SG person\NOM.SG be\3SG.PRS evil\NOM.SG
    'That person is evil.'   [pit090926.13m36s]*e*

10 Derivational morphology

(70) bahás almatj
bahá-s almatj
evil-ADJZ person\NOM.SG
'evil person' [pit090926.13m40s]e

In addition, the nominalized form *bahá-k* 'evil' can be further derived into an adjective *bahágis* 'painful' as in (71).

(71) bahá-k → bahá-gi-s 'painful'
evil-NMLZ evil-NMLZ-ADJZ [0102]

However, as pointed out in detail in §7.1 through §7.3, not all adjectives follow this pattern. In fact, based on the current data, the *-s* suffix marks attributive adjectives (as in (70)) and as well as predicative adjectives, and, synchronically, it is not considered to be productive for either attributive or predicative forms at all.

10.3.2 Ordinal numeral derivation with *-át*

Numerals, a sub-category of adjectivals (cf. §7.9), are subject to derivation. The basic ordinal numerals can be derived by applying the derivational suffix *-át* (or its allomorph *-et*) to the respective cardinal numeral, although the forms *vuostas* 'first' and *mubbe* 'second' are suppletive. Ordinal derivation is discussed in §7.9.1.1 in more detail, including a comparison of cardinal and ordinal numbers in Table 7.7 on page 144.

10.4 Adverbial derivation

Adverbs are not common in the corpus (as opposed to other word classes and phrase types with adverbial functions), but do appear to be derivable from an adjective base using the suffix *-git*. This is dealt with in more detail in §9.1.1.

10.5 Summary of derivational morphology

Table 10.2 on the facing page provides an overview of the derivational morphology discussed in this chapter.

10.5 Summary of derivational morphology

Table 10.2: Summary of derivational morphology discussed in this chapter

type	suffix	base	result	section
nominal	-tj	noun	diminutive	§10.1.1
	-k	noun	characterized by base referent	§10.1.2
		adjective		
		verb		
	-o	verb	the action itself	§10.1.3
	-däddje	verb	person involved in state of affairs	§10.1.4
		noun		
	-vuohta	adjective	characterized by base referent	§10.1.5
		noun		
verbal	-tj	verb	diminutive	§10.2.1
	-st	verb	causative; inchoative	§10.2.2
		noun		
	-d	verb	reflexive; other	§10.2.3
		noun		
	-dall	verb	diminutive; characterized by base referent; etc.	§10.2.4
		noun		
	-duvv	verb	passive	§10.2.5
		adjective	change of state	
		noun		
adj.	-s	noun	attributive adjective	§10.3
	-át	cardinal num.	ordinal num.	§10.3.2
adv.	-git	adjective	adverb	§10.4

11 Phrase types

There are five types of phrases in Pite Saami which form syntactic constituents of other phrases or of clauses:

- verb complex (VC)
- nominal phrase (NP)
- adjectival phrase (AP)
- adverbial phrase (AdvP)
- postpositional phrase (PP)

Table 11.1 summarizes the main syntactic functions of the various phrase types, and the sections of this chapter that deal with them.

Table 11.1: Phrase types and their syntactic functions

	predicate	argument/adjunct/ complement	modifier in NP	modifier in AP
VC	✓			
NP	✓	✓	✓	
AP		✓	✓	
AdvP		✓		✓
PP		✓		

11.1 Verb complex

The Pite Saami verb complex (abbreviated 'VC') consists minimally of a finite verb, and maximally of a finite verb and one or two non-finite verb forms. With the exception of the imperative, the finite verb inflects for tense or mood, number and person, and agrees with the subject. The imperative only inflects for number.

11 Phrase types

In combination with non-finite verb forms, the verbal categories negation, mood, and aspect can also be expressed.

To better describe the distribution of finite and non-finite verbs forms in VCs, verbs are divided into two groupings:

- lexical verbs and the copular verb *årrot* 'be'

- grammatical verbs (the negation verb, the aspectual auxiliary verb *årrot* 'be', and the modal verbs; cf. §13.1.5).

In VCs featuring only one verb form, the finite verb is a lexical verb or the copular verb. In VCs with two or three verb forms, the finite verb is a grammatical verb, while the selection of each non-finite form is determined by the type of verb governing it: the verb of negation triggers the connegative form, the aspectual auxiliary verb triggers either the perfect or the progressive form, and the modal verbs trigger the infinitive form. This is summarized in Table 11.2.

Table 11.2: Verb complex patterns with one, two and three verbs

qty.	verb form or forms				
1	finite verb (lexical/copula)				
2	finite verb (grammatical)	+	non-finite form (lexical/copula)		
	modal verb	+	INF		
	aspectual auxiliary	+	PRF or PROG		
	negation verb	+	CONNEG		
3	finite verb (grammatical)	+	non-finite form (grammatical)	+	non-finite form (lexical/copula)
	aspectual auxiliary	+	modal\PRF or PROG	+	INF
	negation verb	+	modal\CONNEG	+	INF
		+	asp. auxiliary\CONNEG	+	PRF or PROG

The constituent order of the individual verbal components is not strictly set, although the ordering indicated in Table 11.2 is most common. Furthermore, other clause-level components may occur between these verb forms (cf. §12.2 and §13.1.5).

For instance, the examples in (1) and (2) each feature a VC consisting solely of a finite verb. In (1) it is the singular imperative form of the lexical verb *vädtjat* 'fetch', while in (2) it is the encliticized 3SG.PRS form of the copular verb.

11.1 Verb complex

(1)   *vietja   pahparav!*
      [vietja]$_{VC}$ pahpara-v
      fetch\SG.IMP paper-ACC.SG
      'Get some paper!'   [pit090519.316]

(2)   *dun   váre   namma'l*
      d-u-n   váre   namma=[l]$_{VC}$
      DEM-RMT-GEN.SG mountain\GEN.SG name\NOM.SG=be\3SG.PRS
      Sállvo
      Sállvo
      Sállvo\NOM.SG
      'The name of that mountain is Sállvo.'   [pit100404.005]

In (3), there are two VCs. The first VC is *ij…dága*[1] and consists of the finite negation verb and the lexical verb *dáhkat* 'make, do' in its connegative form, but is split by the particle *dä* and the NP argument *aktagav*. The second VC is the verb *váhtjat* 'fetch', here in its 1SG.PRS finite form.

(3)   *ij   dä   aktagav   dága,   mån   viehtjav*
      [i-j]$_{VC1}$ dä   aktaga-v   [dága]$_{VC1}$ mån   [viehtja-v]$_{VC2}$
      NEG-3SG.PRS then nothing-ACC.SG make\CONNEG 1SG.NOM fetch-1SG.PRS
      dav   maŋŋel
      d-a-v   maŋŋel
      DEM-DIST-ACC.SG after
      'It doesn't matter, I'll get that later.'   [pit100404.157]

The example in (4) consists of three VCs. The first, *lin båhtam* 'had come', is headed by the 3PL.PST form of the auxiliary verb *årrot* 'be' and combines with the perfect form of the main lexical verb *båhtet* 'come'. The second and third VCs are both simple VCs consisting only of a finite verb form.

(4)   *jus stalpe   lin   båhtam   elo   sissa, dä*
      jus stalpe   [li-n   båhta-m]$_{VC1}$ elo   sissa dä
      if   wolf\NOM.PL be-3PL.PST come-PRF   reindeer.herd\GEN.SG into   then
      vuolgin   ja   vitjin   davva
      [vuolgi-n]$_{VC2}$ ja   [vitji-n]$_{VC3}$ d-a-vva
      drive-3PL.PST and fetch-3PL.PST DEM-DIST-ACC.SG
      'If wolves had entered the reindeer herd, they went and got him.'
                                                              [pit0906_Ahkajavvre_a.091]

---

[1] The complete phrase *ij aktagav dága* is likely a calque of the Swedish phrase *det gör ingenting* 'that doesn't matter' (lit.: 'that does nothing').

11 Phrase types

A modal verb and a non-finite verb form are illustrated by the VC *máhtta... båhtet* 'can come' in (5). Here, the modal *máhtta* 'can' is the finite verb, and *båhtet* 'come' is in the infinitive form.

(5) båtsoj   máhtta   duv   nala   båhtet
    båtsoj   [máhtta]_{VC} duv   nala   [båhte-t]_{VC}
    reindeer\NOM.SG can\3SG.PRS 2SG.GEN upon come-INF
    'The reindeer can attack you.' (lit: 'come upon you')   [pit080909.048]

Similarly, in (6), the VC *virrten märrket* 'have to mark' contains the finite verb *virrten* 'must' and the infinitive verb form *märrket* 'mark'.

(6) dä   virrten   märrket   dajt   miesijd   dåle
    dä   [virrte-n   märrke-t]_{VC} d-a-jt   miesi-jd   dåle
    then must-1DU.PRS mark-INF   DEM-DIST-ACC.PL calf-ACC.PL now
    tjaktjan
    tjaktja-n
    autumn-INESS.SG
    'Then we have to mark those calves now in the autumn.'   [pit080909.008]

Note that, formally, clauses featuring a modal verb are identical to complement clauses featuring an infinitival predicate; cf. §14.2.1.2.

Finally, the clauses in (7) through (9) provide examples of VCs with three verb forms. In (7), the VC consists of the finite negation verb in 1SG.PRS (*iv*), the aspectual auxiliary *årrot* in connegative form (*lä*), and the lexical verb *gullat* 'hear' in its perfect form (*gullam*). The VC in example (8) contains the finite negation verb 3SG.PRS (*ij*), the modal verb *máhttet* in connegative form (*máhte*), and the lexical verb *adnet* 'have', in its infinitive form. Finally, in (9), the finite aspectual auxiliary *lev* combined with the perfect form of the modal verb *máhttet* 'can' and the infinite complement *ságastit* 'speak' constitute the VC.

(7) dä   iv   lä   åbå   gullam   dav
    dä   [i-v   lä]_{VC} åbå   [gulla-m]_{VC} d-a-v
    then NEG-1SG.PRS be\CONNEG at.all hear-PRF DEM-DIST-ACC.SG
    'I haven't heard that at all.'   [pit090702.203]

(8) ij   vanj   dä   máhte   ilá   stuor dålåv   adnet
    [i-j]_{VC}   vanj   dä   [máhte]_{VC}   ilá   stuor dålå-v   [adne-t]_{VC}
    NEG-3SG.PRS really then can\CONNEG too big fire-ACC.SG have-INF
    'One cannot really have too big of a fire.'   [pit090702.176]

(9) mån   lev   máhttam   sámev   ságastit
    mån   [le-v   máhtta-m]$_{VC}$ sáme-v   [ságasti-t]$_{VC}$
    1SG.NOM be-1SG.PRS can-PRF   Saami-ACC.SG speak-INF
    'I have been able to speak Saami.'   [sje20121009.46m27s]*e*

The corpus does not provide any evidence for three-verb VCs with a modal verb as the finite verb, so whether this logically possible structures is acceptable must be left to future research. However, it is clear that the negation verb is only attested as a finite verb, and can never occur as the second or third verb in a multi-verb VC.

11.2 Nominal phrases

Nominal phrases (abbreviated 'NP') in Pite Saami are divided into two groups:

- full NPs

- pronouns

NPs can function as arguments, adjuncts, predicates, adverbials, dependents of postpositions and possessors or modifiers of other NPs. They consist of at least one nominal component that inflects for case and number. Note that NPs can also be modified by postpositional phrases and non-finite verb forms, but due to a lack of sufficient data, a description of these NP modifiers must be left for future study. Finally, relative clauses also modify an NP; these are covered in §14.2.4.

NPs have the structure illustrated in (10), with optional components in parentheses.

(10)   [(demonstrative) + (other modifier(s)) + nominal + (refl-intensifier) + (rel-clause)]$_{NP}$

Either a noun or a pronoun forms the head of an NP. The demonstrative, the nominal and any attributive reflexive pronoun always inflect for case and number, while generally the other modifiers do not. Other modifiers may be an adjectival phrase, a numeral or an NP in genitive case. An intensifier in the form of a reflexive pronoun (cf. §6.3) can modify a noun phrase as well, and occurs after the head. Finally, the head can be modified by a relative clause, which also occurs after the head. Some examples for possible NP structures are found below.

The only NP in (11) consists solely of the noun *Tjeggelvasav* 'Lake Tjeggelvas'.

(11)   ja dä   vuojnav   Tjeggelvasav
       ja dä   vuojna-v [Tjeggelvasa-v]$_{NP}$
       and then see-1SG.PRS Lake.Tjeggelvas-ACC.SG
       'And then I see Lake Tjeggelvas.'   [pit100404.013]

11 Phrase types

In the example in (12), the NP *dat ello* 'that reindeer herd' consists of a demonstrative and the head noun, and is the subject of the clause. In (13), the subject NP consists of the head noun *ello* 'reindeer herd' and the genitive NP *dáj Skailej* 'of these Skailes'[2] which modifies the head noun.

(12) ja dä såkoj dat ello
 ja dä såko-j [d-a-t ello]$_{NP}$
 and then drown-3SG.PST DEM-DIST-NOM.SG reindeer.herd\NOM.SG
 'And then that reindeer herd drowned.' [pit0906_Ahkajavvre_b.010]

(13) dáj Skailej ello såkoj
 [[d-á-j Skaile-j]$_{NP1}$ ello]$_{NP2}$ såko-j
 DEM-PROX-GEN.PL Skaile-GEN.PL reindeer.herd\NOM.SG drown-3SG.PST
 'These Skailes' reindeer herd drowned.' [pit0906_Ahkajavvre_b.002]

An NP marked for genitive case can also function as a modifier that narrows the reference of the head noun by signifying some characteristic of the head noun's referent, as in (13) above. Similarly, in (14) the genitive NP *mále* 'blood' modifies the head noun *gamsajd* 'dumplings'.

(14) ja dágaj mále gamsajd
 ja dága-j [[mále]$_{NP1}$ gamsa-jd]$_{NP2}$
 and make-3SG.PST blood\GEN.SG dumpling-ACC.PL
 'And one made blood dumplings.' [pit080924.253]

In the example in (15), the NP *nåv edna båtsoj* 'so many reindeer'[3] consists of the AP *nåv edna* 'so many' and the head noun *båtsoj* 'reindeer'.

(15) dä lij nåv edna båtsoj
 dä li-j [nåv edna båtsoj]$_{NP}$
 then be-3SG.PST so much reindeer\NOM.SG
 'There were so many reindeer.' (lit.: 'so much reindeer')
 [pit0906_Ahkajavvre_b.013]

As the example in (16) illustrates, it is possible for more than one modifier to be included in an NP. Here, both APs *guäkte* 'two' and *stuor* 'big' modify the noun head, which is the derived compound *guhkajuolgagijd* 'long-leggers' (referring to moose).

---

[2] *Skaile* is a family name.

[3] Note that the word *båtsoj* 'reindeer' is often marked for singular, even when referring to more than one reindeer.

(16) dä inijmä guäkte stuora guhkajuolgagijd
dä ini-jmä [guäkte stuora guhka-juolga-gi-jd]$_{NP}$
then have-1PL.PST two big long-leg-NMLZ-ACC.PL
'Then we had two big moose.' (lit.: 'long-leggers') [pit090702.331]

If the context is sufficiently clear, it is possible that the head noun is not realized when a demonstrative and/or modifier is present; such cases are referred to as elliptical constructions. Numerals, for instance, can be in elliptical constructions, as in (17), in which the noun referring to 'nets' is not realized, so *gålmát* 'third' composes the entire NP.

(17) ja gålmát sjadda dä Stutjaj
ja [gålm-át]$_{NP1}$ sjadda dä [Stutja-j]$_{NP2}$
and three-ORD become\3SG.PRS then Stutja-ILL.SG
'And the third one is then placed at Stutja.' (referring to 'fishing net')
[pit090702.026-027]

With the exception of the ACC.SG form of *akta* 'one', numerals do not inflect for case and number (cf. §7.9).

Less commonly, an adjectival phrase can be in an elliptical construction, either with or without a demonstrative (cf. §7.1.1). In the absence of a head noun, the adjective in the AP is the host for case and number, and is morphologically a nominal. In the example in (18) includes a demonstrative; here, the head noun referring to a girl is not overt, and the NP only contains the demonstrative *dat* 'that' and the adjective *tjábba* 'beautiful'. The sentence in (19) illustrates a similar structure, but without a demonstrative. In this case, the head noun referring to a piece of candy is not realized, and the NP consists only of the adjective *rupsisav* 'red', which inflects for case and number.[4]

(18) dat tjábba máhtta sáme
[d-a-t tjábba]$_{NP1}$ máhtta [sáme
DEM-DIST-NOM.SG beautiful\NOM.SG can\3SG.PRS Saami\GEN.SG
gielav
giela-v]$_{NP2}$
language-ACC.SG
'That beautiful one can speak the Saami language.' [pit090930a.148]*e*

---

[4] Cf. §7.1.1 for more details about adjectives in elliptical structures.

(19) bårov   rupsisav
    båro-v   [rupsisa-v]$_{NP}$
    eat-1SG.PRS red-ACC.SG
    'I eat the red one.'   [pit090930a.119]e

There are many examples in the corpus of NPs consisting of a pronoun, such as the demonstrative pronoun *dajd* in (20), or the personal pronoun *mån* in (21).

(20) bisij   dajd   såbe   nanne
    bisi-j   [d-a-jd]$_{NP1}$ [såbe]$_{NP2}$ nanne
    fry-3SG.PST DEM-DIST-ACC.PL stick\GEN.SG on
    'He fried those on a stick.'   [pit100404.125]

(21) mån   mähttiv   råhpat   uksav
    [mån]$_{NP1}$ mähtti-v   råhpa-t   [uksa-v]$_{NP2}$
    1SG.NOM   can-1SG.PST   open-INF   door-ACC.SG
    'I could open the door.'   [pit100404.347]

The second NP in (20), *såbe* 'stick', also illustrates a genitive NP functioning as the complement of a PP.

When the head of an NP is a personal pronoun, it is also possible to modify it. For instance, in (22), the 1SG.NOM reflexive pronoun *etj* modifies the 1SG.NOM personal pronoun *mån* as an intensifier. Note that this ordering (modifier following the head) deviates from the general pattern, in which the modifier occurs before the head of the NP.

(22) mån   etj   hålåv   dále navte
    [mån   etj]$_{NP}$ hålå-v   dále navte
    1SG.NOM   REFL\1SG.NOM say-1SG.PRS   now like.that
    'I myself say it like that.'   [pit090910.29m05s]e

Finally, a relative clause can also occur after the head as part of the NP. An example is provided in (23); see §14.2.4 for more on relative clauses.

(23) dá   lä   jisse   gistá   mejd
    d-á   lä   jisse   [gistá   me-jd
    DEM\PROX-NOM.PL be\3PL.PRS precisely glove\NOM.PL REL-ACC.PL
    dålven   gallga   adnet
    dálve-n   gallga   adne-t]$_{NP}$
    winter-INESS.SG shall\3SG.PRS have-INF
    'These are gloves which one has in winter.'   [pit080708_Session08.006]

11.2.1 NPs in adverbial function

Nominal phrases, particularly when referring to time or place, and thus inflected for one of the locative cases (illative, inessive or elative), are often used as temporal or locational adverbials, as in *giesen* 'in summer' in (24), and in *hiejman* 'at home' in (25), respectively. Furthermore, the word *vahkov* 'week' in (25) shows that an accusative NP can function as a temporal adverbial indicating a period of time.

(24) men jáhkav   minniv   giesen
     men jáhka-v   minni-v   [giese-n]$_{NP}$
     but believe-1SG.PRS go-1SG.PST summer-INESS.SG
     'I believe I went in the summer.'   [pit100404.163]

(25) ja Henning   lij   jou hiejman   urrum
     ja [Henning]$_{NP1}$ li-j   jou [hiejma-n]$_{NP2}$ urru-m
     and Henning\NOM.SG   be-3SG.PST well home-INESS.SG   be-PRF
     vahkov
     [vahko-v]$_{NP3}$
     week-ACC.SG
     'And Henning had been home for a week.'   [pit090702.285]

Finally, the deverbal noun *diedon* literally translates as 'in knowledge', and can be used as a modal adverbial meaning 'of course', as in (26).

(26) etja   diedon   ednen   mielkev   ja
     [etj-a]$_{NP1}$ [died-o-n]$_{NP2}$ edne-n   [mielke-v]$_{NP3}$ ja
     self-NOM.PL   know-NMLZ1-INESS.SG have-3PL.PST milk-ACC.SG   and
     vuostav
     [vuosta-v]$_{NP4}$
     cheese-ACC.SG
     'They themselves of course had milk and cheese.'
                                                  [pit080708_Session02.034]

11.3 Adjectival phrases

Adjectival phrases (abbreviated 'AP') in Pite Saami are divided into three groups based on the type of adjective required as head:

- attributive APs (headed by attributive adjectives)

11 Phrase types

- predicate APs (headed by predicative adjectives)
- numeral APs (headed by numerals)

In the first case, the attributive AP is syntactically embedded in an NP whose head noun it modifies. In the second case, the predicative AP ascribes the property it concerns to the entire NP which is the subject of the copular clause which the AP is embedded in. Numeral APs can occur both attributively and predicatively.

The three possible constituent structures of APs are presented in (27).

(27)   attributive AP: [(AdvP) + attributive adjective]$_{AP}$
        predicative AP: [(AdvP) + predicative adjective]$_{AP}$
        numeral AP: [(AdvP) + numeral]$_{AP}$

The only difference in internal structure between the two adjective APs is the choice of adjective: attributive vs. predicative. Numeral APs normally consist only of a numeral, but can be further modified by an adverbial.

Adverbial phrases are not common in APs. The data are quite limited concerning which type of AdvPs are acceptable, and future study is needed in this respect. Examples from the corpus include *ilá* 'too', *nåv* 'so', *huj* 'really', *åbbå* 'completely' and *gajk* 'all'.

Several examples of APs are provided here. In (28), the AP consists only of the attributive adjective *njalga* 'tasty' and modifies *biebmov* 'food', the head of the NP.

(28)   ja   danna lip   bårråm njalga   biebmov
        ja   danna li-p   bårrå-m [njalga]$_{AP}$ biebmo-v
        and   there be-1PL.PRS eat-PRF tasty   food-ACC.SG
        'And we ate tasty food there.'   [pit110517b2.005]

The example in (29) illustrates an attributive adjective modified by an AdvP.

(29)   ja   dat   lä   urrum huj   buorak
        ja   d-a-t   lä   urru-m [huj buorak]$_{AP}$
        and   DEM-DIST-NOM.SG   be\3SG.PRS   be-PRF really good
        giesse
        giesse
        summer\NOM.SG
        'And it has been a really good summer.'   [pit080909.009]

In (30), the predicative adjective *nuorra* 'young' agrees with the subject NP *mánná* 'child' in number.

(30) mánná   lä   nuorra
     mánná   lä   [nuorra]_AP
     child\NOM.SG be\3SG.PRS young\SG
     'The child is young.'   [pit090930a.310]e

As the example in (31) shows, predicative adjectives are syntactically adjectives, as the predicate adjective *buojde* 'fat' is the head of an AP modified by an AdvP (*nåv* 'so').

(31) dä lä   vuosjkuna   nåv buojde
     dä lä   vuosjkun-a   [nåv buojde]_AP
     then be\3PL.PRS perch-NOM.PL so   fat\PL
     'Then the perch are so fat.'   [pit090702.080]

Finally, examples of numeral APs are provided in (32) through (34). In the example in (32), *guäkte* 'two' modifies the NP *dåpe* 'houses'.

(32) dä guäkte   dåpe   lä   danne
     dä [guäkte]_AP dåpe   lä   danne
     then two   house\NOM.PL be\3PL.PRS there
     'Then two houses are there.'   [pit080924.385]

The example in (33) is noteworthy because it shows that the modifying numeral can be inflected as a superlative; here the ordinal numeral *vuostas* is in the superlative form *vuostamos* meaning 'very first', and modifies the NP *guhkajuolgak* 'moose'.

(33) dieda,   mån   vuotjev   vuostamos
     dieda   mån   vuotje-v   [vuosta-mos]_AP
     know\2SG.PRS 1SG.NOM shoot-1SG.PST first-SUPERL
     guhkajuolgagav
     guhka-juolga-ga-v
     long-leg-NMLZ-ACC.SG
     'You know, I shot my very first long-legger.'   [pit080924.079]

Numeral APs can include an adverbial modifier. The adverb *ber* 'only' modifies the numeral *akkta* 'one' in (34).

(34) vuostak lij   ber akkta   rommå
     vuostak li-j   [ber akkta]_AP   råmmå
     first   be-3SG.PST only one   room\NOM.SG
     'Initially there was only one room.'   [pit100310b.051]

11.3.1 APs in adverbial function

While the data in the corpus are quite limited, it appears that APs headed by an attributive adjective can be used adverbially. This is illustrated by *njuallga* 'correct' in (35).

(35) jus galga njuallga dajd njuovvat dä
jus galga [njuallga]_{AP} d-a-jd njuovva-t dä
if will\3SG.PRS correct DEM-DIST-ACC.PL slaughter-INF then
galga dajd valldet ulgus åvdål gádtsastij
galga d-a-jd vallde-t ulgus åvdål gádtsasti-j
will\3SG.PRS DEM-DIST-ACC.PL take-INF out before hang.up-3SG.PST
'If one slaughtered them correctly, then one would take them out before one hung them up.' [pit080909.105]

11.4 Adverbial phrases

An adverbial phrase (abbreviated 'AdvP') has an adverb as its head, and can potentially be modified by a further AdvP, as illustrated in (36)

(36) [(AdvP) + adverb]_{AdvP}

The AdvP in example (37) consists only of the adverb *buoragit* 'well'.

(37) dalloj dä lij, manaj buoragit
dalloj dä li-j mana-j [buoragi-t]_{AdvP}
at.that.time then be-3SG.PST go-3SG.PST good-ADVZ
'At that time it was, it went well.' [pit0906_Ahkajavvre_a.023]

The sentence in (38) shows that an adverb can be further modified by another, preceding adverb. Here, the AP head *buoragit* 'well' is further modified by the adverb *ganska* 'quite'.[5]

(38) viesojmä vanj ganska buoragit dajna
vieso-jmä vanj [[ganska]_{AdvP1} buoragi-t]_{AdvP2} d-a-jna
live-1PL.PST definitely quite good-ADVZ DEM-DIST-COM.SG
guollemijn aj
guollemi-jn aj
fishing-COM.SG also
'We definitely lived quite well with the fishing, too.'
[pit0906_Ahkajavvre_a.164]

---

[5] The adverb *ganska* is a nonce borrowing from Swedish (cf. Swedish *ganska* 'quite').

The example in (39) illustrates a AdvP (*åbbå* 'quite') which modifies the head of an AP (*vuoras* 'old').

(39) men åbbå vuoras lä del dát
men [åbbå]_{AdvP} vuoras lä del d-á-t
but quite old\SG be\3SG.PRS obviously DEM-PROX-NOM.SG
'But this one is obviously quite old.' [pit080708_Session07.006]

Other forms also frequently fulfill an adverbial function; cf. §11.2.1 for nominal phrases, §11.3.1 for adjectival phrases, §11.5 for postpositional phrases and §8.2.2.3 for non-finite (progressive) verb forms.

11.5 Postpositional phrases

A postpositional phrase (abbreviated 'PP') is headed by a postposition, which is always preceded by an NP complement. Any components in this complementing NP which are subject to case inflection inflect for genitive (as well as number). This structure is illustrated in (40). See Table 9.3 on page 188 for a list of postpositions.

(40) [NP_[GEN] + post-position]_{PP}

The complement in a PP can be any valid nominal phrase. A number of examples for various NPs complementing the head of a PP are provided below: a noun with a demonstrative in (41), a single noun in (42), a demonstrative pronoun in (43), a personal pronoun in (44), an interrogative pronoun in (45), and an interrogative NP (46).

(41) mån gillgiv daj gusaj birra ságastit
mån gillgi-v [d-a-j gusa-j birra]_{PP} ságastit
1SG.NOM will-1SG.PST DEM-DIST-GEN.PL COW-GEN.PL about say-INF
'I was going to talk about those cows.' [pit080924.089]

(42) dä mån tjuotjuv Stuornjárga nanne
dä mån tjuotju-v [Stuor-njárga nanne]_{PP}
then 1SG.NOM stand-1SG.PRS big-point\GEN.SG on
Álesgiehtjen
Álesgiehtje-n
Västerfjäll-INESS.SG
'I am standing on 'Big Point' in Västerfjäll.' [pit100404.012]

11 Phrase types

(43) mån virtev tjåtsev bejat dan sisa
mån virte-v tjåtse-v beja-t [d-a-n sisa]$_{PP}$
1SG.NOM must-1SG.PRS water-ACC.SG put-INF DEM-DIST-GEN.SG into
'I have to put water into that.' [pit080909.164]

(44) da lin duv gugu båhtam
d-a li-n [du-v gugu]$_{PP}$ båhta-m
DEM-DIST\NOM.PL be\3PL.PRS 2SG.GEN to come-PRF
'They have come to you.' [pit110329.35m03s]e

(45) mej nanne lä da?
[me-j nanne]$_{PP}$ lä d-a
what-GEN.PL on be\3PL.PRS DEM-DIST\NOM.PL
'What are those on?' [pit110331a.27m28s]e

(46) mikkir gierge nanne?
[mikkir gierge nanne]$_{PP}$
which rock\GEN.SG on
'On which rock?' [pit110331a.110]e

Postpositional phrases can function as clause-level adverbials, often indicating the location of an action, as in *dan giedge nanne* 'on that stone' in (47).

(47) dä Kataridna ja månnå dan gierge
dä Kataridna ja månnå [d-a-n gierge
then Katarina\NOM.SG and 1SG.NOM DEM-DIST-GEN.SG rock\GEN.SG
nanne pruvkojin ståhkåt
nanne]$_{PP}$ pruvko-jin ståhkå-t
on used.to-3PL.PST play-INF
'Katarina and I used to play on that rock.' [pit100404.159]

Note that, to a very limited extent, some postpositions can be used as prepositions, in which case they head a prepositional phrase. However, the data in the corpus concerning prepositional phrases are so limited that no conclusions can be made at this point. See §9.2.2 for the two examples from the corpus.

12 Overview of the syntax of sentences

In describing Pite Saami clauses, it is useful to begin with basic clauses that contain a full predicate and its arguments, complements and/or adjuncts, before moving on to describe complex clauses which consist of two or more clauses linked to one another. Therefore, basic clauses are described in Chapter 13, including declarative, interrogative and imperative clauses. Chapter 14 then deals with complex clauses, covering coordination and subordination.

However, in order to better understand the syntax of sentences, it is sensible to begin with two general discussions that provide a framework for understanding the syntactic descriptions that follow. The first of these, in §12.1 below, covers grammatical relations in Pite Saami. This leads to the second discussion in §12.2, which concerns clause-level constituent ordering, and the likely role that information structure plays in determining this.

12.1 Grammatical relations

Pite Saami is an accusative language because the only argument of an intransitive verb (S) is marked in the same way as the most-agent-like argument of a transitive verb (A): by the nominative case. The most-patient-like argument of a transitive verb (P) is marked differently: by the accusative case. This is illustrated by the following examples, with an intransitive verb in (1) and a (mono-)transitive verb in (2).

(1) så mån   tjielka   sinne vällahiv
    så mån   tjielka   sinne vällahi-v
    so 1SG.NOM sled\GEN.SG in lie-1SG.PST
    'So I lay in the sled.'   [pit100404.303]

(2) dä   almatj   biejaj   risev   dále nåvte
    dä   almatj   bieja-j   rise-v   dále nåvte
    then person\NOM.SG put-3SG.PRS stick-ACC.SG now so
    'Then one places the stick like this.'   [pit100404.216]

12 Overview of the syntax of sentences

The direct object of a ditransitive verb is also in the accusative case, while the indirect object of a ditransitive verb is in an oblique case (usually in the illative case, which prototypically indicates that the noun refers to the goal of a movement), as illustrated in (3).

(3) *mån vaddav suhta buhtsujda biebmov*
mån vadda-v suhta buhtsu-jda biebmo-v
1SG.NOM give-1SG.PRS several reindeer-ILL.PL food-ACC.SG
'I give food to several reindeer.' [pit110413b.157]*e*

Grammatical relations in Pite Saami are thus marked by morphological means. Constituent ordering does not indicate grammatical relations in any way. For instance, in (4) the object precedes the subject.

(4) *ja dáv aj mån vuojnav vinndegest muv*
ja d-á-v aj mån vuojna-v vindege-st muv
and DEM-PROX-ACC.SG also 1SG.NOM see-1SG.PRS window-ELAT.SG 1SG.GEN
dåbest
dåbe-st
house-ELAT.SG
'And I also see this from the window from my house.' [pit100310b.030]

The following section provides more examples illustrating the flexibility of constituent ordering.

12.2 Constituent order at clause level

Clause-level constituent ordering in Pite Saami is not determined syntactically. That being said, in elicited clauses from the corpus, some ordering patterns do occur more frequently than others, and indicate that SVO ordering is preferred in context-free elicited clauses, everything else being equal. This is illustrated by the examples in (5) through (7).

(5) *sån usjuda*
sån usjuda
3SG.NOM think\3SG.PRS
'He thinks.' [pit081011.154]*e*

(6) *mån vuojnav bierdnav*
mån vuojna-v bierdna-v
1SG.NOM see-1SG.PRS bear-ACC.SG
'I see a bear.' [pit080926.01m24s]*e*

12.2 Constituent order at clause level

(7) ålmaj vaddá blåmåv kuijdnaj
ålmaj vaddá blåmå-v kuijdna-j
man\NOM.SG give\3SG.PRS flower-ACC.SG woman-ILL.SG
'The man gives the flower to the woman.' [pit100324.65m25s]*e*

It is possible that this ordering is triggered by typical Swedish constituent ordering, which is generally SVO, as Swedish was often used as the meta-language in elicitation sessions.

More significantly, the part of the Pite Saami corpus consisting of natural language situations confirms the lack of any set constituent ordering based on syntactic criteria.[1] To illustrate this syntactic flexibility, examples of SOV and OSV constituent ordering are provided in (8) and (9), respectively.

(8) mån vuostasj vierbmev biejav Áktjuotjålbmáj
mån vuostasj vierbme-v bieja-v Áktjuotjålbmá-j
1SG.NOM first net-ACC.SG put-1SG.PRS Áktjuotjålbme-ILL.SG
'First I'll put out the net in Áktjuotjålbme.' [pit090702.024]

(9) sågijd mån anav
sågi-jd mån ana-v
birch-ACC.PL 1SG.NOM use-1SG.PRS
'I use birchwood.' [pit090702.149]

The example in (10) has VSO constituent order, and additionally has the nonfinite verb complement (with OV ordering) in clause-final position.

---

[1] Note that Sammallahti claims that at least for North Saami (although it is not entirely clear whether he means North Saami or is generalizing for all Saami languages here), the "order of the main constituents [...] is largely free from formal restrictions and guided by pragmatic principles", but then states that the "basic order is SVO" (Sammallahti 1998: 95). This seems to reflect the data from the Pite Saami corpus to the extent that context-free elicited clauses tend to be SVO, while in fact no syntactic criteria for constituent ordering can be ascertained in natural language. Lagercrantz takes several pages to describe a variety of tendencies in constituent ordering for Pite Saami declarative clauses, even after describing ordering preferences concerning topic and focus within a discourse and summarizing the actual situation by stating quite vaguely that the position of the subject in a clause has a 'certain stylistic effect' ("Die Stellung des Satzgegenstandes hat eine gewisse stilistische Wirkung") (Lagercrantz 1926: 46). Perhaps current descriptions of the syntax of the Saami languages would be better served if linguists would cease trying to force these languages into an inaccurate (but typologically neat) label such as SVO.

12 Overview of the syntax of sentences

(10) *dä galgav mån gåvåjd vuosedit*
dä galga-v mån gåvå-jd vuosedi-t
then will-1SG.PRS 1SG.NOM picture-ACC.PL show-INF
'Then I will show some pictures.' [pit080825.036]

Attempting to determine constituent order patterns is further complicated by the fact that it is sometimes impossible to tell what the constituent ordering is because NPs referring to information provided by context alone are frequently not realized overtly, as in (10) above and (11) through (14) below.

(11) *ber aktak tjårvev adna*
ber aktak tjårve-v adna
only one antler-ACC.SG have\3SG.PRS
'(The reindeer) only has one antler.' [pit100405b.019]

(12) *gallga giesset ulgus*
gallga giesse-t ulgus
will\3SG.PRS pull-INF out
'(The reindeer herder) will pull (the reindeer buck) out.' [pit080909.017]

(13) *mån biejav dut*
mån bieja-v dut
1SG.NOM put-1SG.PRS there
'I'll put (the pole) there.' [pit100404.218]

(14) *ja vadde, Eva-Karin!*
ja vadde Eva-Karin
and give\2SG.IMP Eva-Karin
'And give (me) (a sausage), Eva-Karin!' [pit090519.208]

While person and number markers on the finite verb indicate grammatical information about the subject, there is no overt subject in (11) or (12). The clauses in (12) through (14) are lacking overt objects. The final example is also missing the indirect object.

Indeed, a complete clause can consist of nothing more than an inflected verb, as in the response in (15), which consists of nothing more than the copular verb inflected for 3SG.PRS.

(15) A: *ja tjábba dállke!*
ja tjábba dállke
and beautiful weather\NOM.SG
'and such beautiful weather!'

B: *lä.*
lä
be\3SG.PRS
'yes, it is' (lit.: 'is')[2]

However, there are no examples in the corpus of verb-initial clauses featuring both an overt subject and a VC with a single verb. While there are plenty of examples of the finite verb preceding the subject and most other clausal constituents, some constituent always precedes the verb. Frequently, it is the adverb *dä*, as in (16).

(16) *ja   dä   båhta   reksak*
ja   dä   båhta   reksak
and then come\3SG.PRS ptarmigan\NOM.SG
'And then a ptarmigan comes.'   [pit100404.241]

If the subject is not realized overtly, or if the VC contains more than one verb form, then the finite verb can be clause initial, as in (17) and (18), respectively.

(17) *bisij   dajd   dä   såbe   nanne*
bisi-j   d-a-jd   dä   såbe   nanne
grill-3SG.PST DEM-DIST-ACC.PL then stick\GEN.SG on
'He grilled them then on a stick.'   [pit100404.125]

(18) *ittjiv   mån   mujte*
ittji-v   mån   mujte
NEG-1SG.PST 1SG.NOM remember\CONNEG
'I didn't remember.'   [pit100404.227]

12.2.1 Information structure

Considering the syntactic flexibility described above, it is only reasonable to consider information structure as a constituent ordering strategy. While a thorough investigation of information structure in Pite Saami is beyond the scope of the present study and must be left for more thorough future research, some preliminary observations can be made.

Specifically, declarative clauses typically begin with the topic (frequently the subject in the nominative case) and end with a comment on that topic. If the

---

[2] The source of the example in (15) is a recording collected by linguist Martin Hilpert during a pilot project he completed on Pite Saami in 2005. I am very grateful to him for providing me with his recordings and annotations. Note that Martin's recordings are not included in the Pite Saami documentation corpus.

comment involves a transitive verb, the object or complement clause (the focus) normally follows the verb, as in (6) and (7) above. However, clausal elements in focus can be moved from their 'default' position, which results in significant deviations from the preferred SVO constituent order. This is reflected in constituent interrogative clauses; here, the interrogative pronoun is in focus and always in clause-initial position (cf. §13.2.1).

The short example text presented in (19) and (20) below should serve to give an impression of how information structure may be the driving force behind constituent ordering at clause-level. Here, the speaker is talking about looking inside her mother's shoes after discovering that a mouse had been in them.

(19) ja danne vuojdniv unna jåŋåtjav.
ja danne vuojdni-v unna jåŋå-tja-v
and there see-1SG.PST small lingonberry-DIM-ACC.SG
'And there I saw a little lingonberry.' [pit100404.353]

(20) jahkav skafferijav lä danne adnam,
jahka-v skafferija-v lä danne adna-m
believe-1SG.PRS pantry-ACC.SG be\3SG.PRS there have-PRF
'I think (the mouse) had a pantry there.' [pit100404.354]

In the first clause (19), the topic is *danne* 'there', which refers to the shoes (the topic of the anecdote at this point) and is clause-initial. The constituent *jåŋåtjav* 'lingonberry' is the focus, but it is not particularly significant in the anecdote, and it follows the finite verb *vuojdniv* 'I saw'. However, when particular emphasis is placed on the focus, as in the following clause in (20), the constituent in focus can be fronted. Here, *skafferijav* 'pantry' is in focus, and receives particular emphasis[3] by occurring before the verb complex *lä danne adnam* 'has had there', while the topic (the mouse) is not realized overtly at all, but implied by the context and by the finite verb form inflected for 3SG. This fronting of a constituent is often accompanied by higher acoustic intensity, as is the case here.

---

[3] The NP *skafferijav* 'pantry' probably receives special emphasis because it personifies the behavior of the mouse in a light-hearted way by claiming that a mouse can have a pantry.

13 Basic clauses

A basic clause is a syntactic unit at text-level consisting minimally of a finite verb. In declarative clauses and interrogative clauses, this finite verb is marked morphologically for person, number, tense and/or mood. Aspect can be expressed analytically at the clause level using an auxiliary verb and a non-finite verb form. In all basic clauses, the finite verb agrees in number and, with the exception of imperative mood, in person with the syntactic subject of the sentence, which is a nominal phrase in the nominative case. NPs referring to information provided by context alone are not necessarily realized overtly. As a result, the syntactic subject and other verbal arguments are often not overtly present.

The following sections first present basic declarative clauses with intransitive and transitive verbs, existential clauses, copular clauses and complex verbal constructions consisting of more than one verb (§13.1). Then, §13.2 deals with interrogative clauses, before §13.3 and §13.4 cover syntactic aspects of the imperative mood and the potential mood, respectively.

13.1 Declarative clauses

Declarative clauses are the most common type of clause in the Pite Saami corpus. In the following, declarative clauses with a single verb are dealt with first, covering intransitive and transitive verbs, and two special cases (existential clauses and copular clauses). Then, declarative clauses featuring a modal or auxiliary verb in addition to the lexical head verb are described; because negation is expressed by an auxiliary verb, it is covered in the same section. While constituent ordering is mentioned in the following sections, it mostly refers to tendencies only, and the flexible nature of Pite Saami constituent ordering should always be kept in mind, as discussed in §12.2.

13.1.1 Basic intransitive declaratives

The subject of an intransitive declarative clause is in the nominative case, as in (1) through (3).

13 Basic clauses

(1) *almatj   usjut   ja...*
almatj   usjut   ja
person\NOM.SG think\3SG.PRS and
'One thinks, and...'   [pit100404.172]

(2) *mån   tjájmav*
mån   tjájma-v
1SG.NOM laugh-1SG.PRS
'I laugh.'   [pit100323a.005]e

(3) *dáj   Skaile   ello   såkoj*
d-á-j   Skaile   ello   såko-j
DEM-PROX-GEN.PL Skaile\GEN.PL reindeer.herd\NOM.SG drown-3SG.PST
'The Skaile family's reindeer herd drowned.'   [pit0906_Ahkajavvre_b.002]

13.1.1.1 Clauses with a passive verb

When a transitive verb is passivized,[1] its valency is reduced, and it becomes intransitive. In this, the patient is the subject of the verb complex, and therefore marked by nominative case; the agent may be left out. This is illustrated by the pair of elicited examples in (4) and (5), in which the former is a transitive clause in active voice, and the latter is an intransitive clause in passive voice.

(4) *máná   lä   tsiggim gådev*
máná   lä   tsiggi-m gåde-v
child\NOM.PL be\3PL.PRS build-PRF hut-ACC.SG
'Children have built the hut.'   [pit110518a.28m14s]e

(5) *dat   lä   tsiggiduvvum*
d-a-t   lä   tsiggi-duvvu-m
DEM-DIST-NOM.SG be\3SG.PRS build-PASS-PRF
'That (hut) was built.'   [pit110518a.27m41s]e

Similarly, the example from a narrative in (6) presents an intransitive passive construction.

---

[1] Transitive verbs can be passivized using the derivational suffix *-duvv*; cf. §10.2.5 on derivational morphology and §8.3 on inflectional morphology for passives.

13.1 Declarative clauses

(6) dát lä vanj dä gajk vuorasumos
d-á-t lä vanj dä gajk vuorasu-mos
DEM-PROX-NOM.SG be\3SG.PRS probably then all old-SUPERL\SG
dágaduvvum
dága-duvvu-m
make-PASS-PRF
'This was probably the absolute oldest made.'
[pit0906_Ahkajavvre_a.120]

The NP referring to the agent of an event can optionally occur obliquely in the elative case if the verb is passivized, as in (7).

(7) gåhte lä tsiggiduvvum mánájst
gåhte lä tsiggi-duvvu-m máná-jst
hut\NOM.SG be\3SG.PRS build-PASS-PRF child-ELAT.PL
'The hut has been built by children.' [pit110518a.28m41s]*e*

13.1.2 Basic transitive declaratives

In declarative clauses featuring a monotransitive verb, the subject is in nominative and is typically the agent, while the object is in the accusative case and is typically the patient of the predicate. Examples can be seen in (8) through (10).

(8) ja mån vuojnav muähtagav danne
ja mån vuojna-v muähtaga-v danne
and 1SG.NOM see-1SG.PRS snow-ACC.SG here
'And I see snow here.' [pit100404.020]

(9) danne sáme edne båhtsujd giesen
danne sáme edne båhtsu-jd giese-n
there Saami\NOM.PL have\3PL.PRS reindeer-ACC.PL summer-INESS.SG
'The Saami keep the reindeer there in the summer.' [pit100404.011]

(10) almatj bedja virbmijd ehket
almatj bedja virbmi-jd ehket
person\NOM.SG put\3SG.PRS fishing.net-ACC.PL evening
'One puts out fishing nets in the evening.' [pit100310b.020]

In declarative clauses with a ditransitive verb, the direct object is also in the accusative case and is typically theme, while the indirect object, typically recipient, is normally in the illative case. Examples can be seen in (11) and (12).

13 Basic clauses

(11)   *mån*   *vaddav*   *gålbmå buhtsujda*   *biebmov*
         mån   vadda-v   gålbmå buhtsu-jda   biebmo-v
         1SG.NOM give-1SG.PRS three   reindeer-ILL.PL food-ACC.SG
         'I give food to three reindeer.'   [pit110413b.156]*e*

(12)   *mån*   *vaddav*   *dunje*   *fahtsajt*
         mån   vadda-v   dunje   fahtsa-jt
         1SG.NOM give-1SG.PRS 2SG.ILL glove-ACC.PL
         'I give gloves to you.'   [pit080926.01m01s]*e*

13.1.3 Existential clauses

The verb *gävdnut*[2] is used as an existential verb.[3] The item whose existence is posited is the syntactic subject of the sentence and thus in the nominative case, which *gävdnut* agrees in person and number with. Examples can be found in (13) and (14).

(13)   *váren*   *gävdnu*   *aj*   *juomo*
         váre-n   gävdnu   aj   juomo
         mountain-INESS.SG exist\3PL.PRS also sorrel\NOM.PL
         'There is sorrel in the mountains, too.' (lit.: there are sorrels...)
                                                                                              [pit080924.178]

(14)   *dal* *itjij*   *gävndoj*   *aktak tjårvebielle*
         dal   itji-j   gävndoj   aktak tjårve-bielle
         now NEG-3SG.PST exist\CONNEG any   horn-half\NOM.SG
         'There isn't a single *tjårvebielle*[4] now.'   [pit100405b.021]

     The subject frequently follows the verb because the subject is often the focus of the clause, but as the clause in (15) shows, the subject may occur before the verb if it is the topic and/or is presupposed knowledge (cf. §12.2.1 on information structure).

---

[2] Much like its Swedish counterpart *finnas*, which is a derivation of the verb *finna* 'find', the Pite Saami verb *gävdnut* is derived from the verb *gávdnat* 'find'.

[3] Note that a copular clause containing an adjunct can also be used as an existential; cf. §13.1.4.

[4] A *tjårvebielle* (lit.: horn-half) is a term used to describe a reindeer with only one antler remaining after the other antler has broken off.

(15) motora   vadnasij.   "motora" ij   gävdnu
     motora   vadnasi-j   motora   ij   gävdnu
     motor\GEN.SG boat-COM.PL "motor" NEG\3SG.PRS exist\CONNEG
     sáme   gielan
     sáme   giela-n
     Saami\GEN.SG language-INESS.SG
     '...with motor boats. There is no (word for) "motor" in the Saami
     language.'   [pit080924.482,484]

13.1.4 Copular clauses

There are several types of copular clauses in Pite Saami. All of these feature the copular verb *årrot* 'be' (see §8.5.7 for more details). Copular clauses can be used to express a variety of information about the subject referent, and these are discussed below.

When the complement of the copula is an NP in nominative case, it identifies or classifies the subject referent, as in (16) and (17), respectively.

(16) *Mattijá*   *lij*   *morbror*   *munje*
     Mattijá   li-j   morbror[5]   munje
     Matthias\NOM.SG be-3SG.PST   maternal.uncle\NOM.SG 1SG.ILL
     'Matthias was my maternal uncle.'   [pit0906_Ahkajavvre_a.007]

(17) *mån*   *lev*   *sábme*
     mån   le-v   sábme
     1SG.NOM   be-1SG.PRS   Saami\NOM.SG
     'I am a Saami.'   [pit080813.00m35s]

The complement of a copular clause can be one or more adjectival phrases headed by a predicative adjective which ascribes properties to the subject referent, as in (18).

(18) *buhtsoj*   *lä*   *nav buojde ja tjábbe*
     buhtsoj   lä   nav buojde ja   tjábbe
     reindeer\NOM.PL be\3PL.PRS   so   fat\PL   and beautiful\PL
     'The reindeer are so fat and beautiful.'   [pit080703.014]

The complement of a copular clause can be an NP in the inessive case in which case it describes the location of the subject referent, as in (19).

---
[5] Note that *morbror* is a nonce borrowing from Swedish. Cf. Swedish *morbror* 'maternal uncle'.

13 Basic clauses

(19) måj   lijmen   Fuordnagin
  måj   lij-men   Fuordnagi-n
  1DU.NOM be-1DU.PST Fuordnak-INESS.SG
  'We two were in Fuordnak.' [pit080924.590]

The complement of a copular clause can be an NP in the elative case in which case it describes the material which the subject referent is made of, as in (20).

(20) ja   dát   lä   aj   struvdast
  ja   d-á-t   lä   aj   struvda-st
  and DEM-PROX-NOM.SG be\3SG.PRS also cloth-ELAT.SG
  'And this is also (made) of cloth.' [pit080708_Session08.015]

A copular clause can also function as an existential clause when it includes a temporal adjunct. In such cases, the existence of the subject referent is posited at that particular time indicated by the adjunct. Pragmatically, this usually announces an event connected to the subject referent. Typically, the temporal referent occurs first in the sentence, then the copular verb, and the subject is last (just as with the existential verb *gädvnut*; cf. §13.1.3), as it is usually the focus. This is illustrated by the example in (21).

(21) ja   dále'l   káffa
  ja   dále=l   káffa
  and now=be\3SG.PRS coffee\NOM.SG
  'And now it's coffee (time).' [pit090519.313]

Possession can also be expressed by a copular construction. In such a construction, the possessed NP is the subject of the clause in the nominative case, which the finite verb agrees with in person and number. The possessor NP is in the inessive case. Such a construction is illustrated by the example in (22).

(22) muvne   lä   akta mánná
  muvne   lä   akta mánná
  1SG.INESS be\3SG.PRS one child\NOM.SG
  'I have one child.' [pit080621.30m54s]*e*

In the corpus, such possessive constructions always have the constituent order POSSESSOR+COPULA+POSSESSED. While this type of possessive construction is the native Saamic structure (Bergsland 1977: 9), it is very uncommon in the Pite Saami corpus, and almost exclusively limited to elicitation sessions. The elicitation scenario may have had an effect on the constituent order,[6] but it is more

---

[6] The equivalent Swedish structure is also normally POSSESSOR + VERB + POSSESSED.

likely the case that the constituent order reflects information structure preferences, specifically the tendency for the topic (more often the possessor, which is animate) to come before the focus[7] (more often the possessed, which is inanimate).

In any case, a clause-level construction using the monotransitive verb *adnet* 'have'[8] expressing possession, as in (23), is now the standard in Pite Saami.[9]

(23) ja dä inijmä gusajd
ja dä ini-jmä gusa-jd
and then have-1PL.PST cow-ACC.PL
'And then we had cows.' [pit080924.091]

13.1.5 Multi-verb declarative clauses

Verbs which govern non-finite verbal complements can be classified into three groups based on the type of non-finite complement verb form they co-occur with, as illustrated in Table 13.1. The finite verb occurs before the non-finite lexical

Table 13.1: Verbs accompanied by a non-finite complement verb

	non-finite form of complement
modals	INFINITIVE
aspectual auxiliary	PERFECT / PROGRESSIVE
negation verb	CONNEGATIVE

complement verb, unless the complement is in focus, in which case it can occur before the finite verb. These verb types are dealt with in §13.1.5.1, §13.1.5.2 and §13.1.5.3, respectively.

---

[7] Cf. §12.2.1 on information structure.
[8] Historically, *adnet* meant 'use' or 'keep' (cf. Lehtiranta 2001: 10), but synchronically it is most frequently used to indicate possession in a transitive verb construction which is essentially identical to the equivalent Swedish verb *ha* or the English verb *have*.
[9] While this construction using the transitive verb *adnet* 'have' is clearly not a copular clause, it is worth pointing this out here, particularly for any readers from Uralic studies, because the copular construction (as in the example in (22)) is no longer the true standard for expressing possession at clause level in Pite Saami.

13.1.5.1 Modal verbs

Modal verbs are used to express modality for the event denoted by the verbal complement. The complementing verb is in the infinitive (marked by the suffix *-t*). Modal verbs include *máhttat* 'can, be able to', *ådtjot*[10] 'may, be allowed to', *virrtit* 'must', *hähttut*[11] 'must', *sihtat* 'want' and *gallgat* 'will/shall'. Some examples are provided in (24) through (26).

(24) tjátsev   ådtjobihtet   juhgat   dasste
 tjátse-v   ådtjo-bihtet juhga-t d-a-sste
 water-ACC.SG may-2PL.PRS   drink-INF DEM-DIST-INESS.SG
 'You all may drink water from that.' [pit090519.022]

(25) ja dä del virrtin   allget   bäbbmat
 ja dä del virrti-n   allge-t   bäbbma-t
 and then well must-3PL.PST begin-INF   feed-INF
 'And then they had to start to feed (the reindeer).' [pit100405a.029]

(26) mij   máhttep   ságastit   Bidumsáme   gielav
 mij   máhtte-p   ságasti-t   Bidum-sáme   giela-v
 1PL.NOM can-1PL.PRS   speak-INF   Pite-Saami\GEN.SG   language-ACC.SG
 'We can speak the Pite Saami language.' [pit110517b2.022]

The modal verb *sihtat* 'want' behaves the same when the subject of the complementing verb complex is coreferential with the subject of the matrix clause, as in (27).

(27) mån   sidav   gulijd   adnet
 mån   sida-v   guli-jd   adne-t
 1SG.NOM   want-1SG.PRS fish-ACC.PL have-INF
 'I want to have fish.' [pit090702.012]

However, when the subject of the modal verb *sihtat* is not coreferential with the subject of the complementing verb complex, then a finite verb clause is the complement to the modal verb, as in the negated clause in (28). Note that, here, *sihtat* is in the connegative non-finite form *sida*.

---

[10] The modal verb *ådtjot* 'be allowed to' is homophonous with the full verb *ådtjot* 'get, receive'. This pattern is found in Swedish, as well, with the verb *få* 'be allowed to' and 'receive', and in English, e.g.: 'I get to go to the movies'.

[11] The word *hähttut* 'must' is likely limited to northern dialects of Pite Saami.

(28) dä   ij   del   almatj   sida   nagin
     dä   i-j   del   almatj   sida   nagin
     then NEG-3SG.PRS obviously person\NOM.SG want\CONNEG some
     sadjáj   vuällget
     sadjá-j   vuällge-t
     place-ILL.SG go-INF
     'Then one obviously doesn't want to go anywhere.'   [pit080924.052]

The modal verb *gallgat* 'will' can also be used to locate events in the future, as in (29) through (31) below.

(29) dä   galgav   sámes mujjtemuv   ságastit
     dä   galga-v   sámes mujjtemu-v   ságasti-t
     then will-1SG.PRS some memory-ACC.SG   say-INF
     'Then I will tell (you) a memory.'   [pit100703a.001]

(30) jo, da lä   akta vuoberis,   gallga   giesset   ulgus
     jo   da lä   akta vuoberis[12]   gallga   giesse-t ulgus
     yes then be\3SG.PRS one buck\NOM.SG   will\3SG.PRS pull-INF out
     'Yes, it's a 3-year old reindeer buck, (he) will pull (it) out.'
                                                          [pit080909.016-017]

(31) gallgap   dav   girjev   ådtjot
     gallga-p   d-a-v   girje-v   ådtjo-t
     will-1PL.PRS DEM-DIST-ACC.SG   book-ACC.SG   get-INF
     'We will get that book.'   [pit110517b.022]

The modal verb *gallgat* 'will' is often used in conditional clauses, as in (32).

(32) jus galga   sáme   viesov   valldet, dä   galga
     jus galga   sáme   vieso-v   vallde-t dä   galga
     if will\3SG.PRS Saami\GEN.SG   life-ACC.SG   take-INF then will\3SG.PRS
     mielagav   dal   navt rutastit
     mielaga-v   dal   navt rutasti-t
     sternum-ACC.SG   then so   pull-INF
     'If I choose Saami style, then I will pull the sternum like this.'
                                                          [pit080909.097]

---

[12] Specifically, a *vuoberis* is a three-year-old reindeer buck, but the gloss has been shortened to save space.

13.1.5.2 The aspectual auxiliary verb *årrot*

The auxiliary verb *årrot* 'be' together with a non-finite complement verb is used to mark the perfective and progressive aspects. This auxiliary verb is homophonous with the copular verb, and is also glossed as 'be'. In the perfective aspect, the complement verb is in a non-finite form marked by the suffix *-m* as in (33) and (34), while the progressive non-finite verb is marked by the suffix *-min* as in (35) and (36), respectively.

(33) *denne liv   riegadam*
denne li-v   riegada-m
there be-1SG.PRS be.born-PRF
'I was born there.'   [pit090702.008]

(34) *lä   dån   mannam nagin bále   ja tjuvvum*
lä   dån   manna-m nagin bále   ja tjuvvu-m
be\2SG.PRS 2SG.NOM go-PRF some time\GEN.SG and accompany-PRF
Vistegij?
Visteg-ij
Vistek-ILL.SG
'Have you ever gone and accompanied (them) to Vistek?' [pit080924.630]

(35) *men mån   lev   tjåjvev   ruhtastemin ullgus*
men mån   le-v   tjåjve-v   ruhtaste-min ullgus
but 1SG.NOM be-1SG.PRS stomach-ACC.SG cut-PROG   out
'But I'm cutting out the stomach.'   [pit080909.054]

(36) *nå, mav   lä   låhkåmin?*
nå   ma-v   lä   låhkå-min
well what-ACC.SG be\3SG.PRS read-PROG
'Well, what is he studying?' (lit.: reading)   [pit080924.667]

13.1.5.3 The negation verb

Pite Saami clause negation is expressed by a special finite negation verb. Unlike other verbs, the negation verb does not have an infinitive or any other non-finite form, but is always a finite verb (cf. §8.5.8). As such, it always agrees in person and number with the subject of the clause, and inflects for tense and mood as well.[13] The complement verb occurs in a special non-finite form called the connegative. Examples for the negative verb can be found in (37) through (39).

---

[13] In this respect, Pite Saami differs significantly from for instance North Saami negative clauses in which the main verb and not the finite negation verb inflects for tense (cf. Svonni 2009: 92).

13.1 Declarative clauses

(37) iv jáhke
 i-v jáhke
 NEG-1SG.PRS believe\CONNEG
 'I don't believe so.' [pit090702.411]

(38) ittjij åbbå gävdno vuodja åsstet
 ittji-j åbbå gävdno vuodja åsste-t
 NEG-3SG.PST at.all exist\CONNEG butter\NOM.SG buy-INF
 'There wasn't any butter to buy at all.' [pit080708_Session03.006]

(39) men ijtjin del bårå dan sisste
 men ijtji-n del bårå d-a-n sisste
 but NEG-3PL.PST then eat\CONNEG DEM-DIST-GEN.SG out
 'But they didn't eat out of this.' [pit080708_Session03.019]

In the examples above, the non-finite complement to the connegative verb is a lexical verb. In the following examples in (40) through (42), the complement connegative verb is a modal or auxiliary verb whose own complement then follows in the appropriate non-finite form.

(40) ij vanj dä máhte ilá stuor dålåv adnet
 ij vanj dä máhte ilá stuor dålå-v adne-t
 NEG\3SG.PRS well then can\CONNEG too big fire-ACC.SG have-INF
 'But you can't have too big of a fire.' [pit090702.176]

(41) dä iv lä åbbå gullam dav
 dä i-v lä åbbå gulla-m d-a-v
 then NEG-1SG.PRS be\CONNEG at.all hear-PRF DEM-DIST-ACC.SG
 'I haven't heard that at all.' [pit090702.203]

(42) nej, mån iv lä bårråm, men
 nej mån i-v lä bårrå-m men
 no 1SG.NOM NEG-1SG.PRS be\CONNEG eat-PRF but
 Jåssjå'l bårråm
 Jåssjå=l bårrå-m
 Josh\NOM.SG=be\3SG.PRS eat-PRF
 'No, I haven't eaten (it), but Josh has eaten (it).' [pit090519.147]

While Pite Saami constituent order is generally flexible (cf. §12.2), there are no examples in the corpus of the verb of negation occurring after the negated complement, but instead the connegative complement verb always follows the finite negation verb in a clause.

13.2 Interrogative clauses

Constituent interrogative clauses in Pite Saami are consistently marked as such syntactically, and thus are distinct from declarative clauses. Polar interrogative clauses, on the other hand, do not differ significantly from declarative clauses, although some syntactic constructions are more common than others. The following sections deal first with constituent interrogative clauses, then polar interrogative clauses in more detail.

13.2.1 Constituent interrogative clauses

Constituent interrogative clauses are the only type of independent clause in Pite Saami which is consistently marked syntactically as a clause type. Specifically, every constituent interrogative clause is marked as such by having an interrogative word or phrase in clause-initial position. When it is an interrogative pronoun, it inflects for case and number consistent with its grammatical role in the clause (as with any pronoun), while the humanness of its (expected) referent determines the choice of the root.[14] Some examples can be found in (43) through (46).

(43) *mav dån hålå?*
ma-v dån hålå
what-ACC.SG 2SG.NOM say\2SG.PRS
'What are you saying?' [pit090519.329]

(44) *majd dä viehkedi?*
ma-jd dä viehkedi
what-ACC.PL then help\2SG.PST
'What then did you help (with)?' [pit080924.615]

(45) *gejna dä tjuovvo*
ge-jna dä tjuovvo
who-COM.SG then accompany\2SG.PST
'Who did you go with?' [pit080924.071]

(46) *man mällgadav ana dajd riehpenen*
man mällgada-v ana d-a-jd riehpene-n
how long-ACC.SG have\2SG.PRS DEM-DIST-ACC.PL smoke.hole-INESS.SG
'How long do you have those in the smoke hole for?' [pit090702.168]

---

[14] Interrogative pronouns referring to non-human NPs all feature a *ma-* root, while those referring to human NPs have a *ge-* root. Interrogative adverbs also begin with *g-*. Cf. §6.4.

13.2 Interrogative clauses

Alternatively, the interrogative can be an adverb, as in (47) through (49).

(47)　gukt　lä　　　dát
　　　gukte lä　　　d-á-t
　　　how　be\3SG.PRS DEM-PROX-NOM.SG
　　　'How is it?'　　　　　　　　　　　　　　　　　　　　　[pit080924.130]

(48)　guste　　　dån　　bådá
　　　guste　　　dån　　bådá
　　　from.where 2SG.NOM come\2SG.PRS
　　　'Where are you coming from?'　　　　　　　　　　　　　[pit080924.003]

(49)　gånne dajt　　　　　tjogidä
　　　gånne d-a-jt　　　　tjogi-dä
　　　where DEM-DIST-ACC.PL pick-2PL.PST
　　　'Where did you pick those?'　　　　　　　　　　　　　[pit080924.168]

Assuming that any constituent which is the pragmatic focus can be marked by fronting, as preliminarily asserted in §12.2.1, then the fronting of the interrogative word is consistent with focus-marking. However, for constituent interrogative clauses, fronting is then obligatory. The rest of the clause is constructed syntactically just as freely as any declarative clause would be. While subject-verb inversion can occur, the flexible nature of Pite Saami constituent ordering prevents this from necessarily marking a clause as interrogative.

It is worth noting that the discourse marker *nå*, which can be translated as 'well' or sometimes 'yes', frequently precedes constituent interrogative clauses, as in (50). However, it is not obligatory, nor is it restricted to interrogative clauses. It is likely a discourse marker, perhaps simply indicating the speaker's active interest in the conversation.

(50)　nå　gukte lij　　　Áhkabákten　　　　gu　　dånnå　lidje
　　　nå　gukte li-j　　　Áhkabákte-n　　　 gu　　dånnå　lidje
　　　well how　be-3SG.PST Áhkkabákkte-INESS.SG when 2SG.NOM be\2SG.PST
　　　mánná?
　　　mánná
　　　child\NOM.SG
　　　'Well what was Áhkkabákkte like when you were a child?'　[pit080924.063]

13 Basic clauses

13.2.2 Polar interrogative clauses

Because of flexible constituent ordering in Pite Saami, there is no reliable syntactic test for whether a clause is a polar interrogative. The intonation of polar questions does not seem to differ significantly from any other types of clauses, either. However, polar interrogative clauses frequently have a constituent order in which the finite verb occurs before the subject. Furthermore, this finite verb is generally the first element in a clause. The examples in (51) through (53) illustrate this.

(51) *galga   dån   ságastit enabuv?*
     galga   dån   ságasti-t ena-bu-v
     will\2SG.PRS 2SG.NOM say-INF much-COMP-ACC.SG
     'Are you going to say more?'   [pit0906_Ahkajavvre_b.041]

(52) *suovade   dån?*
     suovade   dån
     smoke\2SG.PRS 2SG.NOM
     'Do you smoke?'   [pit080702b.073]

(53) *lij   sån   uktu jala lij   Halvar   aj   maŋŋen*
     li-j   sån   uktu jala li-j   Halvar   aj   maŋŋen
     be-3SG.PST 3SG.NOM alone or be-3SG.PST Halvar\NOM.SG also along
     'Was he alone or was Halvar also along?'   [pit080924.308]

As with any Pite Saami clause, the syntactic subject does not have to be realized overtly. In such cases, the finite verb is also usually word initial, as in (54).

(54) *udtju   sáme   gielav   danne sagastit?*
     udtju   sáme   giela-v   danne sagasti-t
     may\2SG.PST Saami\GEN.SG language-ACC.SG there speak-INF
     'Were you allowed to speak Saami there?'   [pit080924.351]

However, it is also possible to front other elements which normally occur after the finite verb, as in (55) and (56). Here, the non-finite perfect form of the complement verb immediately precedes the aspect-marking auxiliary verb.

(55) *juhkum   lä   gajtsa   mielkev?*
     juhku-m   lä   gajtsa   mielke-v
     drink-PRF be\2SG.PRS goat\GEN.SG milk-ACC.SG
     'Have you ever drunk goat's milk?'   [pit080924.128]

(56) bårråm lä dån biergov danne?
 bårrå-m lä dån biergo-v danne
 eat-PRF be\2SG.PRS 2SG.NOM meat-ACC.SG there
 'Have you eaten meat there?' [pit090519.130]

13.2.2.1 Polar interrogatives and the question marker

It is possible for polar interrogative clauses to be identified as such by a question marker *gu~gus* following the finite verb. However, the use of the question marker in polar interrogatives is exceptionally uncommon and can hardly be considered obligatory in current Pite Saami usage; this is reflected in the data from the corpus, which contain only three tokens. See §9.1.2.1 for a preliminary discussion of the question marker, including the three tokens from the corpus.

13.3 Clauses in the imperative mood

Clauses in the imperative mood stand out syntactically by lacking an overt subject NP. Furthermore, they are marked by special portmanteau morphemes on the finite verb which express imperative mood as well as the number of the implied subject of the clause, which is always 2nd person. The finite verb tends to be in clause-initial position, as shown by the examples in (57)[15] and (58).

(57) giehto naginav dan Låddávre birra
 giehto nagina-v d-a-n Låddávre birra
 tell\SG.IMP something-ACC.SG DEM-DIST-GEN.SG Låddávvre\GEN.SG about
 'Say something about this Låddávvre!' [pit080924.314]

(58) bieja pirunav bävvdaj
 bieja piruna-v bävvda-j
 put\SG.IMP potato-ACC.SG table-ILL.SG
 'Put the potato on the table!' [pit101208.478]e

Nonetheless, the standard phrase for 'thank you', shown in (59) in dual person, indicates that a constituent other than the finite verb may occur before a finite verb in imperative mood.

(59) gijtov adnen
 gijto-v adne-n
 thank-ACC.SG have-DU.IMP
 'Thank you (two)!' (lit.: have thanks!) [pit101208.292]e

---

[15] *Låddávvre* is the name of a lake.

13 Basic clauses

However, no other examples of such constructions are found in the corpus, and this constituent ordering may be due to this phrase being a common expression and non-productive lexicalized structure calqued from the Swedish expression *tack ska du ha!* (literally 'thanks you shall have!').

The adverb *dåle* 'now' is common in imperative clauses, and is frequently abbreviated to *dål*, as in (60).

(60) årren   dál
     årre-n   dál
     sleep-DU.IMP now
     'Go to sleep now!'   [pit110518a.06m55s]*e*

13.4 Clauses in the potential mood

Aside from featuring a finite verb inflected for the potential mood[16] by the *-tj* suffix, clauses in the potential mood generally lack an overt subject argument, as in (61) and (62).

(61) nå hålåv,   vuolgetjip   del
     nå hålå-v   vuolge-tji-p del
     well say-1SG.PRS go-POT-1PL   obviously
     'Well then I say we really should probably go.'   [pit090702.013]

(62) nä, virtitjav   nuollat
     nä virti-tja-v   nuolla-t
     no must-POT-1SG   undress-INF
     'Oh no, I'll probably have to take off some clothes.'   [pit090519.029]

However, as the clause in (63) makes clear, it is possible to have an overt subject argument.

(63) jus sån   vuosjatja   káfav
     jus sån   vuosja-tj-a   káfa-v
     if 3SG.NOM prepare.coffee-POT-3SG coffee-ACC.SG
     'If he will perhaps make coffee.'   [pit110404.269]*e*

With this in mind, clauses in the potential mood do not differ syntactically from declarative clauses.

---

[16] Cf. §8.1.3.2 on the usage and the morphology of the potential mood.

13.4 Clauses in the potential mood

As mentioned in §8.1.3.2, the potential mood can also be used as a less severe command. This resembles clauses in the imperative mood by also never occurring with an overt subject, as shown in example (64).

(64) *vuosjatja* *káfav*
 vuosja-tj-a káfa-v
 prepare.coffee-POT-2SG coffee-ACC.SG
 'Perhaps you could make some coffee.' [pit110404.267]*e*

14 Complex clauses

Two or more clauses can be conjoined by coordination or subordination. After coordination is covered in §14.1, complement clauses are presented in §14.2.1 and adverbial clauses are dealt with in §14.2.2. Finally, relative clauses which do not form a constituent of a matrix clause, but are instead part of a nominal phrase, are described in detail in this chapter as well (in §14.2.4).

14.1 Clausal coordination

There are several coordinating conjunctions that are used to syntactically join the basic clauses described in Chapter 13. In such cases, a coordinating conjunction occurs between the two clauses it connects. The clauses themselves are otherwise not marked in any way for coordination. The coordinating conjunctions are *ja* 'and', *vala* 'but', *men*[1] 'but', *jala* 'or' and *eller*[2] 'or'. The examples in (1) and (2) illustrate clausal coordination using the coordinators *ja* and *men*, respectively.

(1) mån   anav   Árjepluove   gaptev   nanne, ja Ivan
    mån   ana-v   Árjepluove   gapte-v   nanne ja   Ivan
    1SG.NOM have-1SG.PRS   Arjeplog\GEN.SG   frock-ACC.SG   on   and Ivan
    adna   Arrvehavre   gaptev
    adna   Arrvehavre   gapte-v
    have-3SG.PRS   Arvidsjaur\GEN.SG frock-ACC.SG
    'I have an Arjeplog frock on, and Ivan has an Arvidsjaur frock.'
                                                                 [pit080825.047]

---

[1] Note that *men* is a borrowing from Swedish (< *men* 'but') and is used almost exclusively in the corpus, while the native Saamic word *vala* is only found in a Pite Saami reading based on a Lule Saami translation of the New Testament (recording pit100403). Several examples in Lagercrantz (1926) include *men* (e.g. on p. 20), so it has been part of Pite Saami for at least a century.

[2] Just as with *men*, *eller* is a borrowing from Swedish (< *eller* 'or'); however, the native Saamic word *jala* is rather common as well in the corpus. Furthermore, unlike *men*, *eller* is not mentioned in Lagercrantz (1926), so it seems that *eller* is likely a more recent word-choice development, perhaps due to increased dominance of the Swedish language over the last century.

14 Complex clauses

(2) men ijtjin del bårå dan siste, men
men ijtji-n del bårå d-a-n siste men
but NEG-3PL.PST obviously eat\CONNEG DEM-DIST-GEN.SG out but

ednen biebmojd biergojd ja dåle návte deggara
edne-n biebmo-jd biergo-jd ja dåle návte deggara
have-3PL.PST food-ACC.PL meat-ACC.PL and now like.this such\GEN.PL

sinne
sinne
in

'But they obviously didn't eat out of that, but they had food, meat and so on in such things.' [pit080708_Session03.019]

When *jala* and *eller* function as clausal coordinators in the corpus, they are mostly used to indicate meta-language commentary showing that the second clause is an alternate or amended version of the first clause, as in (3), rather than to provide clause-level alternatives.

(3) dåle'l gámbal dåhpe, jala almatj hållå
dåle=l gámbal dåhpe jala almatj hållå
now=be\3SG.PRS old house\NOM.SG or person\NOM.SG say\3SG.PRS

"unna dåbátj"
unna dåbá-tj
small house-DIM\NOM.SG

'Now this is the old house, or one says "the little house".'
[pit100310b.047-049]

14.2 Clausal subordination

Certain types of Pite Saami clauses can be subordinate to another clause or to a nominal phrase. When embedded at clause-level, a subordinate clause can be either a complement clause or an adverbial clause, depending on whether it fills an argument or an adverbial role. These two types of subordinate clause are described in §14.2.1 and §14.2.2, respectively. Subordinate clauses featuring non-finite verb forms are likely also found in Pite Saami, a possibility which is dealt with briefly in §14.2.3. Finally, relative clauses are covered in §14.2.4.

14.2.1 Complement clauses

A complement clause fills an argument slot of the verbal predicate in the matrix clause it belongs to. There are a variety of complement clause constructions, and

14.2 Clausal subordination

both finite and infinitive predicates are possible. Complement clauses can be marked by a complementizer or can stand in juxtaposition to the matrix clause. The different complement clause marking strategies are summarized in Table 14.1 and described in the following sections.

Table 14.1: Types of complement clause marking

predicate type	subordination strategy
finite	complementizer *att*
	juxtaposition
infinitive	juxtaposition

14.2.1.1 Complement clauses with a finite predicate

Complement clauses with a fully inflected finite predicate are attested using one of two strategies. First, the borrowed complementizer *att*[3] can mark a complement clause. In such cases, the complement clause typically follows the matrix clause. The complementizer is in clause-initial position in the complement clause. Examples can be found in (4) and (5).

(4) *ja dä mån hålåv att sidav bajket*
ja dä mån hålå-v att sida-v bajke-t
and then 1SG.NOM say-1SG.PRS SUBORD want-1SG.PRS poop-INF
'And then I say that I want to poop.' [pit080924.591]

(5) *men mån diedav att háre lä*
men mån dieda-v att háre lä
but 1SG.NOM know-1SG.PRS SUBORD greyling\NOM.PL be\3PL.PRS
jávren
jávre-n
lake-INESS.SG
'But I know that there are greyling in the lake.' [pit100404.052]

Secondly, complement clauses with a finite predicate may be juxtaposed to the matrix clause they belong to. The complement clause typically follows the matrix clause. Verbs hosting such complements include *jáhkket* 'believe', *diehtet* 'know', *hållåt* 'say' and *tuhtjet* 'like'. Examples can be found in (6) through (8).

---

[3] Cf. the Swedish marker *att*, which is also a complementizer.

14 Complex clauses

(6)   *mån*   *jáhkav*   *stuor tjuovtja*   *lä*   *danne*
       mån   jáhka-v   stuor tjuovtj-a   lä   danne
       1SG.NOM believe-1SG.PRS big   whitefish-NOM.PL be\3PL.PRS there
       'I believe there are big whitefish there.'   [pit090702.123]

(7)   *men mån*   *tuhtjiv*   *dat*   *lij*   *nav suohtas*
       men mån   tuhtji-v   d-a-t   lij   nav suohtas
       but   1SG.NOM think-1SG.PRS DEM-DIST-NOM.SG be\3SG.PST so   nice
       tieltajn   *viessot*
       tielta-jn   viesso-t
       tent-INESS.PL live-INF
       'But I think it was so nice to stay in tents.'   [pit080924.644]

(8)   *men hålåv,*   *vuhtjijmä*   *mija*   *sárvav*
       men hålå-v   vuhtji-jmä   mija   sárva-v
       but   say-1SG.PRS shoot-1PL.PST 1PL.NOM moose-ACC.SG
       'But then I say we shot a moose.'   [pit090702.404]

Constituent interrogative clauses can also be juxtaposed complement clauses. As with any such interrogative clause, an interrogative pronoun or other question word occurs as the initial element of the complement clause. This strategy typically coincides with complements of epistemic verbs such as *diehtet* 'know' or *skenit* 'understand'. Some examples are provided in (9) through (11).

(9)   *mån*   *iv*   *diede*   *gåsse gillgin*   *gávnadit*
       mån   i-v   diede   gåsse gillgi-n   gávnadi-t
       1SG.NOM NEG-1SG.PRS know\CONNEG when will-1DU.PRS meet-INF
       maŋep   *bále*
       maŋe-p   bále
       after-COMP time\GEN.SG
       'I don't know when we'll meet next time.'   [pit081011.183]

(10)   *mån*   *iv*   *skene*   *mav*   *dån*
       mån   i-v   skene   ma-v   dån
       1SG.NOM NEG-1SG.PRS understand\CONNEG what-ACC.SG 2SG.NOM
       hålå
       hålå
       say\2SG.PRS
       'I don't understand what you're saying.'   [pit080926.05m14s]e

(11) mån diedav gie lä
 mån dieda-v gie lä
 1SG.NOM know-1SG.PRS who\NOM.SG be\3SG.PRS
 'I know who she is.' [pit090702.460]

While the complement clause typically follows the matrix clause, this does not necessarily have to be the case, as illustrated by (12).

(12) man mälgat lij gu lij hiejman, iv
 man mälgat li-j gu li-j hiejma-n i-v
 how far be-3SG.PST when be-3SG.PST home-INESS.SG NEG-1SG.PRS
 mån diede
 mån diede
 1SG.NOM know\CONNEG
 'I don't know how far it was to get home.' [pit100404.317]

14.2.1.2 Complement clauses with an infinitive predicate

Complement clauses with an infinitive predicate can be juxtaposed to the matrix clause they belong to. The complement clause typically follows the matrix clause. While not particularly common in the corpus, verbs such as *állget* 'begin' and *vajáldahtet/åjaldahtet*[4] 'forget' are accompanied by complement clauses headed by an infinitive verb, as in (13) through (16).

(13) nå gosse dijá älgijdä Örnvikast vuodjet vadnásav?
 nå gosse dijá älgi-jdä Örnvika-st vuodje-t vadnása-v
 well when 2PL.NOM begin-2PL.PST Örnvik-ELAT.SG drive-INF boat-ACC.SG
 'Well when did you start to take the boat from Örnvik?' [pit080924.563]

(14) ja dä del virrtin allget biebmat, fodderijd
 ja dä del virrti-n allge-t biebma-t fodderi-jd
 and then obviously must-3PL.PST begin-INF feed-INF feed-ACC.PL
 vuodjet
 vuodje-t
 drive-INF
 'And so they obviously had to start to feed, to transport the feed.'
 [pit100405a.029]

---

[4] The word *vajáldahtet* 'forget' is likely limited to the northern dialects of Pite Saami, while *åjaldahtet* is preferred in the south.

14 Complex clauses

(15) nä, mån   liv   åjaldahtam valldet   maŋen
     nä mån   li-v   åjaldahta-m vallde-t maŋen
     no 1SG.NOM be-1SG.PRS forget-PRF take-INF with
     'No, I forgot to take it along.'   [pit090519.322]

(16) vajálduhtiv   hållåt,   gu   vusjkonijd   dihkiv...
     vajálduhti-v   hållå-t   gu   vusjkoni-jd   dihki-v
     forget-1SG.PRS   say-INF   when perch-ACC.PL   do-1SG.PST
     'I am forgetting to say, when I did the perch...'   [pit090702.079]

14.2.2 Adverbial clauses

An adverbial clause is a subordinate clause that fills an adverbial function in the matrix clause. Adverbial clauses begin with a subordinating element such as *gu* 'when, once', *jus* 'if', *maŋŋel* 'after', *åvdål* 'before', *innan*[5] 'before' or *gukte* 'how', but otherwise are not marked syntactically as subordinate clauses. The adverbial clause itself is headed by a fully inflected finite verb.

For instance, the example in (17) shows that the adverbial clause can follow the matrix clause.

(17) hihtu   vanj dä   baktjat   innan   mån   stärtiv
     hihtu   vanj dä   baktja-t   innan   mån   stärti-v
     must\2SG.PRS   well then back-INF   before 1SG.NOM start-1SG.PRS
     motorav
     motora-v
     motor-ACC.SG
     'Well you have to back up then before I start the motor.'
                                                          [pit090702.018-019]

In the example in (18), the dependent complement clause *gu lidjin sladjim* 'once they had harvested' precedes the matrix clause *dä båhtin da bajás* 'then they came up'.

(18) gu   lidjin   sladjim,   dä   båhtin   da   bajás
     gu   lidji-n   sladji-m   dä   båhti-n   d-a   bajás
     when   be-3PL.PST   harvest-PRF   then come-3PL.PST DEM-DIST\SG.NOM up
     'Once (the farmers) had harvested, then they (the plants) came up.'
                                                          [pit080924.173]

---

[5] Note that the conjunction *innan* is a borrowing from Swedish and is only attested once in the corpus.

Adverbial clauses introduced by the subordinator *jus* 'if' set a condition for the matrix sentence. Other than this conjunction, there is no special marking for the conditional. The conditional clause can occur before or after the matrix clause, as shown in (19) through (21).

(19) jus gussa   dajd   ulli,   dä   bårre
     jus gussa   d-a-jd   ulli   dä   bårre
     if cow\NOM.PL DEM-DIST-ACC.PL reach-3PL.PRS then eat\3PL.PRS
     dajd,   dija   gamasuijnijd
     d-a-jd   dija   gama-suijni-jd
     DEM-DIST-ACC.PL 2PL.GEN shoe-hay-ACC.PL
     'If the cows reach up to it, then they eat it, your shoe hay.⁶'
                                                              [pit080924.221]

(20) ja   dat   lij   samma, jus del   lij
     ja   d-a-t   li-j   samma jus del   lij
     and DEM-DIST-NOM.SG be-3SG.PST same   if   then be-3SG.PST
     guallbana   vaj bijjadaga   vaj smav
     guallban-a   vaj bijjadag-a   vaj smav
     flat.pine.heath-NOM.PL or high.ground-NOM.PL or small
     biehtsasdaga
     biehtsasdag-a
     pine.forest-NOM.PL
     'And that was the same whether it was flat-pine-heath or higher-ground or small pine-forests.'   [pit100405a.009]

(21) jus galga   njuallga dajd   njuovvat   dä   galga
     jus galga   njuallga d-a-jd   njuovva-t   dä   galga
     if will\2SG.PRS correct DEM-DIST-ACC.PL slaughter-INF then will-2SG.PRS
     dajd   valdet   olgus åvdål gádsastam
     d-a-jd   valde-t olgus åvdål gádsasta-m
     DEM-DIST-ACC.PL take-INF out   before hang-PRF
     'If you slaughter them correctly, then you take them out before hanging (them) up.'   [pit080909.105]

---

⁶ Note that in example (19), 'hay' and both pronouns referring to 'hay' are plural; however, for ease of reading, these are singular in the English translation. *Gamasuäjdne* 'shoe-hay' refers to a special type of grass placed inside shoes to insulate one's feet from cold and moisture.

14 Complex clauses

14.2.3 Other subordinate clauses with non-finite verb forms

The literature on Saami languages often mentions other non-finite verb forms in addition to those mentioned above, which can be considered part of non-finite subordinate clauses often in adverbial function. These include the verb genitive, verb abessive or gerunds, for instance (cf. Sammallahti (1998: 103–104) and Svonni (2009: 67–73) for North Saami, or Spiik (1989: 104–111) for Lule Saami). For Pite Saami, Lehtiranta (1992: 95–106) describes the morphological form for a number of such non-finite forms,[7] but does not go into how these are used syntactically, and only one or two example clauses are provided at all. Lagercrantz (1926) does not describe such verb forms.

With this in mind, it is certainly plausible that Pite Saami can make use of non-finite verb forms other than those mentioned above. However, there is little evidence of such forms in the corpus, and even this is limited to progressive forms in elicitation sessions. For instance, as mentioned in §8.2.2.3, the progressive non-finite verb form can be used adverbially. One example featuring the progressive form *gullamin* 'listening' is repeated here in (22). Even here, it is not clear whether such non-finite forms can include arguments or adjuncts.

(22) *gullamin mån tjálav*
gulla-min mån tjála-v
listen-PROG 1SG.NOM write-1SG.PRS
'I write while listening.' [pit110404.089]*e*

Ultimately, the syntactic behavior of such non-finite verbs, and whether these can be part of subordinate clauses, must be left for future study.

14.2.4 Relative clauses

Pite Saami relative clauses are marked by a clause-initial relative pronoun. The fact that this relative pronoun is always the initial constituent in the relative clause is the only internal syntactic marking for relative clauses; otherwise, relative clauses are ordinary clauses with a fully inflected finite verb. The relative pronoun inflects for case according to the syntactic function it fills within the relative clause, and for the number of the NP that it modifies, as illustrated by (23) through (25).

---

[7] The non-finite forms are also included in the verb paradigms in Lehtiranta (1992: 150–155).

(23) dä   inijmä   aktav   vuoksav   majna   vuojadijmä
     dä   ini-jmä   akta-v   vuoksa-v   ma-jna   vuojadi-jmä
     then   have-1PL.PST one-ACC.SG bull-ACC.SG REL-COM.SG drive-1PL.PST
     muorajd
     muora-jd
     wood-ACC.PL
     'We had one bull with which we transported firewood.'
     [pit0906_Ahkajavvre_a.020]

(24) ja   dä   maŋŋemus   skoterijd   majd   iniga
     ja   dä   maŋŋe-mus   skoteri-jd   ma-jd   ini-ga
     and   then after-SUPERL snowmobile-ACC.PL REL-ACC.PL have-3DU.PST
     '…and the last snowmobiles which they had.'   [pit100404.281]

(25) dä   lä   ájge   ma   lä   urrum
     dä   lä   ájge   ma   lä   urru-m
     then be\3PL.PRS time\NOM.PL REL\NOM.PL be\3PL.PRS be-PRF
     'Those are times which have been.' (i.e.: 'those were the good old days')
     [pit090702.409]

Just as demonstrative and interrogative pronouns, relative pronouns only inflect for singular and plural, but not for dual number, as illustrated by the example in (26).

(26) *måj*   ma   lin   båhtam
     måj   ma   li-n   båhta-m
     1DU.NOM   REL\NOM.PL be-3PL.PST come-PRF
     'We two who had come.'   [pit110329.32m45s]e

Note that the relative pronouns are homophonous with the set of interrogative pronouns referring to non-human NPs.[8] However, not only do relative pronouns have a different syntactic function than interrogative pronouns in general, they are not sensitive to the humanness of the referent, unlike interrogative pronouns. For instance, the relative pronoun *ma* is the same in both (25) above and (27) below, although the former has 'times' as an antecedent and the latter refers to 'young people'.

---

[8] Cf. §6.4 and §6.5 for more on interrogative and relative pronouns, respectively.

14 Complex clauses

(27) dä   lin   nuora   álmatja   ma   lin
     dä   li-n   nuora   álmatj-a   ma   li-n
     then   be-3PL.PST young\PRED.PL people-NOM.PL REL\NOM.PL be-3PL.PST
     riejdnohimen
     riejdnohi-men
     herd-PROG
     'They were young people who were herding.'   [pit0906_Ahkajavvre_b.017]

In the previous examples, relative clauses immediately follow the head of the noun phrase they modify. However, it is possible for a postposition to occur between the modified NP and the relative clause, as illustrated by (28).

(28) dat   lij   duv   gugu masa   båhten
     d-a-t   li-j   duv   gugu ma-sa   båhte-n
     DEM-DIST-NOM.SG   be-3SG.PST 2SG.GEN   to   REL-ILL.SG   come-3PL.PST
     'It was to you they came.'   [pit110329.37m04s]*e*

This shows that it is possible, in this case, for a relative clause to not be embedded syntactically in the modified NP, as the relative clause can occur outside the postpositional phrase which the modified NP is a constituent of. It should be emphasized that only a postposition can split a relative clause from the matrix NP it modifies.

There does not appear to be any restriction on the syntactic function that a relative pronoun can fill within the relative clause. With the exception of abessive and essive, which are rare in the corpus for all nominals, relative pronouns are attested for all grammatical cases, as well as being the dependent NP in a postpositional phrase (in genitive case), as in (29), or similarly as the possessor NP (also in genitive case) modifying a noun, as in (30).

(29) dat   lä   náhppe   man   sisa
     d-a-t   lä   náhppe   ma-n   sisa
     DEM-DIST-NOM.SG   be\3SG.PRS   milking.bowl\NOM.SG   REL-GEN.SG   into
     båhtjen   *buhtsujd*
     båhtje-n   buhtsu-jd
     milk-3PL.PST   reindeer-ACC.PL
     'This is a milking bowl into which they milked reindeer.'
     [pit080708_Session02.003]

14.2 Clausal subordination

(30)   *men dä   lä   danne urrum dat   pluovve*
     men dä   lä   danne urru-m d-a-t   pluovve
     but then be\3SG.PRS there be-PRF DEM-DIST-NOM.SG pond\NOM.SG

     man   namma   lä,   mij   lä   namma
     ma-n   namma   lä   mij   lä   namma
     REL-GEN.SG name\NOM.SG be\3SG.PRS REL\NOM.SG be\3SG.PRS name\NOM.SG

     dan,   dáv   mijá   Árjepluovev
     d-a-n   d-á-v   mijá   Árjepluove-v
     DEM-DIST-GEN.SG DEM-PROX-ACC.SG 1PL.GEN Arjeplog-ACC.SG
     'But here was the pond whose name was, which was the name of that,
     this, our Arjeplog.'   [pit090915.013]

This latter example is clear evidence for such a structure, but it is part of a false-start, as it also contains a semantically-driven self-correction just after the targeted example; however, as the single instance in the corpus for a relative pronoun modifying a noun, it must suffice as evidence at this point.

In summary, relative pronouns can fulfill a variety of syntactic functions in a relative clause. Specifically, relative pronouns can be an argument NP, an adjunct NP, a dependent of a PP, or a possessor of an NP.

Appendix: Inventory of recordings

The inventory on pages 262 through 269 lists recordings collected for the Pite Saami Documentation Project by Joshua Wilbur. Not all recordings have provided examples which are included in this grammatical description, but they were all nonetheless essential in the process of coming to terms with the Pite Saami language, and thus relevant for the present study. The information provided reflects the state of the corpus in June 2014.

These 123 recordings are listed in the order they were created. In the vast majority of cases, the name of each recording indicates the date of recording as well (cf. §1.2.2.1); when this is not the case, the date is indicated in the brief description. To keep the inventory simple, abbreviations are often used for the columns 'genre' and 'medium'; the explanations for these abbreviations are listed below. The column 'words' indicates the current number of transcribed and translated Pite Saami words for each recording; currently, some have only been partly transcribed, and some not at all, particularly newer materials. The column 'brief description' provides a summary of the content of each recording; more detailed descriptions are provided in the metadata available at the archives hosting the materials.

Abbreviations used in the inventory of recordings

column	abbreviation	explanation
media	A	audio only
	A/V	audio and video
genre	conv.	conversation
	elic.	elicitation
	explan.	explanation
	narr.	narration
	perf.	performance
	read.	reading
	writ.	written text

Appendix: Inventory of recordings

name	genre	medium	words	brief description
pit080621	elic.	A	119	Basic phrases, wordlist
pit080622a	elic.	A	168	Verb paradigms (PRS); numbers 1–1000
pit080622b	elic.	A	6	Phrase: "thank you"
pit080627	elic.	A	39	More exact numbers
pit080701a	elic.	A	4	Phrase: "how do you say ___ in Saami"
pit080701b	elic.	A	116	Swadesh list - words: 7–15, 17–21, 27–90, 91–114
pit080702a	elic.	A	25	A few short words/phrases (landscape word,s etc.)
pit080702b	elic.	A	226	Swadesh list words: 115–207; a few short phrases
pit080703	explan.	A/V	334	Descriptions of two pictures: 1: Saami camp 2: Reindeer in the tundra
pit080708_Session01	explan.	A/V	0	Description of reindeer saddle carriers
pit080708_Session02	explan.	A/V	202	Description of reindeer milking
pit080708_Session03	explan.	A/V	136	Description of making butter, butter dishes and other dishes
pit080708_Session04	explan.	A/V	151	Description of a Saami chest
pit080708_Session05	explan.	A/V	14	Description of some traditional Pite Saami objects
pit080708_Session06	explan.	A/V	0	Description of a Saami shirt, reindeer-skin shoes
pit080708_Session07	explan.	A/V	74	Description of some traditional Saami tools: a weaving reed (a sort of mini-loom), a lasso ring and an unfinished sheath
pit080708_Session08	explan.	A/V	164	Description of Saami kids' shoes, two hats, reindeer-fur gloves
pit080708_Session09	explan.	A/V	124	Description of animal traps
pit080708_Session10	explan.	A/V	0	Description of how animal traps work
pit080803a	elic.	A	11	Reindeer antler terms

262

Appendix: Inventory of recordings

name	genre	medium	words	brief description
pit080803b	elic.	A	118	Ordinal numbers 1–10, >10
pit080811b1	elic.	A	4	Numerals (cardinal&ordinal), some verb paradigms
pit080811b2	elic.	A	9	Pronouns (NOM), and other random words
pit080813	elic.	A	163	Verb paradigms
pit080818	elic., explan.	A/V	0	Reindeer-related words; numbers 1–10+ (cardinal), 1–9 (ordinal)
pit080819a	elic.	A	448	Adjective paradigms
pit080819b	elic.	A	1	Word: "sárrge"
pit080819c	elic.	A	17	Phrase: "thank you for today"
pit080825	narr., song	A/V	270	Description of speaker's family and her life in her childhood home; Singing of two hymns
pit080909	explan.	A/V	736	Description of reindeer roundup/slaughter, including footage of reindeer being selected, caught, slaughtered, and commentary on butchering a reindeer
pit080917a	elic.	A	201	Some question words; some noun paradigms
pit080917b	elic.	A	8	Numerals 20–30, 40, 50, 60, 1000, 2000
pit080917c	elic.	A	36	Some noun paradigms; some question word paradigms "what" and "who"
pit080924	conv.	A/V	2440	Conversation about old times in Ákkapakte
pit080926	elic.	A	107	Word list from Pite-saami lessons from 25/26 september 2008
pit081011	elic.	A	355	Random words collected during a previous Pite Saami lesson
pit081012a	narr.	A	0	Descriptions of pictures from photo album, mostly of reindeer and calf marking
pit081012b	elic.	A	0	Random words, mostly resulting from pit081012a

Appendix: Inventory of recordings

name	genre	medium	words	brief description
pit081017	elic.	A	8	Days of the week; months; seasons
pit081021a_Story	read., writ.	A/V	0	Reading of a story by Lars Rensund
pit081021b	elic.	A	0	Demonstratives; some vocabulary from pit080708_Session08
pit081028	elic.	A	29	Words beginning with "sjnj-" (/ʃɲ/)
pit081106	explan.	A/V	0	Description of objects from Saami exhibit at Silvermuseet
pit081111	elic.	A	55	Adjective paradigms; some lexical items
pit090411	song, read., perf., writ.	A/V	0	Reading of scripture, singing of hymn
pit090513	elic.	A	18	Paradigm for noun *sábme* 'Saami'
pit090519	conv.	A/V	1247	A group of language activists have a picnic around a campfire, sometimes discussing words for a word list, but also just chatting
pit090525a	elic.	A	24	Noun paradigms for: sábme (Saami), bena (dog)
pit090525b	elic.	A	77	Six noun paradigms; short discussion of (near) minimal pairs
pit090525c	conv.	A	1	Word *buris(t)*
pit0906_Ahkajavvre_a	explan., narr.	A/V	1105	Description of the history and buildings at Ahkajavvre; performance of how to retrieve fishing nets and fish, and how to gut and wash fish; recorded on 9/10 June 2009
pit0906_Ahkajavvre_b	explan.	A/V	301	Description of the history of Ahkajavvre; recorded on 9/10 June 2009

Appendix: Inventory of recordings

name	genre	medium	words	brief description
pit090625	elic.	A	0	A few words from the loanword typology list, mostly about geographic features
pit090630	conv., narr.	A/V	103	Conversation about a trip to Álesgiehtje/Västerfjäll, driving across Tjeggelvas, going to school in Arjeplog; telling of a ghost story
pit090702	conv., narr.	A/V	2245	Conversation about fishing, hunting moose and preparing food in Álesgiehtje/Västerfjäll and Áhkkabakkte
pit090705	explan., narr.	A/V	0	On the way to and at reindeer calf marking the night of 5-6 July 2009
pit090821	elic., explan.	A	0	A variety of words relating to berries, insects, houses, etc.
pit090822	explan., narr.	A/V	0	Description of a variety of places around the speaker's family homestead
pit090823	explan.	A/V	0	Description of the old house at the speaker's family homestead
pit090826	explan.	A	301	Description of how reindeer herders look for unmarked calves at a round-up
pit090910	elic.	A	101	Reflexive pronouns; some verb paradigms
pit090912	explan., conv., narr.	A/V	0	Video of reindeer slaughter, including first stages of butchering a reindeer
pit090915	explan., narr.	A/V	1848	A guided tour of Arjeplog
pit090926	elic.	A	494	Adjective paradigms

Appendix: Inventory of recordings

name	genre	medium	words	brief description
pit090927	elic.	A	445	Adjective paradigms
pit090930a	elic.	A	829	Adjectives in elliptical NPs; some color adjectives; more adjective paradigms
pit090930b	elic.	A	120	Adjective paradigms
pit091001	elic.	A	281	Adjective paradigms
pit00304	elic.	A	62	Basic random wordlist (from the Leipzig-Jakarta list of basic vocabulary)
pit00308a	elic.	A	10	Some basic elicitation forms, NOM.SG and ACC.SG noun paradigms
pit00310b	narr., explan.	A/V	0	Description of a slide show concerning life in Áles-giehtje/Västerfjäll
pit00323a	elic.	A	481	Verb paradigms
pit00323b	song	A	28	Singing of a lullaby
pit00324	elic.	A/V	291	Expressions for spatial relations (mostly postpositions)
pit00326	elic.	A	0	Postpositions; some basic elicitation of existentials and demonstratives
pit00403	perf., read., writ.	A/V	227	Reading of scripture for Easter church service
pit00404	explan.	A/V	1704	Description of the winter landscape around Áles-giehtje/Västerfjäll, skiing, snowmobiles, playing there as a child, trapping ptarmigan, etc.

Appendix: Inventory of recordings

name	genre	medium	words	brief description
pit100405a	explan., narr.	A	758	Description of the current winter from a reindeer herder's perspective and of the activities that went on at the recording location near Blavvtajåhkå
pit100405b	explan.	A/V	461	Description of different kinds of reindeer
pit100703a	narr.	A	312	Story about waiting for the bus with the narrator's aunt
pit101208	elic.	A	674	Verb paradigms
pit110329	elic.	A	112	Pronoun paradigms (personal, demonstrative, relative, interrogative); a few Saami village lexical items
pit110331a	elic.	A	405	Pronoun paradigms (personal, demonstrative, interrogative, reflexive) for NOM,ACC, GEN,ILL
pit110331b	elic.	A	371	Pronoun paradigms (personal, demonstrative, interrogative, reflexive) for INESS, ELAT, COM
pit110404	elic.	A	530	Verb paradigms
pit110413a	elic.	A	394	Some noun paradigms
pit110413b	elic.	A	382	Noun paradigms; 'båtsoj'; includes numerals and quantifiers
pit110415	elic.	A	158	Kinship vocabulary; paradigm for ålmaj (man)
pit110421	elic.	A	89	Noun paradigms for juällge (leg/foot) and rejjdo (tool)
pit110509a	elic.	A	239	Random verbs; random questions about subordinate clause linking; some noun paradigms
pit110509b	elic.	A	111	Noun paradigms
pit110517a	elic.	A	870	Some verb paradigms; includes some potential forms of verbs
pit110517b1	elic.	A	0	Some verb paradigms
pit110517b2	narr.	A	380	Short narrative about the orthography workshop on the previous weekend

Appendix: Inventory of recordings

name	genre	medium	words	brief description
pit110518a	elic.	A	187	Verb paradigms; discussion of passives
pit110518b	elic.	A	0	Some aspects in verbs; verbs for 'scratch/dig'
pit110519a	elic.	A	0	Some partial verb paradigms; some verbal derivations
pit110519b	elic.	A	47	Some conjunction/subordinators; question particle discussion; some partial noun paradigms
pit110521a	elic.	A	150	Pronoun paradigms: NOM, ACC for personal, most reflexive, demonstrative, question, selection, relative pronouns
pit110521b1	elic.	A	529	Some pronoun paradigms
pit110521b2	narr.	A	8	A short narrative about what speaker did the previous day
pit110522	elic.	A	213	Some verb and noun paradigms
sje20121009	elic.	A	252	random grammatical topics: - DIM allomorphy - contracted verbs (gullut) - NEG.IMP (SG/DU/PL) - DEM - 3-way distinction - Adj vs. Adv - passives - Adj as head of NP - possessive suffixes
sje20121014a	elic.	A	1	Questions meant to elicit suspected differences between Pite Saami dialects
sje20121014b	conv.	A/V	0	Conversation about the old days, topics such as reindeer calves, coffee cheese, eating bear meat, seeing a bear, etc.
sje20121011	elic.	A	178	Questions about DIM suffix allomorphy in nouns; 'contracted' verb paradigm; imperative of negation verb; possessive suffixes, etc.
sje20121014d1	elic.	A	3	NP-syntax, gapping; COMP for Adj; coordination, complementizers
sje20130523	narr.	A/V	763	A narrative about going to church and praying

Appendix: Inventory of recordings

name	genre	medium	words	brief description
sje20130530b	conv.	A	1067	a discussion about words, coffee and other topics while preparing and drinking coffee in the kitchen
sje20131006	conv., explan., narr.	A/V	181	Discussion of the homestead; speaker plays with his granddaughter; describes various traditional sheds on his property
sje20131012a	conv.	A/V	0	Short conversation about Trollforsen and some of the old Saami huts there
sje20131012b	conv., narr., explan.	A/V	0	Tour of the speaker's homestead, gathering reindeer moss, playing with a speaker's granddaughter, tour of pictures and artefacts in the living room
sje20131031	explan., narr.	A/V	0	Description of various things related to driving to check on the reindeer and then a potential moose hunt

Bibliography

Álgu. 2006. *The Álgu database: Etymological database of the Saami languages.* Helsinki: Research Institute for the Languages of Finland. http://kaino.kotus.fi/algu. (accessed 2012.04.17).

Anderson, Gregory D.S. 2013. The velar nasal. In Matthew S. Dryer & Martin Haspelmath (eds.), *The world atlas of language structures online*, Leipzig: Max Planck Institute for Evolutionary Anthropology. http://wals.info/chapter/9.

Austin, Peter K. & Julia Sallabank (eds.). 2011. *The Cambridge handbook of endangered languages* Cambridge Handbooks in Language and Linguistics. Cambridge: Cambridge University Press.

Bengtsson, Nils-Henrik, Marianne Eriksson, Inger Fjällås, Eva-Karin Rosenberg, Valborg Sjaggo & Dagny Skaile. 2011. Insamling av pitesamiska ord. (unpublished).

Bergsland, Knut. 1962. The Lapp dialects south of Lappland. In Paavo Ravila & Paul Ariste (eds.), *Commentationes fenno-ugricae in honorem paavo ravila* (Suomalais-ugrilaisen Seuran toimituksia 125), 27–39. Helsinki: Suomalais-Ugrilainen Seura.

Bergsland, Knut. 1977. Saamen kieli ja naapurikielet. *Virittäjä* 81. 1–11.

Bickel, Balthasar & Johanna Nichols. 2007. Inflectional morphology. In Timothy Shopen (ed.), *Language typology and syntactic description: Grammatical categories and the lexicon*, vol. III, 169–240. Cambridge: Cambridge University Press 2nd edn.

Bird, Steven & Gary Simons. 2003. Seven dimensions of portability for language documentation and description. *Language* 79(3). 557–582.

Bull, Tove, Jurij Kusmenko & Michael Rießler (eds.). 2007. *Språk og språkforhold i Sápmi* (Berliner Beiträge zur Skandinavistik 10). Berlin: Humboldt-Universität.

Bylund, Erik. 1956. *Kolonisering av Pite Lappmark t.o.m. år 1867* (Geographica 30). Uppsala: Uppsala universitet.

Collinder, Björn. 1960. *Comparative grammar of the Uralic languages* A handbook of the Uralic languages. Stockholm: Almqvist and Wiksell.

Dixon, Robert M. W. 2010. *Basic linguistic theory*. Oxford: Oxford University Press.

Bibliography

Feist, Timothy. 2010. *A grammar of Skolt Saami*. Manchester: University of Manchester dissertation.

Gippert, Jost, Nikolaus Himmelmann & Ulrike Mosel (eds.). 2006. *Essentials of language documentation* (Trends in Linguistics: Studies and Monographs 178). Berlin: Mouton de Gruyter.

Grenoble, Lenore A. & Louanna Furbee (eds.). 2010. *Language documentation: Practice and values*. Amsterdam: John Benjamins Publishing Co.

Grundström, Harald & Sune Smedeby. 1963. *Lapska sånger: Texter och melodier från svenska Lappland (sånger från Arjeplog och Arvidsjaur)* (Skrifter utgivna genom Landsmåls- och Folkminnesarkivet i Uppsala 2). Uppsala: Lundequistska bokhandeln.

Grundström, Harald & A. O. Väisänen. 1958. *Lapska sånger: Texter och melodier från svenska Lappland (Jonas Eriksson Steggos sånger)* (Skrifter utgivna genom Landsmåls- och Folkminnesarkivet i Uppsala 1). Uppsala: Lundequistska bokhandeln.

Halász, Ignácz. 1885. *Lule- és Pite-lappmarki nyelvmutatvéanyok és szótár* (Svéd-Lapp Nyelv I). Budapest: Kiadja a Magyar tudományos akadémia.

Halász, Ignácz. 1893. *Népköltési gyüjtemény: A Pite Lappmark Arjepluogi egyházkerületéböl* (Svéd-Lapp Nyeiv. V). Budapest: Kiadja a Magyar tudományos akadémia.

Halász, Ignácz. 1896. *Pite lappmarki szótár és nyelvtan* (Svéd-Lapp Nyelv VI). Budapest: Kiadja a Magyar tudományos akadémia.

Hayes, Bruce P. 1989. The prosodic hierarchy in meter. In Paul Kiparsky & Gilbert Youmans (eds.), *Rhythm and meter*, 201–260. Orlando, FL: Academic Press.

Himmelmann, Nikolaus. 2006. Language documentation: What is it and what is it good for? In Jost Gippert, Ulrike Mosel & Nikolaus Himmelmann (eds.), *Essentials of language documentation* (Trends in Linguistics: Studies and Monographs 178), 1–30. Berlin: Mouton de Gruyter.

Korhonen, Mikko. 1969. Die Entwicklung der morphologischen Methode im Lappischen. *Finnisch-Ugrische Forschungen* 37(2–3). 203–362.

Korhonen, Olavi. 2005. *Báhkogirjje: Julevsámes dárruj, dáros julevsábmáj*. Jokkmokk: Samernas utbildningscentrum.

Krauss, Michael. 1997. The indigenous languages of the North: A report on their present state. In Hiroshi Shoji & Juha Janhunen (eds.), *Northern minority languages: Problems of survival* (Senri Ethnic Studies 44), 1–34. Osaka: National Museum of Ethnology.

Lagercrantz, Eliel. 1926. *Sprachlehre des Westlappischen nach der Mundart von Arjeplog* (Suomalais-ugrilaisen Seuran toimituksia LV). Helsinki: Suomalais-ugrilainen Seura.

Larsson, Lars-Gunnar. 1985. Kriterien zur klassifikazion der lappischen Dialekte in Schweden. In Wolfgang Veenker (ed.), *Dialectologia Uralica. Materialien des ersten internationalen Symposions zur Dialektologie der uralischen Sprachen. 4–7 September 1984 in Hamburg*, 159–171. Wiesbaden: Harrassowitz.

Lehtiranta, Juhani. 1992. *Arjeploginsaamen äänne- ja taivutusopin pääpiirteet* (Suomalais-ugrilaisen Seuran toimituksia 212). Helsinki: Suomalais-ugrilainen Seura.

Lehtiranta, Juhani. 2001. *Yhteissaamelainen sanasto* (Suomalais-ugrilaisen Seuran toimituksia 200). Helsinki: Suomalais-Ugrilainen Seura.

Manker, Ernst. 1947. *De svenska fjällapparna* (STF:s handböcker om det svenska fjället 4). Stockholm: Svenska turistföreningens förlag.

Nespor, Marina & Irene Vogel. 1986. *Prosodic phonology*. Dordrecht: Foris Publishers.

Pulkkinen, Risto. 2005. Missionary work: History. In Ulla-Maija Kulonen, Irja Seurujärvi-Kari & Risto Pulkkinen (eds.), *The Saami: A cultural encyclopedia*, 218–221. Vammala: Vammalan Kirjapaino Oy.

Rensund, Lars. 1982. *Renen i mitten*. Luleå: Norrbottens museum.

Rensund, Lars. 1986. *I samernas land förr i tiden*. Luleå: Norrbottens museum.

Rießler, Michael. 2011. *Typology and evolution of adjective attribution marking in the languages of northern Eurasia*. Leipzig: Institut für Linguistik, Universität Leipzig dissertation.

Ruong, Israel. 1943. *Lappische Verbalableitung dargestellt auf Grundlage des Pitelappischen*. Uppsala: Almqvist och Wiksell.

Ruong, Israel. 1945. *Studier i lapsk kultur i Pite lappmark och angränsande områden* Svenska landsmål och svenskt folkliv. Stockholm: Dialekt- och folkminnesarkivet.

Salminen, Tapani. 2007. Endangered languages in Europe. In Matthias Brenzinger (ed.), *Language diversity endangered* (Trends in Linguistics: Studies and Monographs 181), 205–232. Berlin: Mouton de Gruyter.

Sammallahti, Pekka. 1985. Die Definition von Sprachgrenzen in einem Kontinuum von Dialekten: Die lappischen Sprachen und einige Grundfragen der Dialektologie. In Wolfgang Veenker (ed.), *Dialectologia Uralica. Materialien des ersten internationalen Symposions zur Dialektologie der uralischen Sprachen. 4–7 September 1984 in Hamburg*, 149–158. Wiesbaden: Harrassowitz.

Sammallahti, Pekka. 1998. *The Saami languages: An introduction*. Kárášjohka: Davvi Girji.

Schachter, Paul & Timothy Shopen. 2007. Parts-of-speech systems. In Timothy Shopen (ed.), *Language typology and syntactic description: Clause structure*, vol. 1, 1–60. Cambridge: Cambridge University Press 2nd edn.

Selkirk, Elisabeth. 1980. Prosodic domains in phonology: Sanskrit revisited. In Mark Aranoff & Mary-Louise Kean (eds.), *Juncture*, 107–129. Saratoga, CA: Anma Libri.

Selkirk, Elisabeth. 1984. *Phonology and syntax: The relation between sound and structure*. Cambridge, MA: The MIT Press.

Sjaggo, Ann-Charlotte. 2010. *Från Sulidälbmá till Áhkkábáktte: En ortnamnsguide för norra sidan Piteälven i Arjeplogsfjällen*. Jokkmokk: Ann-Charlotte Sjaggo.

Spiik, Nils Eric. 1989. *Lulesamisk grammatik*. Jokkmokk: Sameskolstyrelsen.

Svonni, Mikael. 2009. *Samisk grammatik: Kompendium*. Tromsø: Universitetet i Tromsø.

Tirén, Karl. 1942. *Die lappische Volksmusik: Aufzeichnungen von Juoikos-Melodien bei den schwedischen Lappen* (Acta Lapponica 3). Stockholm: Nordiska museet.

Valijärvi, Riitta-Liisa & Joshua Wilbur. 2011. The current state of the Pite Saami language: Sociological and linguistic factors. *Nordic Journal of Linguistics* 34(3). 295–329.

Wickman, Bo. 1964. A lappish tale from Arjeplog. In Arne Furumark, Sture Lagercrantz, Asbjørn Nesheim & Geo Widengren (eds.), *Lapponica: essays presented to Israel Ruong, May 26, 1963* (Studia Ethnographica Uppsalensia XXI), Lund: Ohlsson.

Wilbur, Joshua (ed.). forthcoming 2014. *Pitesamisk ordbok samt förslag för en pitesamisk ortografi* (Samica 2). Freiburg: Skandinavisches Seminar, Albert-Ludwigs-Universität Freiburg.

Woodbury, Anthony C. 2011. Language documentation. In Peter K. Austin & Julia Sallabank (eds.), *The Cambridge handbook of endangered languages* Cambridge Handbooks in Language and Linguistics, 159–186. Cambridge: Cambridge University Press.

Name index

Álgu, 143
Anderson, Gregory D.S., 53

Bengtsson, Nils-Henrik, 17
Bergsland, Knut, 4, 236
Bickel, Balthasar, 94
Bird, Steven, 10
Bylund, Erik, 10

Collinder, Björn, 4

Dixon, Robert M. W., 26

Eriksson, Marianne, 17

Feist, Timothy, 38, 75, 134, 165, 186, 190
Fjällås, Inger, 17

Grundström, Harald, 9

Halász, Ignácz, 7–9
Hayes, Bruce P., 26
Hilpert, Martin, 229
Himmelmann, Nikolaus, 10

Korhonen, Mikko, 74
Korhonen, Olavi, 17
Krauss, Michael, 7

Lagercrantz, Eliel, 4, 7–9, 50, 92, 98, 112, 113, 152, 154, 165, 186, 187, 190, 227, 249, 256
Larsson, Lars-Gunnar, 1

Lehtiranta, Juhani, 1, 7–9, 50, 92, 98, 111, 113, 117, 152, 154, 165, 166, 175, 176, 190, 237, 256

Manker, Ernst, 3, 4
Morén-Duolljá, Bruce, 99, 168

Nespor, Marina, 26
Nichols, Johanna, 94

Pulkkinen, Risto, 6

Rankvist, Elsy, 13
Rensund, Lars, 10, 17
Rießler, Michael, 128, 129
Rosenberg, Eva-Karin, 17
Ruong, Israel, 3, 4, 7, 8, 159, 195, 202, 203, 206, 207

Salminen, Tapani, 6, 7
Sammallahti, Pekka, 1, 2, 4, 29, 30, 38, 52, 75, 77, 78, 109, 134, 138, 143, 144, 154, 165, 186, 227, 256
Schachter, Paul, 121
Selkirk, Elisabeth, 26, 30
Shopen, Timothy, 121
Simons, Gary, 10
Sjaggo, Ann-Charlotte, 9
Sjaggo, Valborg, 17
Skaile, Dagny, 17
Smedeby, Sune, 9

Name index

Spiik, Nils Eric, 64, 71, 154, 186, 187, 190, 256
Svonni, Mikael, 134, 154, 186, 190, 206, 240, 256

Tirén, Karl, 9

Väisänen, A. O., 9
Valijärvi, Riitta-Liisa, 6, 7, 9
Vogel, Irene, 26

Wickman, Bo, 10
Wilbur, Joshua, 6, 7, 9
Woodbury, Anthony C., 10

Subject index

adjectival phrase, *see* phrase
adjective, 128–142, 197
    attributive, 128–130, 134, 219
    comparative, 89, 90, 135, 137
    predicative, 129–134, 220
    superlative, 135, 138
adposition
    postposition, 188–189, 258
    preposition, 189–190
adverb, 128, 130, 131, 183–187, 243
adverbial phrase, *see* phrase
affricate, 39, 45–48, 57, 77
agreement, 211, 231, 234, 236, 240
approximant, 56–57
aspect, 153, 155, 212, 231, 240, 244
    perfect, 155, 160
    progressive, 156, 157
aspiration, 37, 38
    postaspiration, 37
    preaspiration, 34, 37, 38, 44, 45, 47, 48, 51, 54–57, 75
assimilation, 79, 164

case, 84–92, 113, 115, 120, 123, 125, 130, 137, 140, 142, 143, 215, 217
    abessive, 83, 90, 92, 97, 108, 258
    accusative, 85, 86, 115, 117, 129, 225, 226, 233
    comitative, 89, 137
    elative, 88, 137, 236
    essive, 83, 91, 92, 108, 189, 258
    genitive, 85, 117, 188, 258
    illative, 86, 226, 233
    inessive, 87, 235, 236
    nominative, 84, 91, 113, 117, 189, 225, 229, 232–236
clause
    adverbial, 254–255
    complement, 214, 230, 237, 250–254
    copular, 88, 234*, 235–237
    declarative, 229, 231–241, 243, 246
    existential, 234–236
    interrogative
        constituent, 230, 242–243, 252
        polar, 186, 244–245
    relative, 218, 256–259
complement
    clause, *see* clause
    phrase, 85, 87, 91, 130, 131, 137, 157, 188, 189, 218, 223, 227, 238, 240, 241, 244
complementizer, 251
conjunction, 25, 190–192
consonant center, 29–31, 38, 43, 44, 50, 54, 55, 60, 70, 169
consonant cluster, 25, 50, 58–63
consonant gradation, 75–78, 96, 99, 100, 102, 105, 106, 155, 161, 163, 166, 168–171, 173, 176,

Subject index

  183
  strong grade, 75, 79, 96, 98, 108
  weak grade, 75, 79, 96, 98, 108,
   166, 183, 201
constituent order, 212, 226–230, 236,
  241, 244, 256
coordination, 249–250

demonstrative, 116, 128, 142, 215
demonstrative pronoun, *see*
  pronoun
derivation, 73, 144, 168, 183, 195
  adjectival, 207–208
  adverbial, 183–184, 208
  nominal, 196–202
  numeral, 144, 208
  verbal, 202–207
devoicing, 36, 57
dialect variation, 3*, 50–52, 60, 64,
  70, 71, 77
diminutive, 168, 196, 202
diphthong, 29, 63–65, 68
documentary linguistics, 10

epenthesis, 70

foot, 26, 28, 34, 74
fricative, 48–52
  voiced dental fricative, 51

geminate, 33, 38, 45, 47, 48, 50,
  54–57, 75, 77
grammatical relations, 225–226

inflection, 73, 81, 92, 94, 113, 115, 128,
  143, 147, 161, 165, 168, 180,
  195
  nominal, 83, 84, 92, 96–99, 108
  verbal, 149, 150, 159–162, 165,
   167, 168

information structure, 229–230
  focus, 227*, 230, 234, 236, 237,
   243
  topic, 227*, 229, 230, 234, 237
instrumental, 90
intensity, 27
interjection, 25, 192–194
interrogative
  pro-form, 123–124
  pronoun, *see* pronoun
  question marker, 186–187, 245
intonation, 35, 244

language contact, 6, 7, 10, 17, 27, 36*,
  43*, 50*, 62*, 66, 112*, 138*,
  138, 143*, 146, 179*, 184*,
  185, 189, 190, 191*, 192, 194,
  199*, 201, 204*, 206, 213*,
  222*, 227, 234–238*, 246,
  249*, 251*, 254*

mood, 149, 151–153, 157, 160, 211, 212,
  231
  conditional, 239, 255
  imperative, 150–152, 158, 159,
   166–168, 211, 212, 231,
   245–247
  potential, 152–153, 159, 165,
   246–247
morphology
  linear, 74
  non-linear, 74–81, 92, 96, 161,
   195
morphophonology, 28, 30, 34, 40,
  60, 62, 83, 91, 149

nasal, 52–54
negation, 153, 157, 179, 212, 231, 240
nominal phrase, *see* phrase

Subject index

noun, 79, 83–112, 197
    case, *see* case
    inflection class, 99–109
    number, 83, 91, 92, 113, 115, 120, 123, 125, 130, 131, 137, 140, 142, 143, 149, 151, 152, 157, 160, 175, 211, 215, 217, 228, 231
    dual, 83, 150, 257
numeral, 143–148, 217, 220
    ordinal, 143, 144, 208

orthography, 17–21

passive, 89, 158, 205, 232
person, 113, 149, 150, 152, 157, 160, 175, 211, 228, 231
phoneme inventory
    consonants, 37
phrase
    adjectival, 143, 190, 217, 219–222, 235
    adverbial, 86, 127, 157, 183, 190, 220, 222–223
    nominal, 118, 128, 130, 137, 190, 215–220, 223, 228, 235, 250, 256
    postpositional, 85, 187, 190, 223–224, 258
    prepositional, 187, 224
    verb complex, 149, 211–215, 232, 238
pitch, 27
plosive, 39, 41–45, 57, 77
possession, 85, 87, 236
    possessive suffixes, 109–112
postposition, *see* adposition
postpositional phrase, *see* phrase
preaspiration, *see* aspiration
preposition, *see* adposition

productivity, 195
pronoun, 25, 113–125, 215
    demonstrative, 115–117, 142, 218, 257
    interrogative, 119–123, 125, 252, 257
    personal, 113–115, 218
    reflexive, 117–119, 215
    relative, 125, 256
prosodic domains, 28, 64
prosodic hierarchy, 26

quantifier, 140

schwa, 70
spacial deixis
    distal, 115, 142
    proximal, 115, 142
    remote, 115, 142
stress, 26–28, 34, 35, 66
subordination, 250–259
suffix
    derivational, 183, 198, 200–202, 204, 205, 207, 208, 232*
    inflectional class, 99, 102, 105, 168–171, 173, 175
    nominal, 92, 94, 113
    portmanteau, 92, 160
    possessive, *see* possession
    verbal, 160
syllable, 26, 34
    syllabic structure, 27, 169, 170, 175, 176
    syllabification, 30, 58

tense, 150, 157, 160, 211, 231
    future, 153, 155, 239
    past, 150, 158, 161, 168
    present, 150, 153, 155, 158, 166*, 166–168

Subject index

trill, 55
typological profile, 22–23

umlaut, 78–79, 96, 99, 100, 161, 163, 168–171, 173, 176

valency, 159
    ditransitive, 86, 226, 233
    intransitive, 206, 225, 232
    passive, *see* passive
    transitive, 85, 205, 225, 230, 233, 237
verb, 79, 149–180, 190, 197, 201
    aspect, *see* aspect
    auxiliary, 178, 240–241
    copular, 87, 130, 178, 212, 228, 235, 240
    finite, 211, 231, 244, 251, 254, 256
    inflectional class, 160–180
    modal, 212, 238–239, 241
    mood, *see* mood
    negation verb, 179, 240–241
    non-finite, 153–155, 160, 211, 231, 237, 240, 244, 250, 253, 256
        connegative, 157, 160, 212, 241
    tense, *see* tense
    valency, *see* valency
verb complex, *see* phrase
vowel harmony, 79–81, 98, 100, 102, 161, 164, 169–171, 173, 175, 176
vowel length, 27

word class (overview), 81